Lauren Sutherland QC called to the bar in 1996 and took silk in 2016. Since being called to the bar she has specialised in clinical and professional negligence, and human rights issues in medical law. She is ranked in both Chambers UK and the Legal 500 for clinical negligence (Band 1). She has written and lectured extensively in the area of personal injury and clinical negligence. For many years, she taught 'consent' to dental and medical students. She was part of the legal team in the land-mark case of *Montgomery v Lanarkshire Health Board* [2015] UKSC 11.

A Guide to Consent in Clinical Negligence Post-Montgomery

A Guide to Consent in Clinical Negligence Post-Montgomery

Lauren Sutherland QC

Law Brief Publishing

Published 2018 by Law Brief Publishing, an imprint of Law Brief Publishing Ltd
30 The Parks
Minehead
Somerset
TA24 8BT

www.lawbriefpublishing.com

Paperback: 978-1-911035-12-1

This book is dedicated to my children

Stephanie, Rachel and Alexander, who

taught me what is important in life

Our greatest glory is, not in never falling,

but in rising every time we fall.

~ Oliver Goldsmith ~

FOREWORD BY
THE RIGHT HON LORD BRODIE

This is a very timely book written by a very well qualified author.

The 2015 decision of the United Kingdom Supreme Court in *Montgomery v Lanarkshire Health Board* significantly re-set, from a legal perspective, the balance in the therapeutic relationship between doctor and patient. While the formulation of the law in what was effectively a unanimous judgment of the Court was entirely consistent with what the General Medical Council, intervening on behalf of registered doctors, had said the law should be, and what Baroness Hale in her concurring judgment said that it had already been decided that the law was, in *Montgomery* the determinations by the courts below, founding on what had been said in the House of Lords in *Sidaway v Board of Governors of the Bethlem Royal Hospital*, had been to very different effect. At first instance and then on appeal, the Court of Session had held that, other than in exceptional circumstances, when determining treatment options a clinician has no duty to discuss with her patient the risks associated with what is proposed, as long as not doing so is accepted as proper practice by a responsible body of medical opinion. That approach was to focus on the doctor and to judge how she had performed her duties by reference to the views of other doctors; in law it was doctors who determined what was best for patients. Post *Montgomery*, that is no longer so.

It has always been the case that, in the much-quoted words of Mr Justice Cardozo, sitting as a then newly appointed member of the New York Court of Appeals: "Every human being of adult years and sound mind has a right to determine what shall be done with his own body…" It follows that any person with mental capacity must consent to any medical treatment she may receive; treatment without consent is wrongful.

What *Montgomery* did was radically to rethink just what should be understood by the notion of "consent to treatment" and to endorse, as the GMC had invited it to do, a model of the therapeutic relationship in which when it comes to deciding on how a case should be managed, the focus is turned on the patient and the patient's rights and responsibilities. Under that model it is first for the doctor fully to explain the options to the patient, setting out the potential benefits, risks, burdens and side effects of each option, including the option to have no treatment. It is then for the patient to weigh up what she has been told by the doctor about potential benefits and risks and then to decide on which option is best for her, taking into account not only the clinical considerations but also any other considerations which are of importance to her. It is the patient and not the doctor who is taken to be best able to make the necessary choices, but only once she has been equipped to do so by the doctor explaining, in a way that the patient can understand, what the available choices may involve.

As was decided in *Montgomery*, where an explanation which a reasonable patient would expect to be given is not given and there is an adverse outcome which would have otherwise been avoided, there may be a claim for damages for clinical negligence. For those who may be concerned with such claims and for those more generally interested in this area of the law, Lauren Sutherland's book provides essential reading. It is a work which, to put it colloquially, does what it says on the tin: it provides a comprehensive guide to the law as to the doctor's duty to disclose sufficient information to enable the patient to make an intelligent choice. Having identified the ethical, philosophical and practical context, it sets out, in comprehensive terms, the law as it stood prior to the Supreme Court's decision, not only in Scotland and England but also in other influential jurisdictions. It details what was argued and decided at each stage in *Montgomery*, fully acknowledging the contribution made by the GMC as representing the medical profession. Importantly, it discusses the difficult question of causation: how is a court to be satisfied that had information which should have been disclosed been disclosed the patient would have made a different decision. Finally, in what inevitably is work in progress, it looks at how the decision in *Montgomery* has been taken forward in the subsequent case-law.

There could not have been a more appropriate author for this significant work than Lauren Sutherland QC. Not only is she a very experienced and truly specialist practitioner in the field of clinical negligence but she was part of Mrs Montgomery's legal team in both the appeal before the Court of Session and the appeal to the Supreme Court. Her analysis of *Montgomery* is that of expert counsel who was involved in the development of the critical and ultimately successful arguments from an early stage. As such it can only be of enormous value to the readership of students, lawyers and health care professional for whom it is intended.

Right Hon Lord Brodie
January 2018

PREFACE

Plato referred to the obligation of the physician to obtain a full case history and give no prescription until such time as they had obtained the patient's understanding and consent. It was only in the case of slaves that physicians owed no explanation or justification for their actions.

For many years, the law in the UK on consent was singularly out of step with other Commonwealth jurisdictions. Now the recent decision of the Supreme Court in the case of *Montgomery v Lanarkshire Health Board* has clarified the position in the UK and firmly recognised the rights of the patient in this area of the law.

Sam Montgomery was born in October 1999. It was not until March 2015 that the Supreme Court issued its decision and he had a final resolution of the claim made on his behalf by his mother, Nadine, against Lanarkshire Health Board. By that time Sam was nearly 16 years old.

The case had made its way from a decision of Lord Bannatyne, in the Outer House of the Court of Session in 2010, through the disappointment of the decision of an Extra Division of the Inner House of the Court of Session (Appeal Court) in 2013, and finally to the longed-for and unanimous victory in the Supreme Court in 2015.

Without Nadine's strength and determination, this process would never have started. She was supported in her journey by a legal team consisting of James Badenoch QC, Colin McAulay QC and myself, and Fred Tyler and Joanna McCormack from Balfour & Manson, Solicitors, in Edinburgh.

Ultimately the case has had far-reaching implications for many, and has led to the introduction of a patient-focused test to the law on consent, and a change in practice. It is hoped that, as has happened in other common-law jurisdictions, the change of focus to a patient-orientated duty of information disclosure will improve the delivery of health care.

The argument advanced in the Supreme Court was developed by the claimant's legal team over many long days, weeks, months and years. There are some who say that the decision of the Supreme Court in *Montgomery* was not necessary as the law had already changed. However, on a proper analysis of the decision the Supreme Court has at last recognised the right of the particular patient to make informed choices about their own health care, that information disclosure to patients should be treated differently in law from issues relating to diagnosis and treatment, and therefore that in law the professional practice test is not an appropriate test to be applied in information disclosure cases. Credit for this change lies with those who put in the hard work to bring this to its ultimate conclusion.

The law is as stated on the basis of the materials available to me on 24th December 2017.

Lauren Sutherland QC
December 2017

ABOUT THIS BOOK

The purpose of this book is to set out in full the legal arguments advanced through the various stages of *Montgomery v Lanarkshire Health Board* to its final conclusion in the Supreme Court.

The intention is to analyse the law on consent prior to the Supreme Court decision in *Montgomery* and the arguments made in *Montgomery* in the Scottish courts and the Supreme Court and to consider the way that the decision has been interpreted by the courts following the decision. The focus on an analysis of the law on consent in other jurisdictions, particularly Australia and Canada, is intentional: the Supreme Court specifically endorsed the twofold test in the Australian case of *Rogers v Whitaker*. It is suggested the approach found in these jurisdictions holds the key to understanding how the Supreme Court wished to develop the law on consent and the test to be applied. Those who wish to advance and develop the law in the UK should be familiar with the decisions of those jurisdictions.

This book is intended equally for students, lawyers, doctors and other members of the health care professions.

ACKNOWLEDGEMENTS

I am indebted to the following people who have all helped me in different ways with this book.

I must thank Colin MacAulay QC for reading many of the chapters and constantly challenging my ideas; Professor Sheila McLean for writing a letter in support of the claimant's legal aid application for the Supreme Court; Right Hon Lord Brodie for reading the book and for his excellent foreword; David Stephenson QC for his suggestions on the GMC chapter; Dr David Lloyd, consultant neonatologist, and Dr Rajan Madhok for giving me a medical practitioner's view and for supporting me throughout; Paula McMillan at New Law in Glasgow for always believing in me; Wendy O'Neill, who encouraged me on my hopeless days; all the library staff working in the Faculty of Advocates library in Edinburgh, and in particular Alistair Johnston, who was a fantastic help with research and who can find things no other person can; the clerks at Ampersand in Edinburgh; David Short at Balfour & Manson; Mark Harvey at Hugh James in Cardiff, who knows everyone everywhere; Andrew Smith QC, for permitting me to use the argument made by him on behalf of the GMC in the Supreme Court; Sarah Royal, deputy chief legal advisor, Office of the Health and Disability Commissioner, Wellington; Margaret Brain of Maurice Blackburn in Australia, who assisted by reading my analysis of Australian consent law; Rebecca Scott, barrister, Harbour Chambers, Wellington; Susanne Raab, Pacific Medical Law in Canada, for reading the Canadian chapter; Hugh Jackson for assisting with the proof reading; Tim Kevan for his gentle support and wise counsel; and finally my beloved father, who always said we would win but sadly died days after the hearing in the Appeal Court in Scotland, and to my children, family and friends who had to put up with me over the many years it took to get to the finish line at the Supreme Court.

TABLE OF CASES

CONTENTS

CHAPTER ONE
THE NATURE OF CONSENT

1.   Introduction

As far back as 1984 the *Handbook of Medical Ethics* published by the British Medical Association under the heading "Consent to Treatment" provided a clear and concise summary of the basic principles of consent:

> *The patient's trust that his consent to treatment will not be misused is an essential part of his relationship with his doctor. For a doctor even to touch a patient without consent may constitute an assault.... Consent is only valid when freely given by a patient who understands the nature and consequences of what is proposed.... Assumed consent or consent obtained by undue influence is valueless.... It is particularly important that consent should be free of any form of pressure or coercion.... No influence should be exerted through any special relationship between a doctor and the person whose consent is sought.... Doctors offer advice but it is the patient who decides whether or not to accept the advice.... The onus is always on the doctor carrying out the procedure to see that an adequate explanation is given.*

Despite this statement, and the fact that the General Medical Council (GMC) has since the 1980s formulated a patient-focused model of consent in its professional guidance, it has taken the courts in the UK some time to bring the law into line with the moral and ethical principles that underpin the obtaining of patient consent.

For many years in the UK the test in information disclosure cases was found in *Sidaway v Bethlem Royal Hospital Governors*. It was not until the decision in *Pearce v United Bristol Healthcare NHS Trust* ([1999] PIQR P53) that the Court of Appeal considered the question of information disclosure in a patient-focused way.

In *Chester v Afshar* ([2004] UKHL 41) it was accepted that the rationale for the duty to provide information was to enable an adult patient of sound mind to make for themselves decisions intimately affecting their own lives and bodies. The surgeon owed a legal duty to warn a patient of possible serious risks involved in a procedure. The only qualification was said to be the wholly exceptional cases where treatment is objectively in the best interests of the patient that the surgeon may be excused from giving a warning.

Lord Steyn declared that the function of the law is to enable rights to be vindicated and to provide remedies when duties have been breached. In "modern law, medical paternalism no longer rules and a patient has a prima facie right to be informed by a surgeon of a small, but well established, risk of serious injury as a result of surgery". The patient's right to an appropriate warning for a surgery "ought normatively to be regarded as an important right which must be given effective protection whenever possible".

Lord Steyn recognised that adequate information disclosure ensures that "due respect is given to the autonomy and dignity of each patient". The departure from traditional causation principles in *Chester v Afshar* was directly linked to the court's appreciation of the fact that the patient's right to autonomy and dignity needed to be protected.

In 2015 the United Kingdom Supreme Court at last focused the law on information disclosure in *Montgomery v Lanarkshire Health Board*. Margaret Brazier commented on the decision and said that it has "swept away the last vestiges of legal endorsement of medical paternalism.... No longer are patients only entitled to be told what doctors think it is appropriate to tell them. The much criticised decision of the House of Lords in *Sidaway v Royal Bethlem Hospital* is consigned to history." It is said that the death of *Sidaway* will attract few mourners (*Medicine, Patients and the Law*, Margaret Brazier & Emma Cave, 6th Edition). The UK law on consent is now in line with other common-law jurisdictions and with the professional guidance formulated by the GMC.

The word "consent" derives from the Latin conjunction of *con* and *sentire*, which mean joint agreement. The GMC uses the term "shared decision making".

In *Philosophical Medical Ethics*, Gillon defined consent as follows:

> [C]onsent means a voluntary, uncoerced decision, made by a suffi-
> ciently competent or autonomous person on the basis of adequate
> information and deliberation, to accept rather than reject some
> proposed course of action that will affect him or her.

In the area of information disclosure there are two main ideals. The first principle is that a decision whether to undergo a medical procedure or not is ultimately the decision of the patient and not the doctor. The second is that every person has the right to determine what shall be done to their body. Both stem from the basic human right of self-determination, which in some countries is constitutionally protected and in others is seen as a basic right to be protected by common law.

On this basis, a patient has the right to determine when, how and in what circumstances they shall be treated. If alternative medical or surgical treatments are available, then this right entitles the patient to decide if they would like treatment and if so which option for treatment they would prefer.

Patient consent is widely regarded as fundamental in the doctor–patient relationship. It is a moral and ethical rule as well as a requirement of the law. It is not simply the satisfaction of a legal formality. It is a necessity to justify the medical procedure proposed. It implies that doctor and patient feel that the treatment proposed is the right and proper one.

Information is required to enable a patient to make a decision. The purpose of information is to enable an individual to gain knowledge to allow them to exercise "choice". In cases of information disclosure, the law tends to focus on the question of alternative procedures, and the risks and benefits of those alternatives. The patient also has the choice to elect for no procedure at all.

Consent must be freely and voluntarily given, on the basis of information (unless rejected) as to the risks and benefits of a proposed treatment. A refusal by a competent adult patient to consent to treatment or a procedure should normally be considered conclusive. The power to exercise a choice in treatment options should also include the power to refuse treatment. To give valid consent, the patient should appreciate the implications of their decision. Consent may be either express or implied from conduct.

The role of the doctor is not confined to diagnosis and treatment. Patient consent is an essential prerequisite of all medical treatment, and not simply the satisfaction of a legal formality. It is a necessity to justify the medical procedure proposed.

Peter Jackson J in *Heart of England NHS Trust v JB* ([2014] EWHC 342 (COP)) held:

> *anyone capable of making decisions has an absolute right to accept or refuse medical treatment, regardless of the wisdom or consequences of the decision. The decision does not have to be justified to anyone. In the absence of consent any invasion of the body will be a criminal assault. The fact that the intervention is well-meaning or therapeutic makes no difference.*

In *Montgomery*, the issue before the Supreme Court was whether Mrs Montgomery should have been advised of the options for delivery of the fetus, and the risks and benefits of each option to enable her to exercise "choice" on which method of delivery she wished.

Her position was that had she been advised of the risks and benefits of elective caesarean section, and had she compared the risks and benefits of that procedure with the risks and benefits of proceeding with vaginal delivery, she would have opted for elective caesarean section.

The Supreme Court was also asked to define the duty of the doctor in circumstances where a patient asked questions or expressed concerns. The arguments advanced in *Montgomery* in the Court of Session and Supreme Court are considered in detail in Chapter 4.

When considering the important changes introduced by the decision of the Supreme Court in *Montgomery* it is necessary to understand the underlying concepts that formed the basis for that decision. It is suggested that the decision was important in a number of respects:

(a) The recognition of the importance of patient autonomy or self-determination in the area of information disclosure to patients.

(b) The recognition that the issue of information disclosure to patients can and should be separated from the question of diagnosis and treatment.

(c) Flowing from (a) and (b) above, the recognition that the *Bolam* or *Hunter v Hanley* (professional practice) tests are inappropriate in the area of information disclosure to patients.

(d) The introduction of a particular patient-focused test in the area of information disclosure in line with the test as formulated in *Rogers v Whitaker*.

(e) The focus on the professional guidance issued by the GMC.

(f) The confirmation that where a patient does ask questions of express concern this comes within the second limb of the test formulated in *Rogers v Whitaker*, imposing a specific duty on the doctor to consider the needs of the particular patient.

Each of the above is analysed below. However, following the decision in *Montgomery* certain basic principles can be said to apply to consent in the context of the legally competent patient:

- A doctor requires the consent of a patient to treat the patient.

- A competent patient has the right to accept or refuse treatment, even treatment that the doctor considers is in the best interests of the patient.

- A doctor cannot impose treatment on the competent patient against the will of the patient no matter how beneficial or necessary the doctor considers the treatment to be.

- A patient's valid consent cannot be substituted by a medical judgement that a treatment is in the patient's best interests.

- A patient's consent is required for any diagnostic, preventative or curative treatment.

- The right to know is not confined to the choice of treatment once a disease is present and has been conclusively diagnosed. Information should be given in respect of procedures that may lead to a diagnosis.

- A patient's consent to a particular procedure is limited to that procedure alone and does not entitle the doctor to extend the procedure because it is medically convenient to do so, or perform a different procedure because the doctor chooses to do so.

- The patient's right to receive information is not dependent on making a request for information.

- Where a patient asks questions, the doctor must answer those questions truthfully.

- The patient must receive information on alternative methods of treatment and the risks and benefits of those options.

- The disclosure of information on alternative treatments and the risks and benefits of those alternatives is not filtered by the use of the professional practice test.

- A doctor does not have to provide a patient with every hypothetical option.

- The principle of autonomy or self-determination does not permit a patient to force a doctor to proceed with treatment or a procedure that the doctor does not consider to be in the patient's best interests.

• The information given to the patient on the risks/benefits of treatment should be accurate.

• A patient may place limits on consent and a doctor should respect those limits.

• A patient may withdraw consent validly given, although the determination of this question may be a matter of fact.

2. The term "informed consent"

In this book the use of the oft-used term "informed consent" is avoided where possible. As long ago as 1988, in her book *A Patient's Right to Know: Information Disclosure, the Doctor and the Law* Professor Sheila McLean argued that this is an inappropriate term to use in this area of the law. She noted that "informed" consent is a doctrine developed in US jurisprudence and was actually specifically designed to expand the liability of doctors.

In the USA, the first hint of the use of the term is found in *Salgo v Leland Stanford Junior University Board of Trustees* (317 P 2d 170 (Cal, 1957)). It was initially held that a doctor had a duty to disclose any facts necessary to form the basis of an "intelligent" consent to the proposed treatment. The court then talked about full disclosure of facts necessary to an "informed" consent.

In the UK, the first mention of "informed consent" was in *Chatterton v Gerson* ([1981] Q.B. 432). In *Sidaway v Bethlem Royal Hospital Governors* Lord Scarman recognised that strictly speaking it is a misnomer to use the term "informed consent". To obtain real or valid consent the patient has to be "informed". There is no concept of uninformed consent. In those circumstances, there simply would be no consent.

The High Court in *Rogers v Whitaker* rejected what the court described as the oft-used and "somewhat amorphous phrase 'informed consent'", as had Lord Scarman in *Sidaway*. It was noted that the Supreme Court of Canada had been cautious in its use of the term "informed consent".

The adoption of the term "informed consent" has led a flawed interpretation of information disclosure. The quality of disclosure is implied from the quality of the decision. When thinking about consent to treatment, it is important to remember that the main focus of self-determination is *choice* rather than consent as would be implied by the term "informed consent".

It has been suggested by some writers that the term "informed consent" should be jettisoned from the discourse in this area of law. The phrase "informed consent" detracts from the aims of autonomy in three main ways. First, it incorrectly focuses on obtaining a patient's consent while in fact a refusal ought to be respected equally; secondly, it also suggests that a refusal must be measured according to a different standard – one that requires more or less disclosure; and, thirdly, it assumes that the doctor's role is to provide the information and the patient's role is to consent.

The preference is to allow patients to make "informed decisions" about the options available to them in which situation consent is obtained. It is suggested that the use of the term "real" or "valid" consent is a more appropriate term to be applied.

In *Law & Medical Ethics* (Mason and McCall Smith's 10th Edition), the writers suggest that the phrase "informed consent" is dropped from use in favour of the term "valid" consent. A term is required which pays due deference to patient autonomy and at the same time provides the doctor with a yardstick for what is expected. The writers recognise that there is a need to ensure that any spirit of confrontation between the medical profession and the public is halted. They favour the therapeutic relationship between doctor and patient described by Teff many years previously. The GMC refer to a "partnership" in medical decision-making.

3.   Patient autonomy

In *Montgomery*, the Supreme Court recognised that the concept of patient autonomy or self-determination was central to the issue of patient consent. The word autonomy derives from the Greek, *auto* meaning "self" and *nomos* meaning "custom" or "law". This principle is regarded by many eminent medical ethicists as an important or premier principle in medical ethics. To respect patient autonomy is to accept that the individual patient has a right to their own opinion, to make their own choices, and to make decisions based on their own personal values and beliefs.

It is generally accepted that human beings are entitled to respect and this is so even when the person is sick. This right is neither lost or suspended simply because they are ill, to be restored at some later point in time when they are well. The rights of the individual patient to information go beyond the nature of their illness and whether there is a cure.

Patient autonomy can only be protected where a patient is able to make a meaningful choice, on the basis of adequate information on the available treatments or therapies and the risks and benefits of each. The patient should have information about alternative procedures or treatments, the risks of those alternatives and also the potential benefits of any treatment or therapy.

The recognition of the right to appropriate disclosure of information and the patient's right to accept or reject therapy is the only way to achieve meaningful consent to treatment, or to validate the withholding of treatment. The doctor is the person who holds the information by nature of his/her education and experience. The patient does not have that information but should be the person who makes the ultimate decision about their own body. As the GMC emphasises, the patient should be an active participant in the decisions made about their own health care.

The principle when properly applied envisages a relationship that is more than one where it is accepted that "doctor knows best". On a proper application of the principle it cannot be said that disclosure of relevant information to patients about their condition of treatment is not required because they may not understand the issues. A patient may be in a vulnerable position and this should not be used as an excuse for eliminating their autonomy.

In 2009, Beauchamp and Childress explained:

> *To respect autonomous agents is to acknowledge their right to hold views, to make choices, and to take actions based on personal values and beliefs. Such respect involves respectful action, not merely a respectful attitude.... Respect, in this account, involves acknowledging the value and decision-making rights of persons and enabling then to act autonomously, whereas disrespect for autonomy involves attitudes and actions that ignore, insult, demean, or are inattentive to others' rights of autonomous action.*

The law has always recognised that the concept of autonomy of the patient is universally important. This was set out clearly by Cardozo J in *Schloendorff v Society of New York Hospital* ((1914) 211 N.Y. 125), where he said:

> *every human being of adult years and sound mind has a right to determine what shall be done with his own body; and a surgeon who performs an operation without his patient's consent commits an assault.*

In *Schloendorff* it was said that individuality and autonomy have long been central values in Anglo-American society and law. In general, the more intense and personal the consequences of the choice and the less direct or significant the impact of that choice upon others, the more compelling the claim to autonomy in the making of a given decision. Under this criterion, the case for respecting patient autonomy and decisions about health and bodily fate is very strong.

In *St. George's Healthcare NHS Trust v S (Guidelines); R v Collins Ex p. S (No.2)* ([1999] Fam.26), a woman who was in labour was advised by medical staff that she required a caesarean section and if she did not agree to this she would die, as would her baby. She refused to consent but despite this the caesarean section was performed and the Court of Appeal held that this was unlawful. The court held that the competent adult patient has the right to refuse treatment even at the risk of death. This right of choice is not limited to decisions which others may regard as sensible. It exists notwithstanding that the reasons for making the choice are rational, irrational, unknown or even non-existent (see also *Re S (Adult: Refusal of Medical Treatment)* [1993] Fam.123; *Re MB (Medical Treatment)* [1997] 8 Med. L.R. 217; *Re T [1992]* 3 W.L.R. 782).

In *Airedale NHS Trust v Bland* ([1993] A.C. 789) the court emphasised that any treatment given by a doctor to a competent patient which involves an interference with the physical integrity of the patient requires consent. Respect must be given to the wishes of the patient even if the doctor does not consider that it is in their best interest.

The principle of beneficence is closely linked with medical practice. It has been recognised as a key ethical norm (Tom L. Beauchamp and James F. Childress, *Principles of Biomedical Ethics*, Oxford University Press, 5th Edition, 2001, p12). This concept is recognised in the Hippocratic Oath and by professional bodies. The basic premise is that doctors are trained to act in a positive way that benefits the patient. This is applicable to the patient's right of autonomy or self-determination. Previously the focus has been on the benefits as determined by the medical profession, and for many years the principle was hijacked as a justification for paternalism. However, properly applied, this duty requires respect for the individual patient's autonomy. The GMC promulgation of "shared decision-making" could be seen as a method of striking a balance between the concept of patient autonomy and the doctor's role as a beneficent practitioner.

The principle of autonomy is a legal rule but is also an ethical principle based on the patient's right to "self-determination". The right to autonomy strictly construed would mean that the patient would be entitled to decide and demand what treatments they should have. However, the law does not permit a patient to dictate to the doctor what treatments they will receive.

A doctor is permitted in law to refuse to perform a procedure requested by a patient where the doctor is of the view that this procedure would not be in the best interests of the patient or could be harmful to the patient. In practice, it is recognised that in this area there is a legitimate restriction on patient choice.

In *R (Burke) v GMC* ([2005] EWCA Civ 1003 [2006] Q.B. 273) the Court of Appeal held that where a competent patient makes it clear that they do not wish to receive treatment which is, objectively, in their best medical interests, it is unlawful for doctors to administer that treatment. Personal autonomy or the right to self-determination prevails. However, it was held that autonomy and the right to self-determination did not entitle a patient to insist on receiving a particular medical treatment regardless of the nature of the treatment. Insofar as a doctor has a legal obligation to provide treatment, this cannot be founded simply on the fact that the patient demands it.

In *R (Burke)* the GMC was concerned that a doctor could be required to provide treatment to a patient, or procure another doctor to provide such treatment, even though the doctor believed the treatment was not clinically indicated. The court endorsed the following propositions advanced by the GMC:

(a) The doctor, exercising their professional clinical judgement, decides what treatment options are clinically indicated for their patient.

(b) The doctor then offers those treatment options to the patient, in the course of which they explain to the patient the risks, benefits, side effects etc. involved in each of the treatment options.

(c) The patient then decides whether they wish to accept any of those treatment options and, if so, which one. In the vast majority of cases they will, of course, decide which treatment option they consider to be in their best interests and, in doing so, they will or may take into account other, non-clinical, factors. However, they can, if they wish, decide to accept (or refuse) the treatment option on the basis of reasons which are irrational of for no reasons at all.

(d) If the patient chooses one of the treatment options offered to him, the doctor will proceed to provide it.

(e) If, however, they refuse all of the treatment options offered to them and instead inform the doctor that they want some form of treatment which the doctor has not offered, the doctor will no doubt discuss that form of treatment with the patient (assuming that it is a form of treatment known to the doctor) but if the doctor concludes that this treatment is not clinically indicated he is not required (i.e. he is under no legal obligation) to provide it to the patient, although he should offer to arrange a second opinion.

In *Consent: Patients and Doctors Making Decisions Together* (2nd June 2008), the GMC provides:

If the patient asks for a treatment that the doctor considers would not be of overall benefit to them, the doctor should discuss the issues with the patient and explore the reasons for their request. If, after discussion, the doctor still considers that the treatment would not be of overall benefit to the patient, they do not have to provide the treatment. But they should explain their reasons to the patient, and explain any other options that are available, including the option to seek a second opinion. (5 d)

This issue was considered recently in the case of an 11-month-old baby called Charlie Gard who suffered from encephalomyopathic mitochondrial DNA depletion syndrome, an extremely rare genetic condition. His parents wanted him to have what was said to be an experimental treatment that was only available in the USA. The doctors at Great

Ormond Street Hospital disagreed with the views of the parents as to the suitability of this treatment. They did not consider that any treatment could reverse the brain damage that Charlie had suffered and that his best interests would be served by withdrawing treatment.

The case went first to the High Court, then to the Court of Appeal, then to the Supreme Court and finally to the European Court of Human Rights (*Gard v United Kingdom* (Admissibility) (39793/17) [2017] 2 F.L.R. 773)) The judge in the High Court found on the evidence that it was not in the child's best interests to have further treatment and ultimately this decision was upheld.

However, the patient does have the absolute right to refuse treatment and that is more consistent with a right to bodily integrity. This is dealt with below. The concepts inherent in this right were stated to be the bedrock upon which the principles of self-determination and individual autonomy are based. It has also been suggested that involving the patient as an active participant in the process does assist in the treatment of the patient.

Other jurisdictions have recognised the principle of autonomy as being fundamental to the question of information disclosure to patients. In Canada, in *Ciarlariello Estate v Schacter* ([1993] 2 S.C.R. 119, 100 D.L.R. (4th) 609 at 618) Cory J said:

> *It should not be forgotten that every patient has a right to bodily integrity. This encompasses the right to determine what medical procedures will be accepted and the extent to which they will be accepted.... This concept of individual autonomy is fundamental to the common law and is the basis for the requirement that disclosure be made to a patient.*

In determining the test to be applied in consent cases in the UK, the Supreme Court recognised the fundamental importance of patient autonomy and the patient's right to make choices about his/her own life. The assessment of a person as legally competent implies that the person is autonomous and as such their decisions should be respected.

There has been a clear shift in focus from medical paternalism to respect for patient autonomy.

In *Montgomery*, Lords Kerr and Reed held:

> *patients are now widely regarded as persons holding rights, rather than as the passive recipients of the care of the medical profession. They are also widely regarded as consumers exercising choices.... It would therefore be a mistake to view patients as uninformed, incapable of understanding medical matters, or wholly dependent upon a flow of information from doctors.* (para 75)

> *The social and legal developments which we have mentioned point away from a model of the relationship between the doctor and the patient based upon medical paternalism.* (para 81)

Lady Hale held:

> *It is now well recognised that the interest which the law of negligence protects is a person's interest in their own physical and psychiatric integrity, an important feature of which is their autonomy, their freedom to decide what shall and shall not be done with their body.* (para 108)

It was noted that under the stimulus of the Human Rights Act 1998 the courts have become increasingly conscious of the extent to which the common law reflects fundamental values. The right to respect for private life is protected by Article 8 of the European Convention on Human Rights. The resulting duty to involve the patient in decisions relating to their treatment has been recognised in judgments of the European Convention on Human Rights, such as *Glass v United Kingdom* ((2004) EHRR 341) and *Tysiac v Poland* ((2007) 45 EHRR 947 at 80).

The GMC was represented at the hearing in the Supreme Court, although it had not been represented at any of the previous hearings. It came into the action as an intervener shortly before the Supreme Court hearing and was able to provide the court with a summary of the position of the GMC on the issue of patient consent. The GMC documentation on *Good Medical Practice* and the documentation on patient consent were provided to the court.

Consent: Patients and Doctors Making Decisions Together provides:

> *For a relationship between doctor and patient to be effective, it should be a partnership based on openness, trust and good communication. Each person has a role to play in making decisions about or care.* (para 3 2008 Guidance)

It is clear that the Supreme Court took account of the view of the professional body in coming to its conclusion:

> *The submission on behalf of the General Medical Council acknowledged, in relation to these documents, that an approach based upon the informed involvement of patients in their treatment, rather than their being passive and potentially reluctant recipients, can have therapeutic benefits, and is regarded as an integral aspect of professionalism in treatment.* (para 78)

The prioritisation of the individual right of autonomy or self-determination by the Supreme Court was the first important change made in *Montgomery*. Patients are now recognised in law as having the right to make choices about their own health. The court understood that the right of the individual patient is distinct from the hypothetical reasonable patient and that an individual patient might legitimately make choices that a hypothetical reasonable patient might not do.

Lord Scarman in *Sidaway* had not gone so far as to focus on the individual patient, and intentionally did not do so. *Pearce* could not in law introduce a specific patient-focused test since the test in *Sidaway* was binding upon the court. *Pearce* did however focus on a "reasonable patient" but did not assume a "reasonable patient in the patient's position". In *Montgomery*, the test now becomes a specific test that recognises the right of the individual patient to receive information and participate in decisions about their own health care. Respect for the patient's right to self-determination demands no less an approach.

4.   The separation of information disclosure

A second important factor in the Supreme Court decision in *Mont-gomery* was the separation of the disclosure of information to patients from the duty of the doctor in areas of diagnosis and treatment. For many years, writers in ethics had suggested that it was essential to make this distinction in the area of information disclosure cases but the courts had failed either to understand or grapple with this issue.

In *Law, Ethics and Medicine* (1984) P.D.G. Skegg said that there is nothing "medical" about the requirement that a doctor must obtain a patient's consent. The requirement to obtain the patient's consent is imposed not in the interests of the patient's health but in the interests of individual liberty.

In *Canterbury v Spence* (464 F 2d 772 (1972) (U.S.C.A., District of Colum-bia)) the court distinguished between those aspects of a doctor's duty that are technical and those that are not:

> *The context in which the duty of risk disclosure arises is invariably the occasion for the decision as to whether a particular treatment procedure is to be undertaken. To the physician, whose training enables a self-satisfying evaluation, the answer may seem clear, but it is the prerogative of the patient, not the physician, to determine for himself the direction in which his interests seem to lie. To enable the patient to chart his course understandably, some familiarity with the therapeutic alternatives and their hazards becomes essential.*

The *Canterbury* test was not accepted in a significant number of US states but it is regarded as a highly influential decision. The court saw formidable obstacles to the acceptance of the notion that the doctor's obligation to disclose is either germinated or limited by medical prac-tice. Patients do require access to medical information to enable them to make a decision but the ultimate decision is often based on more than clinical matters. The doctor is unable to properly evaluate the "patient factors" in a decision-making process.

In *Sidaway*, Lord Scarman understood that there were often non-medical factors which influenced a patient's decision-making and recognised the duty of a doctor to:

> ... *provide his patient with the information needed to enable the patient to consider and balance the medical advantages and risks alongside other relevant matters, such as, for example, his family, business or social responsibilities of which the doctor may be only partially, if at all, informed.*
>
> *The doctor's concern is with health and relief of pain. These are medical objectives. But a patient may well have in mind circumstances, objectives, and values which he may reasonably not make known to the doctor which may lead him to a different decision from that suggested by purely medical opinion.* (paras 885–886)

He recognised the different nature of the doctor's duty and the fact that the ultimate decision should be legal not medical:

> *In a medical negligence case where the issue is as to the advice and information given to the patient as to the treatment proposed, the available options and the risk, the court is concerned primarily with the patient's rights. The doctor's duty arises from the patient's right. If one considers the scope of the doctor's duty by beginning with the right of the patient to make his own decision whether he will or will not undergo the treatment proposed, the right to be informed of significant risks and the doctor's corresponding duty are easy to understand, for the proper implementation of the right requires that the doctor be under a duty to inform his patient of the material risks inherent in the treatment.*

In their research, Faden and Beuchamp suggested that 88% of subjects in their study made decisions based on factors external to the information given (*Decision-Making and Informed Consent: A study of the Impact of Disclosed Information*, Social Indicators Research, 7, 1980).

In Australia, the courts have held that there is a fundamental difference between diagnosis and treatment and the provision of advice and information to a patient. It has long been recognised that, in diagnosis and treatment, the patient's contribution is limited to the narration of symptoms and relevant history. In this scenario, the medical practitioner provides the diagnosis and treatment according to their level of skill. However, with the exception of cases of emergency and necessity, all medical treatment is preceded by the patient's choice to undergo it.

In the information disclosure case, choice is meaningless unless it is made on the basis of relevant information and advice. It has been held in Australia that, because the choice to be made calls for a decision by the patient on information known to the medical practitioner but not to the patient, it would be illogical to hold that the amount of information provided can be determined from the perspective of the practitioner alone, or for that matter the medical profession. It was concluded that whether a patient has been given all the relevant information is not a question to which the answer depends upon medical standards or practices.

In Canada, in *Reibl v Hughes* there was also a recognition of the distinction:

> *Expert medical evidence is, of course, relevant to findings as to the risks that reside in or are a result of recommended surgery or other treatment.... The issue under consideration is a different issue from that involved where the question is whether the doctor carried out his professional activities by applicable professional standards. What is under consideration here is the patient's right to know what risks are involved in undergoing or foregoing certain surgery or other treatment.* (paras 894–895)

In *Montgomery*, it was argued by the claimant that there is an important and crucial distinction between the types of duties owed to patients by treating doctors. The doctor has a duty of care in the performance of treatment, and in making a diagnosis. There is a separate duty to the moral or ethical duty which relates to information disclosure. The provision of information permits patients to make choices about what risks they are prepared to run. Medical choice depends on factors that transcend professional training and knowledge.

The Supreme Court accepted that the doctor's duty in relation to information disclosure is separate and distinct from the duty of the doctor in the area of diagnosis and treatment. They recognised as important the fact that patient choice in this context did not depend exclusively on medical considerations.

They noted the fundamental difference between the doctor's role in diagnosis and treatment and their role in discussing with the patient any recommended treatment and the risks and benefits of the alternatives to treatment. The court held:

> … it is a non sequitur to conclude that the question whether a risk of injury, or the availability of an alternative form of treatment, ought to be discussed with the patient is also a matter of purely professional judgement. The doctor's advisory role cannot be regarded as solely an exercise of medical skill without leaving out of account the patient's entitlement to decide on the risks to her health which she is willing to run (a decision which may be influenced by non-medical considerations). Responsibility for determining the nature and extent of a person's rights rests with the courts, not with the medical profession. (para 83)

> The "informed choice" qualification rests on a fundamentally different premise: it is predicated on the view that the patient is entitled to be told of risks where that is necessary for her to make an informed decision whether to incur them. (para 61)

It is clear from reading the decision in *Montgomery* that the Supreme Court not only highlighted the fundamental principle of patient autonomy or self-determination but also identified that questions of disclosure of information to patients must therefore logically be separated from questions related to the duty of the doctor in diagnosis and treatment. In law, issues of information disclosure are now considered a separate and distinct ground of fault to be dealt with by the courts in a different way from traditional professional negligence. This brings the UK into line with other common-law jurisdictions.

5. The use of the professional practice test

Having identified that the key underlying principle was respect for patient autonomy and self-determination, and consequently that the question of information disclosure must be separated from other aspects of the duty of the doctor, the inevitable result must be that the *Bolam* or *Hunter v Hanley* tests are not applicable to this area of the law. The application of such tests is fundamentally inconsistent with these principles.

Prior to *Montgomery* UK law on patient consent was found in the decision of the House of Lords in *Sidaway v Board of Governors of the Bethlem Royal Hospital and the Maudsley Hospital*. A full analysis of this decision is found in Chapter 2. Kennedy and Grubb argued that Lord Diplock was in the minority in *Sidaway* and that the majority rejected the *Bolam* test in information disclosure cases. Margaret Brazier argued that *Sidaway* simply reaffirmed professional standards. Others concluded that *Bolam* had been retained but modified.

In *Bolam*, the issue of information disclosure was one aspect of the case. In the speech to the jury there was no attempt to distinguish the provision of information from any other aspect of the doctor's duty of care to their patient. It was suggested to the jury that it was acceptable for a doctor to not advise of the risks of a therapy if the doctor felt that it was in the patient's best interests and that the patient would be put off if advised of the risks.

The obligation to make disclosure was not defined in terms of the patient's rights. The effect of the *Bolam* test, pre-*Bolitho*, was that the medical profession was permitted to determine what was acceptable practice in terms of the communication of information to patients without any check.

The problem with using the *Bolam* test in the area of information disclosure is that this this test is more concerned with professional consensus and standards than with the rights of the patient. The peculiarities of the particular patient are not considered and non-medical considerations are irrelevant.

The existence of a discernible custom or practice reflecting a respectable medical consensus must be seriously in doubt. Professor Kennedy (*The Patient on the Clapham Omnibus*, 1984 47 MLR 454) has described it as "an obvious fiction" and "something of a nonsense". The professional standard of disclosure has been said to unreasonably subordinate the interest of the patient to the whim of the medical community. Professor Kennedy identifies the basic moral principle to tell the truth and notes that any exceptions to that principle should not rest on the unarticulated say-so of the doctor.

Sir John Donaldson in the Court of Appeal judgment in *Sidaway* and Lord Scarman in the House of Lords recognised the importance of patient autonomy in the information disclosure case. Lord Scarman praised the *Canterbury* test and was not prepare to accept that professional practice should be determinative in the information case. He focused on the issue of patients' rights. If the professional test were deemed appropriate, then:

> *The implications of this view of the law are disturbing. It leaves the determination of a legal duty to the judgement of doctors.... It would be a strange conclusion if courts should be led to conclude that our law, which undoubtedly recognises the right of the patient to decide whether he will accept or reject the treatment proposed, should permit the doctors to determine whether and in what circumstances a duty arises, requiring the doctor to warn his patient of the risks inherent in the treatment which he proposes.*

Prior to *Bolitho*, decisions following *Sidaway* were inconsistent. The Court of Appeal interpreted *Sidaway* in both *Blyth v Bloomsbury Health Authority* ([1993] 4 Med. L.R. 151 C.A.) and *Gold v Haringey Health Authority* ([1988] Q.B. 481). Both judgments have been heavily criticised by writers.

In *McAllister v Lewisham and North Southwark Health Authority* ([1994] 5 Med. L.R. 343, QBD), whilst endorsing the *Bolam* test Rougier J concluded that there were certain risks that did have to be disclosed irrespective of professional practice. It was held that patients were entitled to be given sufficient information on the risks of an operation to enable them to exercise a balanced judgement. (See also *Smith v Tunbridge Wells Health Authority* ([1994] 5 Med. L.R. 334); *Gascoine v Sheridan* ([1994] 5 Med. L.R. 437); *Doughty v North Staffordshire Health Authority* ([1992] 3 Med. L.R. 81); *Newell and Newell v Goldenberg* ([1995] 6 Med. L.R. 371)).

In *Bolitho v City and Hackney Health Authority* ([1998] A.C. 232) the *Bolam* test was considered, although not in the context of information disclosure. It was recognised that in the vast majority of cases the fact that distinguished experts in the field are of a particular opinion will demonstrate the reasonableness of that opinion. Lord Browne-Wilkinson held that only rarely would the courts conclude that an expert's opinion is not logically defensible. Academic reaction to the decision was mixed.

In *Pearce v United Bristol Healthcare NHS Trust* ([1999] P.I.Q.R P53; (1999) 48 BMLR 118) the Court of Appeal was asked to consider the question of information disclosure. It was submitted on behalf of the claimant that when looking at the question of the adequacy of advice given by a doctor the courts are not confined to follow the test in *Bolam*. The claimant lost her case but Lord Woolf MR held:

> *In a case where it is being alleged that a plaintiff has been deprived of the opportunity to make a proper decision as to what course he or she should take in relation to treatment, it seems to me to be the law ... that if there is a significant risk which would affect the judgement*

of a reasonable patient, then in the normal course it is the responsib-
ility of a doctor to inform the patient of that significant risk, if the
information is needed so that the patient can determine for him or
herself as to what course he or she should adopt.

Pearce was a case where the claimant had a choice between intervention
or not in terms of delivery of her baby. The duty to disclose in this
statement is restricted to a "significant" risk that would affect the judgement of "a reasonable patient". Although reluctant to define "significant", Lord Woolf MR then focused on a 10% risk, which one of
the experts had suggested was the level of risk that would trigger a duty
to disclose. He held that the 0.1–0.2 % risk in this case was not significant.

In this decision, there was focus on statistical probability alone in assessing the significance of the risk. The question of the significance of the
risk appears to be the first question to address. He appeared to accept
the decision of the medical experts on what would be classified as
"significant". He permitted the medical profession to filter what risks
were included for consideration. There was no consideration of "individual patient factors", nor was there any consideration of the
potentially serious consequences should the risk materialise.

More problematically for those who advance a concept of information
disclosure based on the principles of autonomy and self-determination
of the patient, the relevance of the risk in *Pearce* was to an objectively
reasonable patient. There was no suggestion of that the subjective position of the particular patient should be a factor taken into account
when assessing risk. The difficulty with the objective patient approach is
that this does not comply with the patient's right to autonomy or self-
determination, which is the foundation for information disclosure. The
Australian courts have emphasised that it is the individual patient who
matters and not the hypothetical or imaginary reasonable patient.

In Maclean, *Beyond Bolam and Bolitho*, it was said of the decision in
Pearce:

The standard becomes: the doctor must disclose those risks that the reasonable doctor believes the reasonable patient ought to find significant to a decision. This view may be cynical, but the judgement in Pearce, and the court's apparent reliance on percentages and expert assessment of significance, does nothing to dispel that cynicism.

In *Wyatt v Curtis* ([2003] EWCA Civ 1779) the issue was one of causation. However, Sedley LJ interpreted Lord Woolf's test to recognise the patient's subjective appreciation of risks:

Lord Woolf's formulation refines Lord Bridge's test by recognising that what is substantial and what is grave are questions on which the doctor's and the patient's perception may differ, and in relation to which the doctor must therefore have regard to what may be the patient's perception.

The House of Lords in *Chester v Afshar* ([2005] 1 A.C. 134) did recognise that medical paternalism no longer ruled and appeared to endorse the decision in *Pearce*. However, in the information disclosure case the spectre of the professional practice test found in *Bolam* and *Hunter v Hanley* remained.

One recognised justification for withholding of filtering information is the so-called therapeutic privilege (or "therapeutic exception", to use the terminology in *Montgomery*). This concept is dealt with later in this chapter. This is the only recognised justification for withholding information and it is accepted this should be used in rare and exceptional circumstances. If the professional practice test is permitted to be used to determine what options are discussed with a patient and the risks and benefits of those options, this is another situation where information is filtered. This runs counter to the foundation principle that the patient should ordinarily make the choice for themselves. To apply the test to information disclosure ignores the patient's right to self-determination.

In legal systems that take the patient's right of self-determination as a starting point in determining the scope of disclosure, the professional standard is rejected. In *Canterbury v Spence* it was said that:

> *Respect for the patient's right of self-determination … demands a standard set by law for physicians rather than one which physicians may or may not impose on themselves.*

In Australia and Canada, it is recognised that when information patients are given about alternative treatments and the risks of the alternatives is filtered by professional practice this frustrates the principle of patient autonomy.

In 1992 in *Rogers v Whitaker* ((1992) 109 A.L.R. 625; [1993] 4 Med.L.R. 79 (H.C. of Aust.)) the High Court of Australia specifically disapproved *Bolam* in information cases. In Australia, even in the sphere of diagnosis and treatment, which was described as the "heartland of the skilled medical practitioner", the *Bolam* principle has not always been applied.

In the area of provision of advice and information and non-disclosure of risk, the *Bolam* test has been completely discarded in Australia for some time. In *Breen v Williams* ((1996) 138 A.L.R. 259 H.C. (Aust)) it was said that the decision in *Rogers v Whitaker* took away from the medical profession in Australia the right to determine, in proceedings for negligence, what amounts to acceptable medical standards. Professor Jones, in his book *Medical Negligence*, also states that in Australia the High Court rejected the *Bolam* test as an appropriate standard for the disclosure of information by the medical profession.

In *Rogers v Whitaker* the court held that it was for the courts to adjudicate on what is the appropriate standard of care after giving weight to "the paramount consideration that a person is entitled to make his own decisions about his life":

> *… the choice is, in reality, meaningless unless it is made on the basis of relevant information and advice. Because the choice to be made calls for a decision by the patient on information known to the*

medical practitioner but not to the patient, it would be illogical to hold that the amount of information to be provided by the medical practitioner can be determined from the perspective of the practitioner alone or, for that matter, of the medical profession.

Whether a medical practitioner carries out a particular form of treatment in accordance with the appropriate standard of care is a question in the resolution of which responsible professional opinion will have an influential, often decisive, role to play: whether the patient has been given all the relevant information to choose between undergoing and not undergoing the treatment is a question of a different order. Generally speaking, it is not a question the answer to which depends upon medical standards or practices.

The decision in *Rogers v Whitaker* followed the approach favoured by the full Court of the Supreme Court of Australia in the South Australian case of *F v R* ((1983) 33 SASR 189 (FC)). *F v R* was decided two years before *Sidaway* and the court refused to apply the *Bolam* test. King CJ, at 194, explained:

The ultimate question, however, is not whether the defendant's conduct accords with the practices of his profession or some part of it, but whether it conforms to the standard of reasonable care demanded by the law. That is a question for the court and the duty of deciding it cannot be delegated to any profession or group in the community.

King CJ agreed with the approach of the Supreme Court in Canada in *Reibl v Hughes*:

To allow expert medical evidence to determine what risks are material and, hence, should be disclosed and, correlatively, what risks are not material is to hand over to the medical profession the entire question of the scope of the duty of disclosure, including the question whether there has been a breach of that duty ... this is not a question that is to be concluded on the basis of the expert medical evidence alone. The issue under consideration is a different issue from that involved in where the question is whether the doctor carried out his professional activities by applicable standards. What is under consideration here is the patient's right to know what risks are involved in undergoing or foregoing certain surgery or other treatment. [894-895]

Since *Reibl v Hughes* in 1980 the Canadian courts have rejected the professional standard test as a means of deciding whether a patient has been given sufficient information to enable them to make an informed decision on how to proceed.

The Supreme Court of Canada, per Cory J for the majority, in *Arndt v Smith* said of the decision in *Reibl v Hughes*:

Reibl is a very significant and leading authority. It marks the rejection of the paternalistic approach to determining how much information should be given to patients. It emphasises the patient's right to know and ensures that patients will have the benefit of a high standard of disclosure.

In *Montgomery*, the Supreme Court also referred to the Australian case of *Rosenberg v Percival* ([2001] H.C.A. 18; (2001) 178 A.L.R. 577). In *Rosenberg* the court noted that in *Rogers v Whitaker* the *Bolam* test was rejected. Reference was made to the statement by Gaudron and McHugh JJ in *Breen v Williams* ((1996) 186 CLR 71 at 114) where it was held that "Rogers took away from the medical profession in the country the right to determine, in proceedings for negligence, what amounts to acceptable medical standards." In *Rosenberg,* the court also accepted that whether a medical practitioner carries out a particular form of treatment in accordance with the appropriate standard of care is a question in which responsible professional opinion will have an influential, often decisive role to play. Whether the patient has been given all the relevant information to choose between undergoing and not undergoing the treatment is a question of a different order. Generally speaking, it is not a question to which the answer depends upon medical standards or practices.

In *Montgomery*, it was argued that in *Sidaway* the House of Lords had retained the *Bolam* test within the context of the information disclosure case but had created an exception to the application of the test. The argument made in the Supreme Court is set out in detail in Chapter 4.

Submissions were made by the claimant to the Supreme Court that the professional practice test found in *Bolam* and *Hunter v Hanley* had no application to a case based on what information should be disclosed to a patient about options for treatment, and the risks and benefits of those options. Reference was made to other jurisdictions which had recognised the test as inappropriate in information disclosure cases.

It was argued that the *Bolam* test focuses on what doctors do, rather than what they should do. This is questionable in all areas of practice given the advent of other means by which the court can assess the question of negligence, but particularly so in information disclosure cases, where patient autonomy must be respected.

The professional practice test is not a legitimate basis for reaching conclusions which affect the rights of patients. There is no consideration of the patient's interests in the *Bolam* test. In this area of the law the courts have a primary role in delivering independent judgments on how patient autonomy can be respected. The relevant information is not derived from the accepted wisdom of the profession.

If the aim of disclosure is to protect individual autonomy or "choice", this is not a matter appropriately defined by the standard of professional practice (*Hunter v Hanley* or *Bolam* tests). If the issue is solely the execution of technical professional duty, then there is a logic in permitting medical input in the form of expert witness testimony to assist the court in deciding whether the conduct falls below an acceptable standard. This area is not directly a question of a patient's right. However, it is important that such testimony is subject to proper analysis by the courts.

Where the question is one of information disclosure and the rights of the patient, there is no such logical argument. The use of a professional practice test in the area places the question firmly in the hands of the doctor/medical expert. The validity of consent is then tested not by what patients want to know but by what doctors decide that patients can be permitted to know. The standard demanded should be a standard set by law and not one prescribed by doctors by means of practice. Such a standard can never address the right of the individual. Individual patients' health care choices involve profound questions that are distinct for the question of professional practice.

It was argued in *Montgomery* that the medical profession should not be permitted to filter information or to substitute their own best medical judgements for the informed decision of the patient. The duty to provide the patient with information should not be defined by the amount of information the doctor thinks the patient should know but by the information the patient needs to enable them to make an autonomous "choice". Where the focus is to be on options for treatment or the implications of a procedure, it is clear that the question of what should be disclosed cannot be determined in the abstract or indeed by a professional practice test.

In *Montgomery*, the Supreme Court understood that it was being asked to depart from the decision of the House of Lords in Sidaway and to "re-consider the duty of a doctor towards a patient in relation to advice about treatment" (para 4).

The Supreme Court concluded that it was wrong to regard *Sidaway* as an unqualified endorsement of the application of the *Bolam* test to the giving of advice about treatment. Only Lord Diplock adopted that position. On his approach, the only situation – other than the one covered by the *Bolam* test – in which a doctor would be under a duty to provide information to a patient would be where a patient asked questions:

> … *because the extent to which a doctor may be inclined to discuss risks with a patient is not determined by medical learning or experience, the application of the* Bolam *test to this question is liable to result in the sanctioning of differences in practice which are attributable not to divergent schools of thought in medical science, but merely*

to divergent attitudes among doctors as to the degree of respect owed to their patients. (para 84)

It follows that the analysis of the law by the majority in Sidaway *is unsatisfactory in so far as it treated the doctor's duty to advise her patient of the risks of proposed treatment as falling within the scope of the* Bolam *test, subject to two qualifications of that general principle, neither of which is fundamentally consistent with that test.... There is no reason to perpetuate the application of the* Bolam *test in this context any longer.* (para 86)

The Supreme Court then set out the correct test to be applied and pointed clearly to the decision of the High Court of Australia in *Rogers v Whitaker*, where the *Bolam* test was rejected in information disclosure cases. The court recognised that departing from the *Bolam* test would reduce the predictability of the outcome of litigation but felt that respect for dignity of patients required the removal of this test:

It appears to us however that a degree of unpredictability can be tolerated as the consequence of protecting patients from exposure to risks of injury which they would otherwise have chosen to avoid. The more fundamental response to such points, however, is that respect for the dignity of patients requires no less. (para 93)

The Supreme Court correctly identified the problem with a professional practice test in the area of information disclosure:

Furthermore, because the extent to which a doctor may be inclined to discuss risks with a patient is not determined by medical learning or experience, the application of the Bolam *test to this question is liable to result in the sanctioning of differences in practice which are attributable not to divergent schools of thought in medical science, but merely to divergent attitudes among doctors as to the decree of respect owed to their patients.* (para 84)

Lady Hale held (para 115):

Once the argument departs from purely medical considerations and involves value judgements … it becomes clear … that the Bolam test, of conduct supported by a responsible body of medical opinion, becomes quite inapposite.

In correctly identifying and defining the fact that information disclosure to patients can and should be separated from the duty in respect of diagnosis and treatment, and in highlighting the difficulties with the application of a professional practice test, the Supreme Court heralded the death of *Bolam* in this area of the law:

It follows that the analysis of the law by the majority in Sidaway is unsatisfactory, in so far as it treated the doctor's duty to advise her patient of the risks of proposed treatment as falling within the scope of the Bolam test, subject to two qualifications of that general principle, neither of which is fundamentally consistent with that test. It is unsurprising that courts have found difficulty in the subsequent application of Sidaway, and that the courts in England and Wales have in reality departed from it; a position which was effectively endorsed, particularly by Lord Steyn, in Chester v Afshar. There is no reason to perpetuate the application of the Bolam test in this context any longer. (para 86)

In the sixth edition of *Medicine, Patients and the Law* (Margaret Brazier and Emma Cave), under the heading "Bye bye Bolam", it is said that the Supreme Court in *Montgomery* ended decades of judicial deference to medical paternalism and "has forthrightly rejected any role for the Bolam test in information disclosure".

The original GMC guidance on consent in 1998 and the later guidance effective from June 2008 make no reference to any professional practice test as appropriate in limiting the amount of information patients should be given.

In November 2016, the Royal College of Surgeons of London produced guidance on consent entitled *Consent: Supported Decision Making*. The guidance was formulated following the decision in *Montgomery*. There is recognition within the guidance that in law the *Bolam* test no longer applies to the area of information disclosure (consent).

The following key principles are said to underpin consent:

- The aim of the discussion about consent is to give the patient the information they need to make a decision about what treatment or procedure (if any) they want.

- The discussion has to be tailored to the individual patient. This requires time to get to know the patient well enough to understand their views and values.

- All reasonable treatment options, along with their implications, should be explained to the patient.

- Material risks for each option should be discussed with the patient. The test of materiality is twofold: *whether, in the circumstances of the particular case, a reasonable person in the patient's position would be likely to attach significance to the risk, or the doctor is or should reasonably be aware that the particular patient would likely attach significance to it.*

6. Information on alternative therapies

In many health care situations, there are alternatives to the treatment or therapy proposed. The fundamental question is one of information disclosure to enable the patient to make a "choice". There is always the option to provide no treatment at all.

Patient autonomy must also be protected by the recognition of the right of the patient to participate meaningfully in a discussion about the choice of treatment or therapy. The function of disclosure of the information is to place the patient in a position where they can make a decision about whether or not to accept a proposed treatment or therapy. A patient requires information to facilitate the decision-making process.

Full vindication of patient autonomy necessitates placing the final authority regarding important decisions in the hands of a patient who has the capacity and desire to exercise it. The choice of a particular therapy of treatment may involve more than just the medical analysis of risks and benefits. The patient should be permitted to select the therapy most suited to their own emotional, personal or financial situation.

It is argued that doctors should only offer patients treatments or therapies that the treating doctor thinks is suitable. It is said that offering a treatment that the doctor does not consider to be good or the best treatment is not sound medical practice. However, this approach is paternalistic and denies the patient the right to make an informed choice. It is also not consistent with the advice given by the GMC.

As a starting point the patient has to be informed of the alternatives to treatment, and the risks and benefits of those alternatives, including the alternative of no treatment. If there are options for treatment the patient should be advised of these options, and the risks and benefits of each option. In the case of an adult with capacity, treatment is not justified in the absence of consent because it is beneficial to the patient, or in the patient's interests.

In *Canterbury v Spence* it was said that it is:

> *evident that it is normally impossible to obtain a consent worthy of the name unless the physician first elucidates the options and the perils for the patient's edification.*

In *Sidaway*, Sir John Donaldson MR said that the courts cannot "stand idly by of the profession by an excess of paternalism, denies its patient a real choice" between available options.

In *Pearce*, Cranston J held that:

> *The duty to inform a patient of the significant risks will not be discharged unless she is made aware that fewer, or no, risks are associated with another procedure. In other words, unless the patient is*

informed of the comparative risks of different procedures she will not be in a position to give her fully informed consent to one procedure rather than another.

Does this mean that a doctor is required to tell a patient about every conceivable alternative treatment? Only full and complete disclosure would allow a truly autonomous decision to be made. However, it is recognised that such full disclosure would be unreasonable and, in some situations, unhelpful. It has been said that overwhelming a patient with information the patient cannot assimilate is not a means of empowering the patient (Waller, B.N., *The Psychological Structure of Patient Autonomy*).

Patient-centred tests in other jurisdictions do not suggest that all information must be supplied to a patient. In Canada, there is a requirement to advise the patient of alternative methods of treatment and their risks, including the risks of the alternatives.

In *Zimmer v Ringrose* ((1981) 124 D.L.R. (3d) 215 (Alta. C.A.)) it was held that the physician or surgeon should discuss the benefits to be gained from the recommended treatment or operation, the advantages and disadvantages associated with alternative procedures and the consequences of forgoing treatment (see also *Brito v Wooley* [2001] B.C.J. No. 1692 (B.C.S.C)). To discharge their duty of care the doctor must give the patient some yardstick against which the patient can assess the options available to them.

In *Dickson v Pinder* (2010 489 AR 54; 2010 ABQB 269) Yamauchi J talked of a fact-dependent assessment process and held that:

A patient cannot make a meaningful and informed choice to consent to therapy unless that patient knows the consequences of other reasonable alternatives or inaction, and can balance the risks and benefits of the proposed therapy against those alternatives.

Failure to advise the patient of options or alternative treatment/s is recognised as depriving the patient of the right to make a fully informed choice (*Van Mol (Guardian ad Litem of) v Ashmore* (1999) 168 D.L.R. (4ᵗʰ) 637 (B.C.C.A.)) (see also *Walker (Litigation Guardian of) v Region 2 Hospital Corp* (1993 116 D.L.R. (4ᵗʰ) 477), where a 15-year-old was entitled to refuse consent to blood transfusions).

In Canada, it is said that a reasonable alternative may be to delay the procedure either to obtain more information or to try alternative or conservative measures (*Semeniuk v Cox* (2000) 76 Alta. L.R. (3d) 30 (Q.B.)). Similarly, if non-treatment is a reasonable alternative then that too ought to be disclosed (*Haughian v Paine* (1987) 37 D.L.R. (4ᵗʰ) 624; *Sicard v Sendziak*, 2008 ABQB 690; *Guay v Wong*, 2008 ABQB 638). If inaction involves a risk, then logically this is something a patient would want to know.

Advice should include any other reasonable forms of diagnostic testing or medical or surgical management. What is reasonable depends on the risks and benefits of the options, the availability of the option, and whether it is reasonable in the context of the management of the particular patient (*Rayner v Knickle* (1988) 47 C.C.L.T. 141 72 Nfld).

In *Rayner v Knickle* ((1988) 47 C.C.L.T. 141 72 Nfld) the court held that the correct summary of a doctor's duty of disclosure was that he must describe to their patient:

(a) how the procedure is carried out;

(b) the benefits of having the procedure done;

(c) the material or special or unusual risks of having the procedure done or forgoing the procedure;

(d) any alternatives to the procedure; and

(e) the risks associated with the alternatives.

In *Seney v Crooks* ((1988) 166 D.L.R. (4ᵗʰ) 337 (Alta.C.A.)) the court held that the mere fact that a doctor prefers one treatment over another does not relieve them of the obligation to advise of other acceptable and known procedures because "[t]hat is what the duty to inform is all about". A patient should be informed of a known treatment which other doctors in the speciality consider to be superior, even if the doctor does not agree.

In *Van Mol (Guardian ad Litem of) v Ashmore* ((1999) 168 D.L.R. (4th) 637 (B.C.C.A.)) the British Columbia Court of Appeal held that a patient should have been informed about the three surgical alternatives that were being considered to repair a narrowing of her aorta, and the risks and advantages of each of them. It was also held that she should have been informed that she could obtain a second opinion before deciding to proceed with surgery.

There has been a tendency to place emphasis on sufficient information to enable the patient to make "intelligent", "informed" or "balanced" decisions. The GMC guidance does not suggest this to be the case and the test as developed by other common-law jurisdictions does not suggest that every conceivable treatment must be discussed. The doctor must advise the patient of reasonable medical treatments and alternatives to treatment. What is reasonable however is not to be judged by reference to professional practice in relation to selection of options or alternatives (*Hunter v Hanley* or *Bolam*). The patient does not need to be advised of hypothetical possibilities.

Even prior to *Montgomery* there appeared to be an understanding that a doctor was required to advise a patient of the options for treatment. It was not suggested that the information on options of treatment should be subject to the filter of the professional practice test.

In *Birch v University College London Hospital NHS Foundation Trust* ([2008] EWHC 2237) the argument was that information about other options and their comparative risks were essential to discharge the doctor's duty. In this case, it was accepted that there was no discussion about the alternative procedure, namely MRI. There had been a discussion about the risks involved in catheter angiography. The comparative risks between MRI and cerebral angiogram were not discussed. This case was decided before *Montgomery* on the basis of Lord Woolf's formulation in *Pearce*. Cranston J held:

> *the duty to inform a patient of the significant risks will not be discharged unless she is made aware of that fewer, or no, risks are associated with another procedure. In other words, unless the patient is informed of the comparative risks of different procedures she will not be in a position to give her fully informed consent to one procedure rather than another.* (para 74)

In *Nicholas v Imperial College NHS Trust* ([2012] EWHC 591), another pre- *Montgomery* case, it was held that there had been a breach of duty in failing to advise the claimant of her options. The claimant had undergone surgery on her carotid artery. Following surgery, a scan demonstrated that there was a residual flap on the artery. The claimant was advised about the presence of the flap. The surgeon decided not to operate unless there were any further symptoms. There were options for treatment and this was only one of them. The surgeon did not discuss the option of operating again or inserting a stent before further symptoms occurred. The claimant suffered a loss of vision in one eye and then surgery was performed, during which she suffered a stroke. The case failed on causation as the court held that even if properly advised she would in any event have followed the surgeon's advice.

There can be legal liability where there has been no information given, but also where the information given is incomplete or erroneous. Sufficient disclosure is one of the preconditions of a legally acceptable consent.

The earlier GMC guidance, from 1998 (*Seeking Patients' Consent: The Ethical Considerations*), provides that doctors should provide patients with options for management, including the option not to treat. For each option the doctor is advised that they must provide the patient with explanations of the likely benefits and the probabilities of success.

In the GMC guidance *Consent: Patients and Doctors Making Decisions Together* (2 June 2008) there is a direction on what information should be given to patients when deciding whether to consent to treatment, which should include:

- options for treatment or management of the condition, including the option not to treat;

- the potential benefits, risks and burdens, and the likelihood of success, for each option; this should include information, if available, about whether the benefits or risks are affected by which organisation or doctor is chosen to provide care. (9c, e)

In this guidance, a basic model is provided:

The doctor uses specialist knowledge and experience and clinical judgement, and the patient's views and understanding of their condition, to identify which investigations or treatments are likely to result in overall benefit for the patient. The doctor explains the options to the patient, setting out the potential benefits, risks, burdens and side effects of each option, including the option to have no treatment. The doctor may recommend a particular option which they believe to be best for the patient, but they must not put pressure on the patient to accept their advice. (5b)

This document also provides that a doctor should explain the probabilities of success, or the risk of failure of, or harm associated with options for treatment using accurate data. The GMC provides that the doctor must advise the patient of any treatments that may have a greater benefit for the patient than those the doctor or the doctor's organisation can offer (9l).

The issue of options for delivery of the baby was central to the question to be addressed in *Montgomery*. The claimant contended there were two options for delivery, and that Mrs Montgomery should have been advised of the risks and benefits of each option. It was accepted that ultimately the fetus needed to be delivered but this could be done by elective caesarean section or by proceeding to vaginal delivery with a low threshold to opt out and have a caesarean section should any concerns arise during the course of labour. Both were legitimate options.

The parties did not dispute that had Mrs Montgomery requested an elective caesarean section this request would have been acceded to. It was argued it was Mrs Montgomery, not Dr McLellan, who should choose which option to select having been fully advised of the risks of both options. This was the argument recognised by the Supreme Court (para 2). The argument is considered in detail in Chapter 4.

In *Montgomery*, the Supreme Court identified that, in assessing whether a risk was material, the question of alternative treatments, and the risks and benefits of the alternatives, was important to the assessment:

> *the assessment of whether a risk is material cannot be reduced to percentages. The significance of a given risk is likely to reflect a variety of factors besides its magnitude: for example, the nature of the risk, the effect which is occurrence would have upon the life of the patient, the importance to the patient of the benefits sought to be achieved by the treatment, the alternatives available and the risks in those alternatives. The assessment is therefore fact-sensitive, and also sensitive to the characteristics of the patient.* (para 89)

> *it is the doctor's responsibility to explain to her patient why she considers that one of the available treatment options is medically preferable to the others, having taken care to ensure that her patient is aware of the considerations for and against each of them.* (para 95)

> *An adult person of sound mind is entitled to decide which, if any, of the available forms of treatment to undergo, and her consent must be obtained before treatment interfering with her bodily integrity is undertaken. The doctor is therefore under a duty to take reasonable care to ensure that the patient is aware of any material risks involved in any recommended treatment, and of any reasonable alternative or variant treatments.* (para 87)

In *Medical Law and Ethics* (6th edition), Jonathan Herring interprets the decision in *Montgomery* as significant because it requires doctors to discuss reasonable alternatives with patients, although he accepts that this cannot require a doctor to discuss every remedy, including for example alternative medicine remedies.

In *Medicine, Patients and The Law* (6th Edition, para 5.13), Margaret Brazier and Emma Cave state that the decision in *Montgomery* makes it clear that doctors must do more than simply discuss the risks of treatment. Their view is that to enable patients to exercise their right to make their own choices the patient must be aware of the alternatives to treatment.

In November 2016, the Royal College of Surgeons in London issued guidance on consent post-*Montgomery* (*Consent: Supported Decision-Making*) and on the issue of options for treatment it is provided that:

> *Different options for treatment, including the option of no treatment, should be presented side by side and the benefits and material risks should be given objectively.*

> *You should also ensure that options are presented side by side and that the relative risks and benefits of the different options for treatment are discussed. You should not make assumptions regarding the wishes of a patient and what they might perceive as the best option available. You should not assume that the patient has the same set of values, wishes or life priorities as you would have in a similar situation.*

This guidance also provides that surgeons should make patients aware of national guidelines on treatment choices such as NICE (National Institute for Health and Care Excellence) and SIGN (Scottish Intercollegiate Guidelines Network). If the recommendation of the doctor is not in keeping with the current guidelines the doctor must explain the reason for not following current standard guidelines.

The guidance notes that *Montgomery* has changed the focus of the consent process from one in which the surgeon would explain the procedure to the patient and obtain their consent to proceed to one in which the surgeon sets out the treatment options and allows the patient to decide.

7.   Risks that should be disclosed

The pre-*Montgomery* test on what risks should be disclosed was found in *Sidaway*, as innovated by the decision in *Pearce*. It was recognised that in any option for treatment if there was a "significant risk" that would affect the judgement of a reasonable patient then a doctor required to inform the patient of that risk.

There is no duty to disclose all risks however remote they may be, which would do nothing but frighten the patient. In the Australian case of *F v R*, King CJ stated that a doctor is not expected to spend an inordinate amount of time conjuring up fanciful fears in the mind of the patient by stressing risks which are not sufficiently substantial to be a factor in the decision-making of a reasonable person.

In other common-law jurisdictions, the issue of disclosure of information has been considered in detail. Chapter 3 provides an analysis of the main cases of significance on the basis that this is informative of the approach to be used in applying the test found in *Montgomery* given that the Supreme Court explicitly adopted the test in *Rogers v Whitaker*.

In Australia, whether a risk is material is essentially a question of fact to be addressed by the court. All relevant facts should be considered, taken into account and weighed in the balance (*Tai v Saxon* (WA FC, 8 February 1996, unreported, BC9600521)).

In *Rogers v Whitaker* the court concluded that there was a duty to warn of a material risk inherent in the proposed treatment. A risk is material if, in the circumstances of the particular case, a reasonable person in the patient's position, if warned of the risk, would be likely to attach significance to it (the objective limb) or if the medical practitioner is or should reasonably be aware that the particular patient, if warned of the risk, would be likely to attach significance to it (the subjective limb).

The first limb of the test applies objective criteria and focuses on the requirements of a reasonable or ordinary person in the patient's position. The second, subjective limb recognises that a patient may not be reasonable and allows the courts to consider the particular patient and their requirements or fears (reasonable and unreasonable). This is subject to the caveat that the medical practitioner is or ought to be aware of those considerations. If a patient had special needs or concerns and this was known to the doctor, this would indicate that special or additional information is required.

In Canada, material risks are significant risks that pose a real threat to the patient's life, health or comfort (*White v Turner* (1981) 31 O.R. (2d) 773 (Ont.H.C.J.)). In assessing materiality, a court in Canada will balance the severity of the potential result with the likelihood that it will occur. The risk of stroke, paralysis or death has been considered to be material.

In *Dickson v Pinder*, at para 74, Yamauchi J summarised the categories of risks that must be disclosed:

A medical practitioner must disclose a risk, where the patient would not know of the risk and either:

(a) *The risk is a likely consequence, and the injury that would result is at least a slight injury, or*

(b) *The risk has serious consequences, such as paralysis or death, even where that risk in uncommon but not unknown.*

In Australia and Canada, the likelihood of the risk occurring is seen as a distinct concept from the gravity of the risk. The courts consider the likely occurrence of the risk against the consequences of the risk should it occur. The requirement for disclosure is reduced where the risk is remote. However, greater disclosure is required where the consequences of the risk are significant.

The courts in Australia have in some cases classified risks to be material, even where the likely occurrence of the risk is statistically low (see *Bloodworth v Health Authority* [2000] NSWSC 1234). In *Hribar v Wells* ((1995) 64 SASR 129) the likelihood of the risk was less than 1 in 1000. The court held that applying a mathematical formula to assess the magnitude of the risk is not likely to be helpful.

In the Australian case of *F v R* it was emphasised that to allow medical statistics to confine or extend the scope of the proper standard of care would mean handing over the scope of the duty of disclosure to expert medical evidence.

The materiality of risk should not be measured by reference to a certain minimum percentage below which no duty arises irrespective of the consequences of that risk materialising. The courts in many common-law and civil jurisdictions have declined to answer the question of disclosure based simply on the statistical probability of a risk occurring.

In *Rosenberg v Percival*, Gummow J considered that a slight risk of serious harm may satisfy the test of materiality, while a greater risk of less harm might not.

In *Rogers v Whitaker*, the gravity of the loss of sight in the patient's eye was increased in the situation where the claimant was blind in one eye.

In *Haughian v Paine* the Saskatchewan Court of Appeal held that the issue of materiality cannot be reduced to numbers for all cases. Statistics are but one factor to be taken into account.

In *Videto v Kennedy* ((1981) 125 D.L.R. (3d) 127 (Ont.C.A.)) the Ontario Court of Appeal set out the principles that could be derived from the decision in *Hopp v Lepp* and *Reibl v Hughes*. On the issue of the law to be applied in such cases, the following principles were said to apply:

- The question of whether a risk is material and whether there has been a breach of the duty of disclosure should not be determined solely by the standards of the profession.

- The duty of disclosure embraces what the surgeon knows or ought to know that the patient deems relevant to their decision whether or not to undergo the treatment.

- If a patient asks specific questions he is entitled to be given reasonable answers.

- A risk which is a mere possibility does not ordinarily have to be disclosed, but if its occurrence would have serious consequences it should be treated as a material risk.

- The patient is entitled to be given an explanation of the nature of the operation and its gravity. Subject to this, other inherent dangers such as the dangers of anaesthetic or the risks of infection do not have to be disclosed.

- The scope of the duty and whether it has been breached must be decided in the circumstances of each case.

- The emotional condition of the patient may in certain cases justify the surgeon in withholding or generalising information which otherwise should be more specific.

- The question of whether a particular risk is a material risk and whether there has been a breach of duty is a matter for the trier of fact.

In *Rogers v Whitaker* it was noted that the "nature of the treatment" is a factor relevant to the question of materiality. The court approved the judgment in *F v R*, where it was said that the more drastic or complex the intervention to the patient's physical make-up, the greater the need to keep the patient informed as to the risks of the treatment. The suggestion appears to be that the courts are less likely to find risks material in routine or common procedures than more complex procedures.

The GMC guidance provides useful guidance to doctors on discussing side effects, complications and other risks and this is useful for the courts in considering whether there has been a breach of duty (*Consent: Patients and Doctors Making Decisions Together* (2 June 2008), paras 28–36). The guidance provides that clear, accurate information about the risks of any proposed investigation or treatment should be presented in a way patients can understand to help them make informed decisions. The focus should be on the individual patient's situation and the risks relevant to them (para 28).

The doctor should identify the adverse outcomes that may result from the proposed options, including the potential outcome of taking no action. The suggestion is that risks can take a number of forms but will usually be assumed to include side effects, complications, or a failure of an intervention to achieve a desired aim. Included in the risks to be discussed are common risks with minor side effects, but also rare but serious adverse outcomes possibly resulting in permanent disability or death (para 29).

The guidance focuses on the "individual patient" and advises that doctors should consider the nature of the patient's condition, their general health and other circumstances. These are variable factors that may affect the likelihood of adverse outcomes occurring (para 30).

The doctor should do their best to understand the patient's views and preferences about any proposed investigation or treatment, and the adverse outcomes they are most concerned about. A doctor should not make assumptions about a patient's understanding or risk or the importance that they attach to different outcomes. These should be discussed with the patient (para 31).

It is specifically provided that a doctor must tell a patient if an investigation or treatment might result in a serious adverse outcome, even if the likelihood of that is small. Patients should also be told of less serious side effects or complications if they occur frequently (para 32).

Information should be given in a balanced way and without bias, and clear and simple language should be used. Doctors are required to keep up to date with developments in their own area of practice, which may affect their knowledge and understanding of the risks associated with the investigations or treatments they provide (paras 33–36).

The duty of the doctor is to provide information to the patient. The patient needs to know the options and alternatives and the risks and benefits of each option to enable them to make an informed choice on which option they would like.

Following the adoption of the test in *Rogers v Whitaker* in *Montgomery*, the scope of the doctor's duty to disclose information will be influenced by a number of factors:

(a) the reasonable options available for the particular patient, taking account of the patient's condition and needs;

(b) the nature and factual occurrence of risk in each option or alternative with specific reference to the patient;

(c) the potential benefit to the patient of each option or alternative;

(d) the consequences should the risk materialise.

Where there is a risk of grave or irrevocable consequences, the requirements for information disclosure are particularly high. Substantial or material risks must stand at the fore of any duty of disclosure. What is a material risk for the individual patient will depend on the facts and circumstances of the individual case. However, the question of information disclosure is not reduced simply to a question of statistics.

In *Montgomery* it was held that:

> … *the assessment of whether a risk is material cannot be reduced to percentages. The significance of a given risk is likely to reflect a variety of factors besides its magnitude: for example, the nature of the*

risk, the effect which is occurrence would have upon the life of the patient, the importance to the patient of the benefits sought to be achieved by the treatment, the alternatives available and the risks in those alternatives. The assessment is therefore fact-sensitive, and also sensitive to the characteristics of the patient. (para 89)

The courts will continue to require expert evidence to assist on what in fact the treatment options were for the individual patient. However, the question is not what options the reasonable body of practitioners would discuss as that is a filter to information. It is not a filter recognised by the GMC or in the decision of the Supreme Court in *Montgomery*.

Expert evidence is also relevant in relation to the risks and benefits of each option and the factual occurrence of risk in each. The courts will require assistance on the probable consequence/s should the risk materialise. What is "material" in each case should be determined by the courts and is not simply a question of statistics or medical judgement alone. The *Bolam* or *Hunter v Hanley* tests are not relevant to the question. The question must by necessity include non-medical information of issues that are relevant and important to the individual patient when exercising choice.

8.   Rational choices

In firmly embracing the doctrine of autonomy or self-determination this must include the right of the individual patient to act in a way that may seem to the doctor to be irrational. The right to self-determination necessarily includes the right to act irrationally. In any event, the concept of what is a rational decision is fraught with difficulty in the context of patient choice of treatment. What is a medically rational decision may in fact be irrational for a particular patient. A patient may choose to reject treatment for legitimate reasons unknown to the heath provider. A decision that appears irrational to a doctor may make perfect sense in the context of the individual patient's religious or personal beliefs.

A doctor should not assume that simply because a patient does not wish to proceed with a treatment the doctor considers to be in the patient's best interests that the patient does not have capacity. An irrational decision is a decision which is so outrageous in its defiance of logic or accepted moral standards that no sensible person who had applied their mind to the questions to be decided could have arrived at it. Panic, indecisiveness and irrationality in themselves do not amount to incompetence but they may be symptoms or evidence of incompetence.

Peter Jackson J in *Heart of England NHS Trust v JB* ([2014] EWHC 342 (COP)) noted that "common strategies for dealing with unpalatable dilemmas-for example indecision, avoidance or vacillation-are not to be confused with incapacity". It was said:

> *The temptation to base a judgement of a person's capacity upon whether they seem to have made a good or a bad decision, and in particular upon whether they have accepted or rejected medical advice, is absolutely to be avoided. That would be to put the cart before the horse or, expressed another way, to allow the tail of welfare to wag the dog of capacity. Any tendency in this direction risks infringing the rights of that group of persons who, though vulnerable, are capable of making their own decisions. Many who suffer from mental illness are well able to make decisions about their medical treatment, and it is important not to make unjustified assumptions to the contrary.*

In *Re B (Consent to Treatment: Capacity)* ([2002] EWHC 429) it was held that patients must not be found to lack capacity because their decisions appear irrational. However, if the patient is incapable of weighing up the issues or appreciating the consequences of their decisions, then that may mean that they lack capacity. It was held that:

> *The doctors must not allow their emotional reaction to or strong disagreement with the decision of the patient to cloud their judgement in answering the primary question whether the patient has the mental capacity to make the decision.*

In *Re C (Adult Refusal of Treatment)* ([1994] 1WLR 290) a patient in Broadmoor who had been diagnosed as suffering from chronic paranoid schizophrenia refused medical treatment. He was suffering from an ulcerated foot which had become gangrenous and the advice from his doctors was that he should undergo an amputation from below the knee to save his life. He refused to consent to the amputation but agreed to conservative management and his condition did improve. The hospital refused to give an undertaking that the leg would not be amputated at some point in the future and he applied for an injunction to prevent amputation without his written consent. Thorpe J was satisfied that the claimant had understood and retained all of the relevant information and he had arrived at a clear choice. It was held that his right of self-determination had not been displaced.

A patient's capacity may be reduced temporarily owing to the effect of illness or drugs. A patient may be unable to process information due to panic. In *The Mental Health Trust v DD (By her Litigation Friend, The Official Solicitor) Bc* (Number 2) ([2014] EWCOP 11) it was held that the patient was unable to weigh the information when she refused consent to a caesarean section (see also *A Local Authority v E* [2012] EWHC 1639 (COP); *A NHS Trust v X* [2014] EWCOP 35).

In *F v F* ([2013] EWHC 2683 (Fam)), which considered a refused of the measles, mumps and rubella vaccine because it contained animal products, it was considered that neither child was able to give a balanced view and both were overly focused on the ingredients without being able to balance that with other considerations.

In the early guidance, the GMC recognised the right of the patient to refuse a medical intervention even if that refusal would result in harm to themselves or in death. The GMC considered the question of the apparently irrational decision in its guidance. In *Consent: Patients and Doctors Making Decisions Together* (2 June 2008), the GMC emphasises that the patient decides whether to accept an option and they have the right to accept or refuse an option for a reason that may seem irrational to the doctor, or for no reason at all. Doctors should ensure that the patient is aware that they have the right to refuse treatment (para 42):

You must respect a patient's decision to refuse an investigation or treatment, even if you think their decision is wrong or irrational. You should explain your concerns clearly to the patient and outline the possible consequences of their decision. You must not, however, put pressure on a patient to accept your advice. (para 43)

9. Where a patient asks questions

Prior to *Montgomery*, the law recognised that where a patient asks a question they are entitled to a truthful answer. The issue was *obiter* in *Sidaway* but their Lordships did consider the issue.

Lord Diplock was of the view that if a patient asked questions a doctor would tell them "whatever it was the patient wants to know". There was no restriction using the professional practice test.

Lord Templeman was of a similar view:

Mrs Sidaway could have asked questions. If she had done so, she could and should have been informed that there was an aggregate risk of between 1% and 2% of some damage either to the spinal cord or to a nerve root resulting in injury which might vary from irritation to paralysis.

Lord Scarman implied that a doctor should answer truthfully to any direct questions. Lord Bridge held that a specific question must be answered truthfully.

Prior to *Sidaway*, Lord Denning in instructing a jury in *Hatcher v Black* (The Times, 2 July 1954) had suggested that if a doctor told a patient a lie and this was condoned in terms of the *Bolam* test there could be no criticism of the doctor.

In *Lee v South West Thames Regional Health Authority* ([1985] 2 All E.R. 385), Sir John Donaldson MR appeared to suggest that a doctor had discretion in this area. He left the question to the clinical judgement of the doctor to decide what information should be given and what information should be withheld.

In *Blyth v Bloomsbury Health Authority* ((1989) 5P.N. 167) the trial judge rejected the claimant's evidence that she had asked a series of questions. The Court of Appeal accepted the evidence of the medical experts, who said that they would not have given the claimant any more information than she had been given. There was no suggestion in this case that information had been deliberately withheld on the basis that it would be harmful. The court considered that the *Bolam* test must be applied in this area despite the dicta in *Sidaway*.

In Australia, where a patient asks questions the duty is clear. In *F v R*, King CJ held that if the claimant had asked a direct question the doctor would have a duty to give full and frank advice.

In *Rogers v Whitaker* it was held that where a patient asks questions and the nature of the questioning reveals their concerns or personal fears this can be said to satisfy the materiality test. Provided it can be demonstrated that the risk was foreseeable, the Australian courts have attached little significance to the fact that it might be very unlikely to occur (*Rogers v Whitaker* and *Chappel v Hart*).

In *Rogers v Whitaker* the High Court explained:

> *Even if a court were satisfied that a reasonable person in the patient's position would be unlikely to attach significance to a particular risk, the fact that the patient asked questions revealing concern about the risk would make the doctor aware that **this patient** did in fact attach significance to the risk. Subject to the therapeutic privilege, the question would therefore require a truthful answer.*

In Canada, in *Hopp v Lepp* ((1980) 112 D.L.R. (3d) 67) Laskin CJ held that where a patient asks specific questions these questions must be answered. It was provided that without being questioned the doctor should disclose the nature of the operation, its proposed gravity, any material risks and any special or unusual risks. If a risk were small or a mere possibility, it could still need to be disclosed if there were serious consequences should it occur.

Prior to *Montgomery*, where a patient asked direct questions, applying *Sidaway* there appeared to be an exception to information filtered by means of the *Bolam* test. Applying these principles, the patient who asked direct questions could be entitled to more information than the patient who did not. The response of a doctor to a question is not filtered by a professional practice test.

The Supreme Court in *Montgomery* recognised this unsatisfactory and illogical situation:

> *The significance attached in* Sidaway *to a patient's failure to question the doctor is however profoundly unsatisfactory. In the first place, as Sedley LJ commented in* Wyatt v Curtis *[2003] EWCA Civ 1779, there is something unreal about placing the onus of asking upon a patient who may not know there is anything to ask about. It is indeed a reversal of logic: the more a patient knows about the risks she faces, the easier it is for her to ask specific questions about those risks, so as to impose on her doctor a duty to provide information: but it is those who lack such knowledge, and who are in consequence unable to pose such questions and instead express their anxiety in more general terms, who are in the greatest need for information. Ironically, the ignorance which such patients seek to have dispelled disqualifies them from obtaining the information they desire.* (para 58)

> *Why should the patient's asking a question make any difference in negligence, if medical opinion determines whether the duty of care requires that the risk should be disclosed? The patient's desire for the information, even if made known to the doctor does not alter medical opinion. The exception, in other words, is logically destructive of the supposed rule.* (para 59)

One of the issues before the court in *Montgomery* was what the response of the doctor should be if a patient asked questions or expressed concerns. The argument is set out in detail in Chapter 4. Mrs Montgomery had said that she had raised specific concerns with Dr McLellan about the increasing size of the baby, and concerns about whether the baby would be too big to be delivered vaginally. Dr McLellan was of the view that this was not a specific question about exact risks. She accepted that had Mrs Montgomery asked a specific question she would have answered truthfully and told her about shoulder dystocia and cephalopelvic disproportion.

In the Outer House of the Court of Session and in the Appeal Court in Scotland it was accepted that following the speech of Lord Bridge in *Sidaway* a doctor must, when questioned specifically by a patient about risks involved in a particular treatment proposed, answer truthfully and as fully as the questioner required. However, in *Montgomery* it was held that the concerns were of a general nature only and this did not require a full and honest disclosure of factual information.

The Supreme Court recognised that the approach in *Sidaway* to the issue of questions can lead to the drawing of excessively fine distinctions between questioning, on the one hand, and expressions of concern failing short of questioning on the other hand.

The Supreme Court held that the doctor's duty of care takes its precise content from the needs, concerns and circumstances of the individual patient, to the extent that they are or ought to be known to the doctor. It was noted in *Rogers v Whitaker* that the doctor was aware that the patient was already blind in one eye prior to surgery, giving the risk greater significance, but she was anxious about risks. On this basis:

> *Expressions of concern by the patient, as well as specific questions, are plainly relevant. As Gummow J observed in Rosenbery v Percival (2001) 205 CLR 434,459, courts should not be too quick to discard the second limb (i.e. the possibility that the medical practitioner was or ought reasonably to have been aware that the particular patient, if warned of the risk, would be likely to attach significance to it) merely because it emerges that the patient did not ask certain kinds of questions. (para 73)*

It appears following the decision in *Montgomery* that a doctor does have to answer a patient's questions truthfully. With reference to the decision of the High Court of Australia in *Rogers v Whitaker* ((1992) 175 CLR 479, paras 486–487), the Supreme Court asked why the patient's asking a question should make any difference to negligence and concluded: "The exception, in other words, is logically destructive of the supposed rule". The court held that expressions of concern by the patient, as well as specific questions, are plainly relevant and appeared to link this to the second limb of the test in *Rogers v Whitaker*. Given that the Supreme Court has said that the test on information disclosure is ultimately found in the decision of *Rogers v Whitaker*, it seems reasonable to conclude that a doctor must answer a patient's question truthfully.

The GMC has provided guidance on the issue. As far back as 1998, in its *Seeking Patients' Consent: The Ethical Considerations*, the GMC provided that doctors must respond honestly to patients' questions and answer as fully as the patient wishes. If a patient asks about other treatments, or other institutions or doctors providing treatment, these questions should also be answered honestly. This approach continues in the 2008 guidance (*Consent: Patients and Doctors Making Decisions Together* (2 June 2008), para 12).

10. Patient understanding

The simple fact of imparting information does not of itself ensure that a patient makes an informed decision.

Prior to *Montgomery*, UK courts had held that the professional duty requires more than simple disclosure In *Lybert v Warrington Health Authority* ([1996] P.I.Q.R. P45; (1995) 25 BMLR 91) it was held that the warning had to be sufficiently clear and comprehensible and reasonable steps had to be taken to ensure that the information was understood.

Poor communication of risks could amount of a breach of the duty to inform (*Cooper v Royal United Hospital Bath NHS Trust* [2005] EWHC 3381). The doctor does have to have regard to the particular patient's condition and if the patient is affected by medication or other factors the doctor should take account of this when providing information (*Smith v Salford Health Authority* [1994] 5 Med.L.R 321 QBD; (1994) 23 BMLR 137).

The patient's right to receive information should be tested independently from the ability of the patient to understand the information. It is recognised that the doctor fulfils their duty by making the appropriate disclosure in a reasonable way to facilitate patient understanding.

In *Deriche v Ealing Hospital NHS Trust* ([2003] EWHC 3104) the doctor was aware that a patient had already been advised of the risks of chickenpox. The question was how far the doctor could rely upon the earlier counselling. It was held that the doctor should not simply have relied upon the notes but should have checked that the patient had been made aware of risks that were potentially serious for her baby.

In *Canterbury v Spence* (464 F 2d. 772 (1972) (U.S.C.A., District of Columbia)) it was held:

> *In duty to disclose cases, the focus of attention is more properly on the nature and content of the physician's divulgence than the patient's understanding and consent. Adequate disclosure and informed consent are, or course, two sides of the same coin. The former is the sine qua non of the latter. But the vital enquiry on duty to disclose relates to the physician's performance of an obligation, while one of the difficulties with analysis in terms of "informed consent" is its tendency to imply that what is decisive is the degree of the patient's comprehension.*

In *Smith v Tunbridge Wells Health Authority* ([1994] 5 Med. L.R. 334) Moorland J held that the doctor's duty to inform included the use of appropriately simple language and take reasonable care to ensure that their explanation of the risks is intelligible to the particular patient:

> *When recommending a particular type of surgery or treatment, the doctor, when warning of the risks, must take reasonable care to*

ensure that his explanation of the risks is intelligible to his particular patient. The doctor should use language, simple but not misleading, which the doctor perceives from what knowledge and acquaintance- ship that he may have of the patient (which may be slight), will be understood by the patient so that the patient can make an informed decision as to whether or not to consent to the recommended surgery or treatment. (para 339)

It is also important to take account of the patient's general condition at the time the information is disclosed (*Smith v Salford Health Authority* [1994] 5 Med. L.R. 321, QBD; *Lybert v Warrington Health Authority* [1996] P.I.Q.R. 45).

In *Cooper v Royal United Hospital Bath NHS Trust* ([2005] EWHC 3381), as a result of poor communication and lack of coordination between treating doctors the claimant was confused about her options. It was held that there was liability for misleading the claimant and depriving her of the right to choose the treatment she would prefer.

However, in *Al Hamwi v Johnston* ([2005] EWHC 206) a claimant mis- understood the information given. It was held that she had been correctly presented with factually accurate information and the doctor's obligation did not extend to ensuring that the patient had understood the information.

The courts in Canada and Australia have considered this issue in the context of a patient-focused test and these judgments are worthy of review in this area. In Canada, the duty of disclosure includes a duty to take reasonable steps to ensure that a patient actually understands the information. (*Ciarlariello Estate v Schacter* [1993] 2 S.C.R. 119). Where a discussion about risks takes place immediately prior to surgery or where a patient is affected by drugs this may affect adequate disclosure. Where a doctor uses terminology which is highly technical or difficult to understand, the Canadian courts have found this to be an inadequate communication of information.

Canadian courts have also considered the question of communication of information where the patient's first language is not English (*Adan v Davis* [1998] O.J. No.3030 (Gen. Div.) (QL)). In *Reibl v Hughes*, Laskin CJC said that it must have been obvious to the doctor that the claimant had some difficulty with the English language and in that situation he should have made certain that he was understood. The question is whether the patient's linguistic ability is at a level which allows them to understand the information upon which the consent is to be based.

The early guidance from the GMC provided that the doctor should discuss treatment options with the patient at a time when the patient is best able to understand and retain the information. Guidance is given on the appropriate way to present information to patients (para 13).

In *Consent: Patients and Doctors Making Decisions Together* (2 June 2008), the GMC provides that a doctor should check whether the patient has understood the information they have been given, and whether or not they would like more information before making a decision (para 11).

How a doctor discusses the patient's diagnosis, prognosis and treatment options are recognised to be important. The guidance provides that doctors should:

- Share information in a way that the patient can understand and, whenever possible, in a place and at a time when they are best able to understand and retain it

- Give the patient time to reflect, before and after they make a decision, especially if the information is complex or what is being proposed involves significant risks (para 18a, d)

Doctors should give information to patients in a balanced way and it is suggested in the GMC guidance that a doctor may need to support their discussions with patients by using written material, or visual or other aids. If this is done, the guidance states "you must make sure the material is accurate and up to date" (paras 19, 20).

Doctors should check whether patients need any additional support to understand information, to communicate their wishes or to make a decision. Wherever practical, arrangements should be made to give the patient any necessary support. The type of support envisaged is: using an advocate or interpreter; asking those close to the patient about the patient's communication needs; or giving the patient a written or audio record of the discussion and any decisions that were made (para 21).

If a doctor feels that limits on their ability to give patients the time or information they need is seriously compromising their ability to make an informed decision, the GMC suggests that they should raise their concerns with their employer or contracting authority (para 25). Reference is made to *Good Medical Practice* and the explanatory guidance, *Raising and Acting on Concerns about Patient Safety*.

In *Montgomery*, the Supreme Court provided that a doctor had a duty to take reasonable care to ensure that a patient was aware of material risks involved in any recommended treatment, and of any reasonable alternative or variant treatments (para 87):

> *the doctor's advisory role involves dialogue, the aim of which is to ensure that the patient understands the seriousness of her condition, and the anticipated benefits and risks of the proposed treatment and any reasonable alternatives, so that she is then in a position to make an informed decision. This role will only be performed effectively if the information provided is comprehensible. The doctor's duty is not therefore fulfilled by bombarding the patient with technical information which she cannot reasonably be expected to grasp, let alone by routinely demanding her signature on a consent form.* (para 90)

This statement brings the law into line with professional guidance issued by the GMC.

11. The right to refuse treatment

A competent adult patient has an absolute right to choose whether to consent to medical treatment, to refuse it or to choose one rather than another of the treatments being offered (*Re T (Adult: Refusal of Medical Treatment*) [1992] 4 All ER 645, C.A.). There is some overlap in this area with the right of a patient to make an irrational choice, dealt with above.

In *Heart of England NHS Foundation Trust v JB* ([2014] EWHC 342 (COP)) it was held that the right to decide whether or not to consent to medical treatment is one of the most important rights guaranteed by the law. The freedom to choose is what it means to be a human being:

> *For this reason, anyone capable of making decisions has an absolute right to accept or refuse medical treatment, regardless of the wisdom or consequences of the decision. The decision does not have to be justified to anyone.... The fact that the intervention is well-meaning or therapeutic makes no difference.*

In *Re C (Adult: Refusal of Treatment)* ([1994] 1 W.L.R. 290), a 68-year-old paranoid schizophrenic refused to consent to a below-the-knee amputation. He had a gangrenous right foot and his doctors thought that his chances of survival were low without amputation. He sought an injunction restraining the hospital from amputating his leg. The court said that the question was whether as a result of his chronic mental illness he did not sufficiently understand the nature, purpose and effects of the proposed amputation.

In *Re MB (Medical Treatment)* ([1997] 8 Med. L.R. 217), the Court of Appeal set out a list of factors to be taken into account in deciding whether a patient was competent to make a decision about medical treatment.

In *Re W (A Minor) (Medical Treatment: Court's Jurisdiction)* ([1993] Fam. 64) a 16-year-old with anorexia nervosa was doubted to have sufficient understanding to enable her to make an informed decision to refuse treatment.

In *Re E (Medical Treatment: Anorexia)* ([2012] EWHC 1639 (COP)), a 32-year-old woman with anorexia nervosa had a settled wish to die. It was held that as a result of her condition she lacked capacity to accept or refuse treatment in relation to interventions relating to forcible feeding.

In *Re KB (Adult) (Mental Patient: Medical Treatment)* ((1994) 19 B.M.L.R. 144), the patient's condition was such that she would die within 14–21 days without nasogastric feeding. She had been diagnosed as suffering from anorexia nervosa and detained under the Mental Health Act. It was concluded that she was not competent to refuse consent. In this case the requirement for nasogastric feeding was inter-linked with her mental illness, unlike the situation in *Re C* (see also *Re B (Adult, Refusal of Medical Treatment)* [2002] 2 All ER 449).

Religious objection can be a legitimate reason for a patient to refuse treatment. The courts have supported the rights of Jehovah's Witnesses to refuse blood products on religious grounds.

In the Canadian case of *Malette v Shulman* ((1990) 67 D.L.R. (4th) 321, Ont C.A.) an unconscious patient arrived at a casualty department after a road traffic accident. The doctor was aware that she carried a card saying that she was not willing to accept blood products. Despite this, he administered blood products and he was found liable in battery. It was held:

> *The principles of self-determination and individual autonomy compel the conclusion that the patient may reject blood transfusions even if harmful consequences may result and even if the decision is generally regarded as foolhardy.... To transfuse a Jehovah's Witness in the face of her explicit instructions to the contrary would, in my opinion, violate her right to control her own body and show disrespect for the religious values by which she has chosen to live her life.*

In *Re T (Adult: Refusal of Treatment)* ([1993] Fam.95) the principles set out in *Malette v Shulman* were seen to be correct. However, it must be noted that this relates to the refusal of blood products by a competent adult.

In *Re E (A Minor)* ((1990) 9 BMLR 1) A 15–year-old Jehovah's Witness who was seriously ill with leukaemia was made a ward of court and a transfusion was ordered against his wishes. The judge accepted that he was intelligent, mature for his age and well informed about his choices. However, it was held that he lacked insight into the process of dying. Following the transfusion his condition went into temporary remission but at 18 he relapsed and again refused a transfusion. On this occasion his wishes were complied with and he died.

In *An NHS Foundation Hospital v P* ([2014] EWHC 165), emergency treatment was authorised for a 17-year-old who had taken an overdose of paracetamol. She had a history of self-harm and if the treatment was not administered within a specific time period she would suffer serious injury or death. The treatment was authorised despite the fact that she was thought to have capacity under the Mental Health Act.

There have been a number of cases where the courts have forced a mother to undergo a caesarean section against her wishes. In *Re S (Adult: Refusal of Medical Treatment)* ([1993] Fam. 123) a woman refused to consent to a caesarean section on religious grounds. There was a serious risk to both mother and baby if her wishes were adhered to. The court granted a declaration that it would be lawful to perform the caesarean section, although this caused much controversy at the time as she was not found to be incompetent.

In *Re MB (Medical Treatment)* ([1997] 8 Med. L.R. 217) the Court of Appeal made it clear that in the case of a competent pregnant woman the patient had the absolute right to refuse medical treatment. The fact that the baby might die as a result of the refusal being upheld was not relevant. In this case the mother was found on the facts to be incompetent.

In *St. George's Healthcare NHS Trust v S; R. v Collins and Others Ex p. S* ([1999] Fam. 26) the Court of Appeal reaffirmed the view that a court has no jurisdiction to order a competent woman to undergo medical treatment, even if there is a risk to the life of the fetus. Where a mother retains her capacity, her consent is a prerequisite for treatment.

Doctors are not under a duty to persuade or attempt to persuade patients to change their minds if the doctor considers the decision made by them to be unwise (*Al Hamwi v Johnston, The North West London Hospitals NHS Trust*). A patient's consent may be vitiated by pressure of duress from another person (*Re T (Adult)* [1992] 4 All ER 649).

The GMC guidance *Consent: Patients and Doctors Making Decisions Together* (2 June 2008) provides:

> *If, after discussion, a patient still does not want to know in detail about their condition or the treatment, you should respect their wishes, as far as possible. But you must still give them the information they need in order to give their consent to a proposed investigation of treatment. This is likely to include what the investigation or treatment aims to achieve and what it will involve, for example: whether the procedure is invasive; what level of pain or discomfort they might experience, and what can be done to minimise it; anything they should do to prepare for the investigation of treatment; and if it involves any serious risks.* (para 14)

> *If the patient insists that they do not want even this basic information, you must explain the potential consequences of then not having it, particularly if it might mean that their consent is not valid. You must record the fact that the patient has declined this information. You must also make it clear that they can change their mind and have more information at any time.* (para 15)

12. Is there a duty to ensure the patient makes "the right decision"?

The doctor is under no duty to ensure that the patient chooses what the doctor considers is the "right option". In *Attwell v McPartlin* ([2004] EWHC 829) it was recognised that there was no scope for a duty to "push". It was recognised that it was for the patient, not the doctor, to decide whether the risks of any particular treatment or procedure are acceptable.

The High Court has held that there is a duty to present information in such a way that the patient's right to make their own decision is usurped.

In *Consent: Patients and Doctors Making Decisions Together* (2 June 2008) the GMC provides that a doctor may recommend a particular option which they believe to be best for the patient, but they must not put pressure on the patient to accept their advice (para 5b). Information should be given in a balanced way.

13. The therapeutic exception

For many years, the question of "therapeutic privilege" loomed large in consent cases. There appeared to be some confusion whether this applied in the UK and if so how it was defined. In theory, this doctrine permits a doctor to filter information to the patient. As a general rule, the courts have recognised that therapeutic reasons for narrowing the scope of information disclosure are only legally acceptable in rare circumstances.

It has been argued that a justification for not telling the patient the whole truth is in conflict with the "do no harm" principle or "bene-volent deception". The doctor justifies the fact that they have not advised the patient of all the risks of a procedure on the basis they do not wish to frighten or distress the patient. Once a view prevails that patients generally do not want to know the truth, rationalisations can be readily created which serve to justify this position.

The patient does have a right to waive their right to information. However, this does not entitle the doctor to decide to filter information disclosure because the doctor thinks it is in the patient's best interest to do so. The doctrine should never be used to entice a patient to accept treatment which he might, if properly informed, refuse.

Professor Kennedy has said that the device of therapeutic privilege pays lip service to the principle of truth-telling and self-determination, while it creates a discretionary exception which is quite capable of swallowing these principles when the doctor decides the occasion requires it.

In *AB v Leeds Teaching Hospital NHS Trust* ([2004] EWHC 644) it was argued that giving families information about the retention of organs might cause them distress and perhaps psychiatric harm. Gage J held that this was something that needed to be considered on a case by case basis.

In both Canada and Australia the courts do recognise that there may be instances in which a doctor is not required to fully consent a patient (*Reibl v Hughes*; *Hopp v Lepp*). This is dealt with in detail in Chapter 3 and the cases from both jurisdictions are of assistance to those in the UK attempting to define situations where it is acceptable not to communicate risks to patients.

In Canada, it had been thought the exception had its foundation in "therapeutic privilege". However, in *Meyer Estate v Rogers* it was held that there was no defence of therapeutic privilege in Canada. It was felt that therapeutic privilege is an American exception to the rule that doctors are required to inform their patients of the risks associated with a proposed procedure following the decision in *Canterbury v Spence* (464 F 2d 772 (1972) at paras 788 and 789).

In Australia and Canada, it is recognised that doctors need not disclose information to a patient if by doing so he may do more harm to the patient than any benefit to be gained from the treatment. Where the emotional condition of the patient is such that a detailed disclosure would cause the patient extreme anxiety the doctor may be justified in withholding information. It has been suggested in Canada that the so-called therapeutic privilege should be construed very narrowly and applied in only the most exceptional circumstances.

It was accepted that there could be cases where a patient is unable or unwilling to accept bad news from a doctor. In those circumstances a physician is obliged to take reasonable precautions to ensure that the patient has communicated their desire not to be told, or that the patient's health is so precarious that such news will undoubtedly trigger an adverse reaction that will cause further unnecessary harm to the patient.

In the Australian case of *Battersby v Tottman* ((1985) 37 SASR 524) it was held that a doctor would be in breach of their duty to the patient if he withheld from a mentally normal and emotionally sound patient information as to a material risk simply because he found that the patient might make an unwise decision, perhaps based upon unreasonable considerations, not to undergo treatment.

In *Canterbury v Spence* it was held that privilege does not accept the paternalistic notion that the physician may remain silent simply because divulgence might prompt the patient to forgo therapy that the physician feels the patient really needs.

In *Consent: Patients and Doctors Making Decisions Together* (2 June 2008) it is provided by the GMC that information may be withheld if the doctor believes that giving it would cause the patient serious harm. In this context "serious harm" means more than that the patient might become upset or decide to refuse treatment. Where a decision is made to withhold information from the patient the reason must be recorded within the medical records and the doctor must be prepared to explain and justify the decision. The decision must also be reviewed and consideration must be given to whether information can be given to a patient at a later date without causing serious harm (paras 16, 17).

The Supreme Court in *Montgomery*, in departing from the professional standard, expressly acknowledged a role for what it called the "therapeutic exception". A doctor would be entitled to withhold information reasonably considered detrimental to the patient's health (para 88) or in circumstances of necessity. However, the court did warn that that this exception must not be abused or used to prevent patients from making decisions that the doctor might see as contrary to the patient's best interests (para 91).

The scope of this therapeutic exception remains undefined by the Supreme Court. However, it seems clear that any reason given for withholding information must relate to the particular patient in question, and not be based on patients generally.

In *Medicine, Patients and the Law* (6th Edition), Margaret Brazier and Emma Cave note that the Supreme Court in *Montgomery*, in departing from the professional standard, expressly acknowledges a role for what they call the "therapeutic exception". They are of the view that the Supreme Court endorsed the right of the doctor to withhold information reasonably considered to be detrimental to the patient's health or in circumstances of necessity. Any defence must now be based on cogent reasons relating to the welfare of that particular patient, and not just on the patient's age or the surgeon's view on the minimal risk.

14. Emergencies

In an emergency situation where the patient is unable to give consent and there is no available evidence of a patient's own wishes, a doctor has authority to act in the best interests of the patient and do whatever is necessary to preserve life.

In *Re F (Mental Patient: Sterilisation)* ([1990] 2 A.C. 1, at para 52) it was recognised by Lord Bridge that this authority is necessary otherwise doctors and other health care professionals would otherwise face an intolerable dilemma in the emergency situation.

Some members of the medical profession assume that if an adult patient is unable to consent it is appropriate to obtain consent from a member of their immediate family. In law, the consent of the patient in this situation cannot be obtained from a family member. The law does not recognise anyone else as having the legal capacity to give or refuse consent on behalf of the competent adult patient.

There is some confusion amongst medical ethicists of the justification for this principle. There have been three potential justifications advanced in the UK to permit treatment of an unconscious patient in an emergency situation. One argument is that consent is implied, as the unconscious patient if conscious would probably consent to life-saving treatment. Another is that there is no "hostile touching" in this situation and the medical professional's actions are acceptable in the ordinary conduct of daily life (*Wilson v Pringle* [1987] Q.B. 237). In *Re F (Mental Patient: Sterilisation)* ([1988] Fam.52) this concept was doubted to be accurate.

The final argument justifying treatment is based on the principle of necessity. It is recognised in law that where a person acts out of necessity this legitimates an otherwise wrongful act. However, the treatment undertaken must not be more extensive that is required by the exigencies of the situation.

In *Re F (Mental Patient: Sterilisation)* ([1990] 2 A.C. 1) it was provided that treatment of a temporarily incapacitated patient in an emergency will be lawful if it is in the best interests of the patient, but only if carried out in order to save their life or to ensure improvement or prevent deterioration in their physical or mental health.

In *Williamson v East London and City Health Authority* ((1998) 41 BMLR 85), the claimant had consented to the removal and replacement of a leaking breast implant. During surgery, the condition was more significant than had been anticipated and a subcutaneous mastectomy was performed by the surgeon. It was held that consent to such an extensive procedure had not been obtained and damages were awarded despite the fact that it was accepted that an operation would have been required at some point in the future.

In Canada, there is a distinction made between procedures which would have been unreasonable to postpone. In *Murray v McMurchy* ([1949] 2 D.L.R. 442) a fibroid was discovered during the course of a caesarean section and the doctor removed it. The doctor argued that it was a potential danger if the patient became pregnant again. It was held that it was not unreasonable to postpone the operation, and there was no immediate threat to the patient.

In *Marshall v Curry* ([1933] 3 D.L.R. 260) the Canadian courts found that it was unreasonable to postpone the procedure and there was no liability. The claimant had sought damages for battery against the surgeon who removed a testicle in the course of a hernia operation. The court held that the removal of the testicle was necessary and it would not have been reasonable to put the procedure off to another day.

In Australia, in *Candutti v ACT Health and Community Care* ([2003] ACTSC 95) the doctor proceeded to perform a laparotomy to sterilise the patient when problems arose during the course of laparoscopic ster-ilisation. There was no reason why the doctor could not have halted the laparoscopic sterilisation and obtained the consent of the patient.

The early guidance from the GMC provided that a doctor may provide medical treatment in an emergency, provided that the treatment is immediately necessary to save life or avoid significant deterioration in the patient's health. However, the doctor should respect the terms of any valid advance refusal (para 18).

The later GMC guidance, *Consent: Patients and Doctors Making Dec-isions Together* (2 June 2008), provides that where an emergency arises in a clinical setting and it is not possible to find out a patient's wishes the doctor can treat them without their consent provided the treatment is immediately necessary to save their life or to prevent a serious deteri-oration in their condition (para 79). The treatment provided must be the least restrictive of the patient's future choices.

15. Fraud or misrepresentation

Where there is coercion, fraud or misrepresentation there is no consent. In *Sidaway v Bethlem Royal Governors* ([1984] Q.B. 493) Sir John Donaldson MR said:

> *It is only if the consent is obtained by fraud or misrepresentation of the nature of what is to be done that it can be said that an apparent consent is not a true consent.*

Where there is a deliberate lie or a dishonest answer to a direct question from a patient this can be seen to be evidence of bad faith vitiating consent. In *Re T (Adult: Refusal of Treatment)* ([1993] Fam.95) it was said that misinforming a patient, whether or not innocently, and the withholding of information which is expressly or impliedly sought by the patient may well vitiate either a consent or a refusal of treatment.

In *Appleton v Garrett* ([1997] 8 Med L. Rev. 75), a dentist was held liable in battery despite the fact that the patient had agreed to what was being done. The dentist performed extensive restorative dental work on healthy teeth for financial gain. Dyson J held that the defendant had committed a battery. The patient's consent for work on the healthy teeth was not "real".

In *R v Tabassum* ([2000] Lloyd's Rep. Med.404, C.A.) the defendant told three women that he was conducting a survey into breast cancer and persuaded the women to allow him to examine their breasts. He was found guilty of indecent assault and the Court of Appeal upheld the conviction.

In Canada, fraud or misrepresentation by a doctor about the procedure is seen to affect the validity of patient consent. In *Reibl v Hughes*, in delivering the judgement of the Supreme Court Laskin CJC held:

> *unless there has been misrepresentation of fraud to secure consent to the treatment, a failure to disclose the attendant risks, however serious, should go to negligence rather than battery.*

Australian law distinguishes between the negligent failure to warn a patient who consents to treatment and the fraudulent procurement of consent for non-therapeutic purposes.

In *White v Johnston* ([2015] NSWCA 18) the allegation was that the dental treatment the claimant received amounted to an assault as he was aware that the treatment was unnecessary and ineffective and there was no therapeutic purpose in the treatment given. When a medical practitioner is solely motivated by an unrevealed non-therapeutic purpose, the patient's consent is not valid. Where the question is whether a medical practitioner has fraudulently procured a patient's consent, the onus lies upon the patient to establish fraud. The court said that there were some situations where a patient's *prima facie* consent will not be an answer to assault and battery. Reference was made to *Rogers v Whitaker*, *Reibl v Hughes* and *Chatterton v Gearson*, where it was said that if information is withheld in bad faith the consent is vitiated by fraud (see also *Dean v Phung*).

In *R v Mobilo* ([1991] 1 VR 339 (Supreme Court of Victoria)), a radiographer performed an ultrasound trans-vaginally rather than trans-abdominally. The woman knew what was to be done and there was a benefit in the examination performed. It was alleged that the procedure was performed for sexual gratification and the defendant was convicted of rape, which was overturned on appeal. The Supreme Court of Victoria held that the sexual motive was irrelevant as the patient had consented.

In *R v Bolduc and Bird* ((1967) 63 DLR (2d) 82) a majority of the Canadian Supreme Court held that a patient had given valid consent to an intimate examination by a doctor in the presence of a friend whom the patient believed was a medical intern.

Following the decision in *Montgomery*, it is arguable that if fraudulent or inaccurate information is given by a doctor this is evidence that the patient has not in fact been able to exercise an informed choice and, on that basis, has not consented.

16. Consent forms

Patients are normally asked to sign a pre-prepared written consent form prior to surgical procedures. The form will certify that doctors have explained the proposed operation, investigations or treatment to the patient. The legal consequences of the signature depend on the facts surrounding the signature and the information given to the patient.

In *St. George's Healthcare NHS Trust v S* ([1999] Fam.26) the Court of Appeal held that where a competent patient refuses consent the advice given to the patient should be recorded. If the patient is unwilling to sign a written confirmation of their refusal this should also be recorded in writing.

Such forms are evidence that the patient has signed the form but are not evidence that the patient has been given full information about the options and the risks and benefits of the procedure. There is no presumption that simply because a patient has signed a consent form that the patient has given valid consent. Equally, the absence of a signature does not mean a patient has not consented.

In *Chatterton v Gerson* ([1981] Q.B. 432) Bristow J said that:

> *getting the patient to sign a pro forma expressing consent to undergo the operation "the effect and nature of which have been explained to me" ... should be a valuable reminder to everyone of the need for explanation and consent. But it would be no defence to an action based on trespass to the person if no explanation had in fact been given. The consent would have been expressed in form only, not in reality.*

In *Re T (Adult: Refusal of Treatment)*, Lord Donaldson MR said:

> *It is clear that such forms are designed primarily to protect the hospital from legal action. They will be wholly ineffective for this purpose if the patient is incapable of understanding them, they are not explained to him and there is no good evidence (apart from the*

patient's signature) that he had that understanding and fully appreci-
ated the significance of signing it.

In *Coughlin v Kuntz* ((1987) 42 C.C.L.T. 142 (B.C.S.C.); affirmed [1990] 2
W.W.R. 737, 745 (B.C.C.A.)), the patient had signed a consent form but
it was held that the patient did not understand and appreciate the
nature of the procedure and as such there was no valid consent. In this
case, the procedure was novel, unique and under investigation by the
College of Physicians and Surgeons.

The absence of a signature on a consent form or an ineffective signature
does not inevitably mean the patient has not consented to the
procedure. It will depend on the facts and circumstances of the case.

In *Taylor v Shropshire Health Authority* ([1998] Lloyd's Rep. Med. 395) it
was held that an ineffective signature on a consent form does not necessarily indicate that the patient has not given valid consent. Popplewell J
regarded the consent form as "pure window dressing" (see also *Newbury v
Bath District Health Authority* (1998) 47 B.M.L.R. 138).

In *Williamson v East London & City Health Authority* ([1998] Lloyd's
Rep. Med. 6) an earlier signed consent form was amended to reflect the
true nature of the procedure performed. The amendments were not
signed and it was held that this strongly pointed to the fact that she had
not been present when it was amended.

Normally the consent form will specify the procedure the patient
consents to. If there is a variant of the procedure during the course of
surgery it is a question of fact whether the consent form is sufficient.
Normally supplementary procedures would require additional consent.

Some of the older consent forms had a standard clause to the effect that
the patient consented to such further or alternative operative measures
of treatment as may be found necessary during the course of the operation or treatment. This type of clause would now be considered highly
questionable.

In *David v Barking, Havering and Brentwood Health Authority* ([1993] 4 Med. L.R. 85), the claimant signed a consent form authorising the administration of a general anaesthetic for her surgery. During the procedure, the anaesthetist administered a caudal block and following surgery the claimant was unable to move her legs or control her bladder. She did make a recovery but had some residual disability. She alleged that she was not consented for the caudal block since she had not been informed about it. It was held that she had been given sufficient information about the anaesthetic to have consented to the caudal block.

Care must be taken to ask a patient to sign consent forms when they are not affected by sedation or other medication. In *Kelly v Hazlett* ((1976) 75 D.L.R. (3d) 536 (Ont. H.C.)) the patient signed the consent form after the administration of a sedative. In this case, it was held that the patient had appropriately consented as she had a knowledge of the nature and character of the procedure. However, Morden J commented that the validity of the consent in such a situation must be open to question.

In *Consent: Patients and Doctors Making Decisions Together* (2 June 2008), the GMC provides that before accepting a patient's consent the doctor should consider whether they have been given all the information they want or need, and how well they understand the details and implications of what is proposed (para 44). The guidance provides:

> *You must use the patient's medical record or a consent form to record the key elements of your discussion with the patient. This should include the information you discussed, any specific requests by the patient, any written, visual or audio information given to the patient, and the details of any decisions that were made.* (para 51)

In November 2016, the Royal College of Surgeons in London issued guidance on consent following *Montgomery* and in relation to the consent form provided:

- Consent should be written and recorded. If the patient has made a decision, the consent forms should be signed at the end of the discussion. The signed form is part of the evidence that the discussion has taken place, but provides no meaningful information about the quality of the discussion.

- In addition to the consent form, a record of the discussion (including contemporaneous documentation, of the key points of the discussion, hard copies or web links of any further information provided to the patient, and the patient's decision) should be included in the patient's case notes. This is important even if the patient chooses not to undergo treatment.

17. Conclusion

For many years, a patient's right to information has been circumscribed by what doctors as a professional body thought they should be told. Courts in many countries had endorsed this paternalistic approach and this denied patients the right to make their own health care decisions. Since the 1980s an increasing number of common- and civil-law jurisdictions have moved away from the professional standards of disclosure to patient-based ones.

The decision in *Montgomery* has had a significant impact on the area of information disclosure to patients and at last brought the UK law into line with other common-law jurisdictions. UK lawyers should ask the question why the law in the UK has steadfastly adhered to a professional practice test in this area which had been rejected from around the 1980s by many other jurisdictions.

The medical profession cannot now collectively determine by its own practices how much information a patient is entitled to receive when making decisions about their own health. In recognising the rights of patients, the Supreme Court has also emphasised the individual responsibility of patients in making decisions about their own health.

The liability of the doctor will be determined on the basis of what information they gave to the patient prior to or during the treatment.

What the reasonable doctor should have told the patient in question will need to be viewed against the background of the specific facts and circumstances of the individual case.

It may be reasonable to suggest as a starting point that a doctor does have to advise a patient of the factual reasonable options for treatment and the risks and benefits of those options. It can be assumed that an individual patient will want at least as much information as the reasonable patient would require. Thereafter the doctor must look at the factual circumstances of the patient in front of them and assess whether additional information is required to enable *this* patient to make a choice.

Where a patient asks specific questions, or has concerns under the second limb of the test in *Rogers v Whitaker* there is an additional responsibility imposed on the doctor to address any issues raised.

In the Justice KT Desai Memorial Lecture 2017 (*Law of medicine and the individual: current issues. What does patient autonomy mean for the courts?*), Lady Justice Arden hailed the arrival of an informational right for patients which is not dependent on medical judgement. She concluded that following the decision in *Montgomery* "the pendulum has swung decisively from paternalism at one end to autonomy at the other":

> *Montgomery is for me a landmark decision because of its focus on the patient and the patient's right to know. It represents a paradigm shift in the role of the doctor. The same will apply to the clinicians. The doctor or clinician is no longer wholly in control of the treatment options. The patient herself must be fully involved in those choices. This is an important point of principle because patient autonomy is an aspect of individual liberty. The patient should be in a position to make decisions about his or her body, and to give her fully informed consent to any intrusions into it. (There is a parallel here between patient autonomy and privacy. The patient is entitled to protection by the law for his or her private space.)*

The GMC has for many years produced guidance recognising the rights of patients in this area and this guidance appears to have been largely ignored by the courts, which have been content to allow the medical profession to dictate what they decide individual patients should be told by reference to a generalising standard and ignoring their own professional guidance.

As far back as 1998, in *Seeking Patients' Consent: The Ethical Considerations*, the GMC provided:

> *Successful relationships between doctors and patients depend on trust. To establish that trust you must respect patient's autonomy-their right to decide whether or not to undergo any medical intervention.*
>
> *Patients must be given sufficient information, in a way they can understand, to enable them to exercise their right to make informed decisions about their care.*
>
> *Patients have a right to information about their condition and the treatment options available to them.*
>
> *When providing information you must do your best to find out about patients' individual needs and priorities.*
>
> *It is for the patient, not the doctor, to determine what is in the patient's own best interests.*

The guidance has been regularly updated but the theme has essentially remained unaltered. The guidance sets out the professional standard expected from a doctor in respect of information disclosure.

There have been significant changes in the nature of the relationship between the doctor and patient and this was recognised by the Supreme Court. The days where patients were seen as passive participants in decisions about their own care made entirely by the doctor are long gone. The GMC talks about mutual decision-making, with patients as active participants.

In *Montgomery*, the Supreme Court made reference to the GMC guidance in identifying the ethos of professionally acceptable disclose of information to patients:

> *Work in partnership with patients. Listen to, and respond to, their concerns and preferences. Give patients the information they want or need in a way they can understand. Respect patients' right to reach decisions with you about their treatment and care.*

The basic model is a partnership between doctor and patient:

> *The doctor explains the options to the patient, setting out the potential benefits, risks, burdens and side effects of each option, including the option to have no treatment. The doctor may recommend a particular option which they believe to be best for the patient, but they must not put pressure on the patient to accept their advice. The patient weighs up the potential benefits, risks and burdens of the various options as well as any non-clinical issues that are relevant to them. The patient decides whether to accept any of the options and, if so which one.*

In Australia, when considering the cases of *Rogers v Whitaker* and *Chappel v Hart*, it was said:

> *Technical proficiency henceforth will be only part of the health care practitioner's necessary arsenal of skills. It must be accompanied by sophisticated communication skills, and this is an important step forward for consumers.... The doctor must engage in "real dialogue" with the patient. (*Freckleton, I., *The New Duty to Warn*, 1999)

In his article "Informed Consent and Other Fairy Stories" ((1999) 7 Med. L.R. 103), Professor Michael A. Jones commented following the decision in *Sidaway* on a perceived imbalance of power in the doctor–patient relationship:

> *Part of the imbalance between doctor and patient is due to the patient's lack of information, and, on one view, it is the function of*

the law to redress the imbalance by providing patients with the "right" to be given that information, or perhaps more accurately imposing a duty on doctors to provide it. There are some within the medical profession who appear to resent the notion that informed consent is part and parcel of "patient rights"-a patient with rights is a lawsuit waiting to happen. On the other hand, a patient with no rights is a citizen who is stripped of his or her individuality and autonomy, as well as her clothes, as soon as she walks into the surgery or the hospital.

Professor Jones noted that the law can have a powerful and galvanising role in how the doctor–patient relationship operates. The "happy ending" as he saw it would be found if the iterative process between case law and professional guidance were to lead to the creation of a more substantive "right" to information and choice for patients. The decision of the Supreme Court in *Montgomery* will achieve this aim if properly applied by the courts.

Although the issue of consent formed a central part of the argument in *Bolam*, *Sidaway* provided the first opportunity for the House of Lords to examine consent, and the duty of the doctor to disclose information. *Sidaway* was also concerned with the extent of the doctor's duty to volunteer information about the risks of treatment.

Prior to *Sidaway* there had been a number of first-instance decisions that addressed the issue of a doctor's duty to provide information to their patients. (*O'Malley-Williams v Board of Governors of the National Hospital for Nervous Disease* ([1975] 1 B.M.J. 635 (Bridge J)); *Wells v Surrey AHA* (1978 The Times, 29 July); *Sankey v Kensington and Chelsea and West-minster AHA* (2 April 1982, unreported QBD)).

In *Chatterton v Gerson* ([1981] Q.B. 432) and *Hills v Potter* ([1983] 3 All E.R. 716) the courts did make some attempt to define what information should be disclosed to make consent meaningful. In *Chatterton*, Bristow J applied the *Bolam* test and held that it was the doctor's duty to "explain what he intends to do, and its implications, in the way a careful and responsible doctor in similar circumstances would have done" (para 6-034). It was considered that if there were a real risk inherent in the procedure a doctor had a duty to warn the patient of that risk.

The same approach was adopted in *Hills v Potter*, where there was an inherent risk of paralysis in the operation even if it had been performed with due skill and care. It was held that the proper standard of disclosure was the *Bolam* test. It was doubted whether there was a distinction in the medical context between advice on the one hand and diagnosis and treatment on the other. In *Hills v Potter* it was not accepted that by adopting the *Bolam* principle the court in effect abdic-ated its power of decision to the doctors. It was provided that a court must be satisfied that the standard contended for on their behalf accords with that upheld by a substantial body of medical opinion, and that the body of opinion is both respectable and responsible and experienced in this particular field of medicine.

In this period the courts in the UK clung to the simplistic professional test, which placed weight on medical judgement. They did not appear to seriously contemplate any departure from the test. The emphasis was not on the rights of the patient. The medical profession was permitted to "judge" not only issues of technical negligence but also what information a patient was permitted to receive. The disclosure of risks inherent in the proposed treatment was seen as a product of the doctor's duty of care rather than as a product of the patient's right to self-determination.

2. The background facts

In *Sidaway* there was a clear opportunity for a superior court to consider the issue of information disclosure and recognise the fact that the disclosure of information to patients is a matter distinct from technical expertise or diagnosis.

The claimant in *Sidaway* had suffered from persistent pain in her neck and shoulders. She was advised she should have an operation on the spine and this would relieve her pain. She was given some general warnings about the possibility of disturbing a nerve root, and the consequences should this occur. She was not warned of the possibility of damage to the spinal cord. The risk of spinal cord damage was less than 1%. One consequence of damage to the spinal cord was paralysis.

The claimant sustained severe damage resulting in partial paralysis. It was not suggested that the surgery was performed negligently. The claimant argued that she should have been advised of the risk of paralysis, and that had she been advised of the risk she would not have proceeded with the surgery. At that time a responsible body of medical opinion would not have advised of the risk of spinal cord damage. The initial trial judge, and the Court of Appeal, held that there was no negligence as the doctor had acted in accordance with the professional practice test as found in *Bolam*. The claimant then appealed to the House of Lords.

3.   The decision

The House of Lords in *Sidaway* affirmed the opinion of the Court of Appeal. There were a number of distinct strands in the speeches delivered by their Lordships but what is clear was that there was not a unanimous endorsement of *Bolam* principles in the context of a professional negligence case based on a failure to consent a patient. It is important in considering the impact of *Montgomery* to consider and analyse the views expressed by the court in this case.

Lord Diplock

Lord Diplock considered that any alleged breach of a doctor's duty of care towards their patient, whether it related to diagnosis, treatment or advice, should be determined by applying the *Bolam* test:

> *The merit of the* Bolam *test is that the criterion of the duty of care owed by a doctor to his patient is whether he has acted in accordance with a practice accepted as proper by a body of responsible and skilled medical opinion.... To decide what risks the existence of which a patient should be voluntarily warned and the terms in which such warning, if any, should be given, having regard to the effect that warning may have, is as much an exercise of professional skill and judgement as any other part of the doctor's comprehensive duty of care to the individual patient, and expert medical evidence on this matter should be treated in just the same way. The* Bolam *test should be applied.* (para 895)

According to Lord Diplock, the duty to inform was not a separate duty but part of the overarching duty of care owed by the doctor to the patient. The content of this duty was set out in *Bolam*. The doctor's duty in obtaining a patient's consent was to provide the patient with that information which a responsible body of doctors would judge to be appropriate. If doctors decide to withhold information, it was not for the courts to gainsay them. The extent and limits of the duty of the doctor to disclose information was determined by analysis of expert evidence of contemporary professional practice. He declined to draw any distinction between the exercise or technical skill and information disclosure. On his analysis, if the patient has any right at all it is the right to be treated as the doctor thinks best.

Lord Diplock did suggest that if a patient manifested an attitude by means of questioning that suggested they wished information it would be the duty of the doctor to tell the patient whatever it was the patient wanted to know. There was in his view no obligation to provide a patient with unsolicited information about risks. He said:

> *The only effect that mention of risks can have on the patient's mind, if it has any at all, can be in the direction of deterring the patient from undergoing the treatment which in the expert opinion of the doctor it is in the patient's interest to undergo.* (para 896)

In this statement, he appears to endorse a test in which a patient who asks questions is entitled to different (more) information than a patient who does not.

Lord Bridge of Harwich

Lord Bridge of Harwich developed the second strand of that argument and, with some variation, Lord Templeman agreed. Lord Bridge (with whom Lord Keith of Kinkel concurred) relied on *Bolam*. It seems clear that his view was that the duty went slightly further than a simple *Bolam* approach. He recognised that a conscious adult of sound mind was entitled to decide for themselves whether or not they will submit to a particular course of treatment proposed by the doctor.

He recognised the logical force of the North American jurisprudence, particularly the principles found in *Canterbury v Spence* (464 F.2d 772 (1972) (U.S.C.A., District of Columbia)) and *Reibl v Hughes* ([1980] 114 D.L.R. (3d) 1 (S.C.C.)). He made reference to one of the best known statements of patient rights in information disclosure by Laskin CJC in *Reibl v Hughes*. He regarded it as impractical in application. Like Lord Diplock he emphasised the patient's lack of medical knowledge, their vulnerability to making irrational judgements, and the role of "clinical judgement" in assessing how best to communicate to the patient significant factors necessary to enable the patient to make an informed decision (para 899).

Lord Bridge failed to distinguish between the exercise of the technical role and information disclosure. He said that the duty must "primarily" be a matter of clinical judgement. However, he recognised that applying the *Bolam* test without qualification to the question of disclosure of risks carried a danger of medical paternalism which might not be controlled by the courts. He was of the view that, even in a case where no expert witness in the relevant field condemns the non-disclosure as being in conflict with accepted and responsible medical practice, it may be open to a judge to come to the conclusion that a disclosure of risk was so obviously necessary to the informed choice on the part of the patient that no reasonable prudent medical man would fail to make it.

Lord Bridge then provided one example of the type of case where he thought a doctor would have a duty to advise irrespective of professional practice. He said that the kind of case he had in mind was an operation involving a substantial risk of grave adverse consequences. In that situation, the doctor would be under a duty to advise the patient, whatever the prevailing medical view. The example he gave was one where there was a 10% risk of stroke following surgery, as was found in *Reibl v Hughes*. In such a case, in the absence of some cogent clinical reason why the patient should not be informed, a doctor, recognising and respecting their patient's right of decision, could hardly fail to appreciate the necessity for an appropriate warning:

> *But even in a case where, as here, no expert witness in the relevant medical field condemns the non-disclosure as being in conflict with accepted and responsible medical practice, I am of the opinion that the judge might in certain circumstances come to the conclusion that disclosure of a particular risk was so obviously necessary to an informed choice on the part of the patient that no reasonably prudent medical man would fail to make it. The kind of case if have in mind would be an operation involving a substantial risk of grave adverse consequences, as, for example, the ten per cent risk of a stroke from*

the operation which was the subject of the Canadian case of Reibl v
Hughes *114 DLR (3d) 1. In that case, in the absence of some cogent
clinical reason why the patient should not be informed, a doctor,
recognising and respecting his patient's right of decision, could hardly
fail to appreciate the necessity for an appropriate warning.* (para
900)

Lord Templeman

The speech of Lord Templeman equivocates between an acceptance of
Bolam and a potential for something more. He approached the issue on
the basis of an orthodox common-law analysis. He stated the doctor
had a duty to act in the "best interests of the patient" and provide the
patient with information which would enable the patient to make a
balanced judgement. He said that a patient might make an unbalanced
judgement if he is deprived of adequate information.

He recognised a difference between general and special dangers. A
doctor might warn a patient of a danger which may be special in kind
or magnitude, or special to the patient. As regards the former, a simple
and general explanation should be enough to alert the patient. In relation to special dangers, there was a duty to inform.

Like Lord Diplock and Lord Bridge, he focused on the imbalance
between the knowledge and objectivity of the doctor, and the ignorance
and subjectivity of the patient. He did appear to accept that it was the
right of the patient to decide whether or not to submit to treatment
recommended by the doctor, and even to make an unbalanced and irrational judgement. It is not entirely clear what he was proposing but it
cannot be said that he views the duty as one solely defined by the *Bolam*
test.

Lord Scarman

The approach of Lord Scarman was the most patient-orientated
approach. He agreed with the final decision of the court but took a
radically different view and gave primacy to the right of the patient. His

view did not ultimately prevail; however, his speech is worthy of consideration as this was the speech referred to by the Supreme Court in *Montgomery*.

Lord Scarman said that the decisive question for the court was whether the doctor had overlooked or disregarded their patient's right to determine for themselves whether or not to have the operation which had resulted in partial paralysis by withholding from them the information necessary to make a prudent decision.

Lord Scarman focused on the issue of rights. In his view, the doctor's duty arose from the patient's rights. He dissented from the majority in his approach on the application of the *Bolam* test. He was concerned that the application of the *Bolam* test to the issue of what information a patient was entitled to receive would leave too much to the discretion of the medical profession. The test did not allow the question to be addressed from the perspective of the patient. He concluded that a patient had a right to know what treatment entails so as to be able to make a reasoned choice and thus give valid consent. He considered this to be a basic human right protected by the common law. He said:

If one considers the scope of the doctor's duty by beginning with the right of the patient to make his own decision whether he will or will not undergo the treatment proposed, the right to be informed of significant risk and the doctor's corresponding duty are easy to understand, for the proper implementation of the right requires the doctor to be under a duty to inform the patient of the material risks inherent in the treatment. (para 888)

If, therefore, the failure to warn a patient of the risks inherent in the operation which is recommended does constitute a failure to respect the patient's right to make his own decision, I can see no reason in principle why, if the risk materialises and injury or damage is caused, the law should not recognise and enforce a right in the patient to compensation by way of damages. (paras 884–885)

Lord Scarman recognised that the duty to provide information was of a different order from the duty to take care in treatment, and as such this was not a matter to be decided on the basis of evidence as to prevailing medical practice:

> *The doctor's concern is with health and the relief of pain. These are medical objectives. But a patient may well have in mind circumstances, objectives, and values which may lead him to a different decision from that suggested by a purely medical opinion.*
> (paras 885–886)

Lord Scarman chose as his guide the case law which had evolved in the USA and Canada, particularly *Canterbury v Spence* and *Reibl v Hughes*. The *Canterbury* propositions in his opinion reflected "a legal truth which too much judicial reliance on medical judgement tends to obscure".

He did not adopt the rights-based approach reflected in the North American doctrine of informed consent, but he was persuaded of the underlying correctness of the argument. According to his approach, the law can expect doctors to provide the patient with sufficient or adequate information to make a considered decision. He concluded that there was room in UK law for a legal duty to warn a patient of significant risks inherent in the treatment proposed. He considered that the patient's right to decide for themselves was a basic human right protected by the common law. Courts should not allow medical opinion on what was best for a patient to override the right of the patient to make their own decision. The court should determine the scope of the duty and also decide whether the doctor has acted in breach of their duty.

Lord Scarman also focuses on the concept of materiality. Information is material, and thus the doctor would have a duty to disclose it to the patient, if it were something which the particular patient would wish to know, or if it were that which a reasonable patient, in the particular patient's circumstances, would wish to know. The test of materiality was whether, in the circumstances of the particular case, the court was satisfied that a reasonable person in the patient's position would be likely to attach significance to the risk, or cluster of risks, in deciding whether to undergo the proposed treatment. What was relevant was the likely incidence of injury and the degree of harm threatened.

Lord Scarman said that responsible medical judgement may provide the law with an acceptable standard in determining whether a doctor has complied with their duty of care in diagnosis or treatment. However, he considered that the issue of whether there was a duty to warn and the scope of that duty was of a different nature.

Lord Scarman envisaged that that the duty to inform also extended to information about alternatives:

> *To the extent that I have indicated I think that English law must recognise a duty of the doctor to warn his patient of risk inherent in the treatment which he is proposing: and especially so, if the treatment be surgery. The critical limitation is that the duty is confined to material risk. The test of materiality is whether in the circumstances of the particular case the court is satisfied that a reasonable person in the patient's position would be likely to attach significance to the risk. Even if the risk be material, the doctor will not be liable if upon a reasonable assessment of his patient's condition he takes the view that a warning would be detrimental to his patient's health.* (paras 889–890)

He did recognise that the decision as to what is a material risk should be addressed with reference to the particular patient. However, he rejected this test as being utopian, preferring the "prudent patient" test. He also permitted the defence that a doctor may reasonably withhold information from a patient if they considered that it was in the patient's best interest to do so.

4.   Cases following the decision in Sidaway

Following *Sidaway* the Court of Appeal adopted a restricted approach to the doctor's duty to disclose in *Blyth v Bloomsbury Health Authority* ([1993] 4 Med. L.R. 151, C.A.) and *Gold v Haringey Health Authority* ([1988] Q.B. 481). In these cases, there was preference for the most paternalistic of the speeches in *Sidaway* determining the doctor's duty with reference to the reasonable professional standard. What was important was the doctrine seen to be emerging from *Sidaway*, and, if there was an extension of *Bolam*, what that might be.

Blyth v Bloomsbury Health Authority (heard in 1985 and reported in 1993) considered the nature of the duty of the doctor where it was asserted that a patient had asked questions. The Court of Appeal considered that the question of what a claimant should be told in response to specific questions could not be divorced from the *Bolam* test, any more than when no inquiry was made. In this case the court appeared to go further than *Sidaway* in extending *Bolam* principles to a request for information from a patient.

In *Gold*, the claimant underwent a sterilisation operation, which failed and she conceived a fourth child. She argued that the defendants were negligent in failing to warn her of the risks of failure. The rate of failure was 20–60 per 10,000. The trial judge found the defendants to be negligent despite the fact that there was evidence that a substantial body of doctors would not have advised of the risk. He also took the view that the *Bolam* test did not apply in the non-therapeutic context. The decision was reversed by the Court of Appeal. The Court of Appeal came down firmly in favour of *Bolam simpliciter*. Lloyd LJ (with whom Watkins and Stephen Brown LJJ agreed) chose to rely exclusively on the speech of Lord Diplock in *Sidaway*. It was stated that it was open to the House of Lords in *Sidaway* to adopt the doctrine of "informed consent" favoured in the USA and Canada but that they had declined to follow that path (see *Loveday v Renton* [1990] 1 Med LR 117).

In *Eyre v Measeday* ([1986] 1 All ER 488) the claimant asserted that she had not been advised of the risk of failure of her sterilisation procedure.

The claim was founded on breach of contact. In rejecting the claim, it was held that in withholding the information the doctor was following a practice accepted by current professional standards.

In *McAllister v Lewisham and North Southwark HA* ([1994] 5 Med LR 343) Rougier J accepted that the *Bolam* test was the appropriate standard for determining disclosure of information. However, he held that, in the absence of "cogent clinical reason" justifying withholding information, there were certain risks that ought to be disclosed irrespective of professional practice. With reference to the judgment of Lord Bridge in *Sidaway*, he held:

> *within certain limitations, a patient is entitled to be given sufficient information on the risks of an operation to allow him or her to exercise a balanced judgement; after all it is their life that is going to be affected.* (para 351)

In *Pearce v United Bristol Healthcare NHS Trust* ([1999] P.I.Q.R. P53), Lord Woolf MR relied primarily upon Lord Bridge's approach in *Sidaway*. This case concerned an expectant mother whose baby had gone over term. Her consultant obstetrician took the view that she should wait and have a normal delivery, rather than proceed to caesarean section at an earlier date. The mother was not warned of the risk the baby could die *in utero*, which is in fact what happened. The question was whether she should have been warned of that risk to assist her in selection of the option for delivery. The level of the increased risk – 0.1–0.2% – was not considered to fall within the category of significant risk.

The Master of the Rolls (with whom Roch and Mummery LJJ agreed) concluded that if there was a significant risk that would affect the judgement of a reasonable patient then, in the normal course of events, it was the responsibility of the doctor to inform the patient of that risk. Lord Woolf said he rejected any reliance on precise percentages of risk, accepting that there may be exceptional circumstances where the duty to warn did not apply. In determining what to tell a patient the doctor had to take account of all relevant considerations, which included the ability of the patient to comprehend what was said, and the physical and mental state of the patient at the time. It was said:

> *In a case where it is being alleged that a plaintiff has been deprived of the opportunity to make a proper decision as to what course he or she should take in relation to treatment, it seems to me to be the law ... that if there is as significant risk which would affect the judgement of the reasonable patient, then in the normal course it is the responsibility of the doctor to inform the patient of that significant risk, if the information is needed so that the patient can determine for him or herself as to what course he or she should adopt.* (para 59)

The decision in *Pearce* has been said to have informed the decision in *Sidaway*. It includes consideration of the interest of the patient, which the *Bolam* test does not do, and holds that risks should be disclosed if they are significant to the reasonable patient. It is not the test formulated in *Montgomery*.

In *Wyatt v Curtis* ([2003] EWCA Civ 1779) there was around a 1% risk that chickenpox in pregnancy might result in significant brain damage. Sedley LJ stated:

> *Lord Woolf's formulation refines Lord Bridge's test by recognising that what is substantial and what is grave are questions on which the doctor's and the patient's perception may differ, and in relation to which the doctor must therefore have regard to what may be the patient's perception. To the doctor, a chance in a hundred that the patient's chickenpox may produce an abnormality in the foetus may well be an insubstantial chance, and any abnormality may in any case not be grave. To the patient, a new risk which (as I read the judge's appraisal of the expert evidence) doubles, or at least enhances, the background risk of a potentially catastrophic abnormality may well be both substantial and grave, or at least sufficiently real for her to want to make an informed decision about it.* (para 16)

In *Chester v Afshar* ([2004] UKHL 41; [2005] 1 A.C. 134; [2004] 3 W.L.R. 927 HL) the House of Lords revisited consent, but principally in the context of causation. However, it is relevant to consider the majority's comments regarding the patient's right to autonomy. Lord Bingham of Cornhill said that the doctor in question had been under a duty to warn the patient of a small (1–2%) risk that the proposed operation might lead to a seriously adverse result. The rationale of the duty was to enable an adult patient of sound mind to make for themselves decisions that intimately affected their own lives and bodies.

In *Chester v Afshar* Lord Steyn cited with approval Lord Woolf MR's judgment in *Pearce*. He emphasised that in modern law medical paternalism no longer rules, and that a patient has a *prima facie* right to be informed by a surgeon of a small but well established risk of serious injury. He went on to identify patient autonomy and dignity as the legal interests protected by the obligation to obtain informed consent. There was recognition that during the 20 years since *Sidaway* the importance of personal autonomy had been more and more widely recognised. It was also noted that, when making a decision that might have a profound effect on health and well-being of a patient, that patient was entitled to information and advice about possible alternative or variant treatments.

In *Chester*, Lord Hope found the duty to disclose in the speeches of Lord Bridge and Lord Templeman in *Sidaway*. In discussing the question of causation, Lord Hope acknowledged the highly subjective significance of the risk.

In *Al Hamwi v Johnston and North West London Hospitals NHS Trust* ([2005] EWHC 206 (Q.B.) [2005] Lloyd's Rep Med 309) it was said that advice should be balanced and tailored to the individual patient. Reference was made to the GMC guidance on consent.

In *Birch v University College London Hospital NHS Foundation Trust* ([2008] EWCH 2237 (Q.B.)) the court held that a patient should be told of the comparative risks of alternative procedures. Cranston J relied on *Pearce* and *Chester*. He explained that the obvious rationale was patient autonomy and respect for the reality that it was the patient who must bear any consequences if a risk transforms itself into a reality.

In Scotland, Lord Caplan was asked in *Moyes v Lothian Health Board* ([1990] 1 Med. L.R. 463) to consider what was essentially a causation argument in a consent case. The claimant had suffered a stroke whilst undergoing angiography. It was accepted that angiography carried a risk of significant neurological symptoms (including stroke), even in a healthy patient. The risk was 0.2–0.3%. The claimant claimed that she should have been warned of the risk of stroke. In her situation, the risk of stroke was increased as a result of her hypersensitivity and history of migraine. The Health Board contended that she had been warned about the risk of stroke generally, but not that the risk was increased owing to her hypersensitivity and history of migraine. The stroke which occurred was actually caused by an embolism and the Health Board argued there was no causal connection between the failure to warn and the injury. Lord Caplan accepted the claimant's argument that had she been advised of the cumulative risks of the procedure she would not have gone ahead.

In *Smith v Tunbridge Wells Health Authority* ([1994] 5 Med.L.R.334) Moreland J took the view that the doctor, when warning of risks, must take reasonable care to ensure that their explanation of the risks was intelligible to their patient. The very fact of consent and the speed of the consent were thought by the court to be indicative that a risk of impotence was not communicated to this young man. Mooreland J suggested that the doctor should use language which was understandable by the patient. This is stated in the current GMC guidance on consent.

In *Smith v Salford Health Authority* ([1994] 5 Med. L.R. 321 QBD) the experts were all agreed that the risks of paralysis from the surgery, or indeed death, should have been explained and in doing so there was a failure in care. In this case the claimant failed on the causation argument. (See also *Doughty v North Staffordshire Health Authority* [1992] 3 Med LR 81; *Newell and Newell v Goldenberg* [1995] 6 Med LR 371).

In *McAllister v Lewisham and North Southwark Health Authority* ([1994] 5 Med. L.R. 343, QBD) the claimant was left with the impression that there were no risks in proceeding with surgery for a large AV malformation. In fact, the risks associated with the operation were significant. The evidence was to the effect that many neurosurgeons would not have attempted the surgery.

In *Jones v North West Strategic Health Authority* ([2010] Med.L.R.90) Nicol J relied on Lord Woolf's approach in *Pearce*. His interpretation of the test is even closer to the spirit of the prudent patient test. His view was that the role of the expert was to define the nature and quantify the likelihood of the risks relevant to the claimant's case. He relegated the experts to the role of factual advisors to the court.

In *Meiklejohn v St George's Healthcare NHS Trust, Homerton University Hospitals Foundation Trust* ([2014] EWCA Civ 120) the court considered the duty to advise and warn about diagnosis, treatment and possible side effects was to be decided with reference to the *Bolam* test. It was said that there was no duty to warn of a possible alternative diagnosis that was not reasonably suspected.

5.   Comment

In Brazier's opinion, the *Sidaway* decision in no way concluded the debate on the role of the law in determining how much information patients must be provided with in order to give consent to a procedure. She felt that their Lordships were too readily convinced by arguments that enhancing patient autonomy might in some way damage their health. She argued that they also failed to take account of the complex nature of the doctor–patient relationship and much of debate in the UK on the development of effective health care.

The difficulty with the decision in *Sidaway* is how it was interpreted by the courts in subsequent cases up to the point of the decisions in *Pearce*, *Wyatt* and finally *Montgomery*. Following *Sidaway* most lawyers agreed that the *Bolam* test was the starting point for the court. The majority did appear to embrace the test and only Lord Scarman felt that it was inappropriate in the consent setting. What then of the cases where the *Bolam* test did not assist a claimant? It is clear from the view of the majority in *Sidaway* that the *Bolam* test was not the end of the matter. There was some recognition by Lords Bridge of Harwich, Keith of Kinkel, Templeman and Scarman of the right to self-determination.

The difficulty is finding consistency on the test to be applied in the case of "the exception" to the professional practice test because it was expressed in different ways by their Lordships. What seems clear is that Lord Diplock was the only judge in *Sidaway* who applied the *Bolam* test without exception. Indeed, Lord Scarman in 1986, when giving a lecture at the Royal Society of Medicine, stated that Lord Diplock was in a minority of one ((1986) 79 J Roy Soc Med 697).

In the application of the *Bolam* test in *Sidaway* it was recognised that the courts may need to deal with conflicts in medical opinion. In fact, Lord Bridge anticipated the *Bolitho* argument (*Bolitho v City and Hackney Health Authority* [1998] A.C. 232) when he talked about conflicts of medical evidence and the fact that the courts would resolve those conflicts. However, he specifically stated that, even in a case where there was no expert evidence to condemn the non-disclosure of information, there were certain circumstances in which a judge could come to a conclusion that disclosure of a particular risk was so obviously necessary to an informed choice on the part of a patient that no reasonably prudent medical man would fail to make it.

Decisions immediately following *Sidaway* were disappointing. It has been said that the decision in *Gold* was an irritating exercise in totally misplaced judicial paternalism which confirmed, following *Sidaway*, that some judges still clung to the opinion that less inquisitive patients are entitled to know only what doctors think they should be told. Professor Ian Kennedy was surprised and somewhat saddened by the *Gold* decision and observed that the court missed the very critical issue that for a patient to give proper consent they need to understand not only the risks but also the alternatives (The Times, 24 April 1987).

In England and Wales, although *Sidaway* was binding upon the courts, in most cases the lower courts had tacitly ceased to apply a strict *Bolam* test in relation to consent cases. Some exceptions were demonstrated by

Meiklejohn v St George's Healthcare NHS Trust, Homerton University Hospitals Foundation Trust.

In *Pearce*, the Master of the Rolls did refer to Lord Bridge's speech in *Sidaway*, but the approach can also be seen to be consistent with some of the views expressed by Lord Templeman as well as the test favoured by Lord Scarman. Lord Woolf MR's speech provides an analysis of what is required. He does however reject reliance on case law from other common-law jurisdictions. He also makes reference to "a significant risk which would affect the judgement of a reasonable patient". In doing so he is clearly applying an objective reasonable patient test to the question of materiality.

Professional guidance from the GMC goes further than the reasonable patient test and states that a doctor requires to find out about the patient's individual needs and priorities. The focus is on the patient as an individual and not simply the reasonable patient. The problem with only an objective test, as suggested in *Pearce*, is that it ignores the right of the individual patient to make a decision that is not reasonable. This is not the patient-centred test applied in *Rogers v Whitaker* and analysed in Chapter 3.

In *Chester v Afshar* there were relevant observations on the decision of the Master of the Rolls in *Pearce*. *Chester v Afshar* clearly embraces the right of the patient to have information about risks to enable them to make informed decisions.

Whilst there was some lack of clarity in the early decisions in the courts, elsewhere in the late 1990s there was recognition that there needed to be significant changes in the way health care was delivered. In 1998 the Bristol Royal Infirmary Inquiry was set up to investigate the deaths of babies undergoing heart surgery. The report was published in 2001 and Professor Ian Kennedy QC demanded that the NHS learn from the lessons of Bristol and act upon them. This report emphasised the central role of consent in the provision of medical care. The theme was a partnership involving patients.

Professor Kennedy concluded that in a patient-centred health care service patients must be involved, wherever possible in decisions about their treatment and care. He emphasised that the patient and the professional should meet as equals with different expertise. The education and training of all health care professionals should be imbued with the idea of this partnership.

In 1997 the Senate of Surgery of Great Britain and Ireland published *The Surgeon's Duty of Care*, which imposed on surgeons a duty in relation to patient information as rigorous as now provided for in *Montgomery*. There was also clear guidance issued by the General Medical Council. This period also saw the Human Rights Act 1998, of which Articles 2, 3, 5 6, 8 and 12 may all have relevance in different situations involving patient consent.

The Scottish courts were bound to follow the decision in *Sidaway*. The difficulty for the pursuer in *Montgomery* was the lack of consistency and clarity in *Sidaway* on what test should be applied by the courts to the exception to the professional practice test that the majority had recognised should exist. Because of this lack of clarity, it was possible for the defenders to take an extract from what Lord Bridge said in isolation and argue that the test should be focused on "adverse outcome" rather than anything else. They did not consider what had been said by all of their Lordships on the exception. They argued in *Montgomery* that the occurrence of brain damage or cerebral palsy was the adverse outcome to be considered. They suggested that shoulder dystocia was not an adverse outcome, and so the significant risk of shoulder dystocia was not relevant to the assessment. This argument was successful at first instance and on appeal but was rejected by the Supreme Court.

Lord Bridge had in fact started the passage by saying that in certain circumstances a judge may come to the conclusion that disclosure of a particular risk was so obviously necessary to an informed choice on the part of the patient that no reasonably prudent medical man would fail to make it. He then gave as one example an operation involving a substantial risk of grave adverse consequences such as a 10% risk of stroke. This was only one example of a situation where a judge could conclude the *Bolam* test could be set aside.

In *Montgomery* in the Supreme Court it was submitted on behalf of the claimant that the *Hunter v Hanley* or *Bolam* test had no appropriate application to the standard required when providing information to a patient. The appropriate test was the patient-focused test found in *Rogers v Whitaker*.

The decision in *Montgomery* has now clarified the test to be applied, and firmly removed the *Hunter v Hanley* and *Bolam* tests from the question of information disclosure to patient. The full argument is set out in Chapter 4. It has been said that the more weight that is attached to the individual patient's own will the more patient-centred the approach becomes. Prior to *Montgomery*, even with the view expressed in *Pearce*, these tests were relevant to the question of consent. Removal of the professional practice test is an extremely important development as it changes the way doctors and lawyers will view the issue of consent and rightly recognises the right of the patient to self-determination.

It is also arguable that following *Montgomery* the Supreme Court has embraced a twofold test not found in the words of Lord Woolf in *Pearce* and it is for this reason that agents now seeking to apply *Montgomery* must understand the approach formulated in Canada and Australia. The tests applied in both countries are set out in full in Chapter 3.

To quote from the GMC, the focus is now on patients making "informed decisions". To speak of "informed consent" as recognised by Lord Scarman in *Sidaway* is a misnomer. The requirement that consent be informed is only one component of valid consent. If the patient has not been given full information about the treatment options (including the option of no treatment), and the risks and benefits of those options, the patient cannot make an "Informed decision" to consent. Where this information is missing, a patient cannot make a reasoned choice. There is no valid consent.

The Supreme Court has said that the correct position in relation to the risks involved in treatment can now be seen to be substantially as per the approach adopted by the High Court of Australia in *Rogers v Whitaker*. The test in *Pearce* is subject to the refinement made by the High Court of Australia, which, it is suggested, is now the test to be applied in information disclosure. The court concluded there was a duty to warn of a material risk inherent in the proposed treatment. A risk is material if, in the circumstances of the particular case, a reasonable person in the patient's position, if warned of the risk, would be likely to attach significance to it (the objective limb), or if the medical practitioner is or should reasonably be aware that the particular patient, if warned of the risk, would be likely to attach significance to it (the subjective limb).

In 1985, Lord Scarman did recognise the importance of the rights of the patient and the importance of a patient-focused test but stopped short of the test now formulated by the Supreme Court in *Montgomery*. The Supreme Court has now clarified the position and come down in favour of a test that recognises the right of the individual patient to make decisions about their own health care.

CHAPTER THREE
THE APPROACH TO CONSENT
IN OTHER JURISDICTIONS

1.   Introduction

In the 1980s, Canada introduced a patient-focused test to their consent law, and in 1992 the Australian High Court in *Rogers v Whitaker* introduced what was at the time the most patient-orientated doctrine of consent amongst the common-law jurisdictions.

In *Montgomery*, the Supreme Court was provided with an analysis of the main cases on consent in other common-law jurisdictions. Those representing the claimant considered that, in deciding whether a patient-focused test should be introduced into the UK law on consent, the Supreme Court should consider how other jurisdictions had approached this question and analyse how they had formulated the legal test to be applied. It was also important to assess whether the test was workable in medical practice in the other jurisdictions.

In the decision issued by the Supreme Court in *Montgomery* there was reference to the principles found in the Canadian case of *Reibl v Hughes*, the Australian case of *Rosenberg v Percival* and in particular the decision of the High Court of Australia in *Rogers v Whitaker*.

The UK Supreme Court in *Montgomery* specifically referred to the judgment of Mason CJ and Brennan, Dawson, Toohey and McHugh JJ in *Rogers v Whitaker* and noted that the Australian court had identified the basic flaw involved in approaching all aspects of a doctor's duty of care in the same way:

> *Whether a medical practitioner carries out a particular form of treatment in accordance with the appropriate standard of care is a question in the resolution of which responsible professional opinion will have an influential, often a decisive, role to play; whether the patient has been given all the relevant information to choose between*

> *undergoing and not undergoing the treatment is a question of a different order.* **Generally speaking, it is not a question the answer to which depends upon medical standards or practices.** *Except in those cases where there is a particular danger that the provision of all relevant information will harm an unusually nervous, disturbed or volatile patient, no special medical skill is involved in disclosing the information, including the risks attending the proposed treatment.* (para 71)

The Supreme Court in *Montgomery* noted that the High Court of Australia in *Rogers v Whitaker* also reformulated the test of the materiality of a risk so as to encompass the situation in which the doctor knows or ought to know that the "actual" patient would be likely to attach greater significance to a risk than the hypothetical reasonable patient might do:

> *a risk is material if, in the circumstances of the particular case, a reasonable person in the patient's position, if warned of the risk, would be likely to attach significance to it or if the medical practitioner is or should reasonably be aware that the particular patient, if warned of the risk, would be likely to attach significance to it.* (para 72)

In embracing *Rogers v Whitaker* the UK Supreme Court reinforced the principle that the doctor's duty of care takes its precise content from the needs, concerns and circumstances of the individual patient, to the extent that they are or ought to be known to the doctor.

Following *Rogers v Whitaker*, expressions of concern by the patient, as well as specific questions, were held to be "plainly relevant" to consideration of the issue. The Supreme Court in *Montgomery* noted:

> *As Gummow J observed in* Rosenberg v Percival *(2001) 205 CLR 434, 459, courts should not be too quick to discard the second limb (i.e. the possibility that the medical practitioner was or ought reasonably to have been aware that the particular patient, if warned of the risk, would be likely to attach significance to it) merely because it*

emerges that the patient did not ask certain kinds of questions. (para 73)

The decisions from common-law jurisdictions that have sought to apply a patient-focused test to the issue of consent are vital for UK lawyers and UK courts in deciding how to apply the test in the post-*Montgomery* era. Other jurisdictions have been grappling with the concept of a patient-focused test in litigation since the 1980s and have encountered, and in some situations resolved, the questions that UK lawyers are at present trying to resolve.

The UK Supreme Court specifically referred to the patient-focused test as defined in *Rogers v Whitaker*, *Rosenberg v Percival* and *Reibl v Hughes* and stated that it did intend to go further than the test proposed by Lord Woolf in *Pearce v United Bristol Healthcare NHS Trust* ([1999] PIQR P53):

> *The correct position, in relation to the risks of injury involved in treatment, can now be seen to be substantially that adopted in* Sidaway *by Lord Scarman, and by Lord Woolf MR in* Pearce, **subject to the refinement** *made by the High Court of Australia in* Rogers v Whitaker. (para 87)

Although the decision in *Sidaway* was binding in the UK it was recognised that following the decision in *Pearce* English courts had tacitly ceased to apply a strict *Bolam* test and focused on what would affect the judgement of the "reasonable patient".

It is important to note the language of the test formulated by Lord Woolf:

> *that if there is a significant risk which would* **affect the judgement of a reasonable patient,** *then in the normal course it is the responsibility of the doctor to inform the patient of that significant risk, if the information is needed so that the patient can determine for him or herself as to what course he or she should adopt.*

In *Montgomery*, the Supreme Court went further than *Pearce* and endorsed a reasonable patient in the patient's position test. There is also the addition of a particular patient test focused on the peculiarities of the particular patient known to the doctor. This second limb of the test is not found in *Pearce* and is derived from *Rogers v Whitaker*.

Many of the UK decisions following *Montgomery* are inconsistent and some only appear to focus on a test formulated on the basis of a "reasonable patient" in the position of the claimant. This is dealt with in Chapter 7. It is suggested that the test formulated by the Supreme Court in *Montgomery* is a twofold test and it is vital that those developing the case law in the UK recognise this and have a clear understanding of the cases (particularly in Australia) where this test is developed and explained.

2.   **Australia**

a.   **Standard of care**

In Australia, it is for the court to determine whether conduct conforms to the standard of reasonable care determined by the law. In Australia, the basic underlying principles on what conduct amounts to medical negligence under common law are similar to that found in the UK.

In *Naxakis v Western General Hospital* ([1999] HCA 22), it was said that the test of medical negligence is not what other doctors say they would or would not have done in similar circumstances. In the context of a medical negligence claim, the standard of care of a doctor or other health care provider is that of an ordinary skilled person exercising and professing to have that special skill.

Following a review of the law of negligence (*Commonwealth of Australia, Panel of Eminent Persons (Chair: D Ipp) Review of the Law of Negligence Report 2002*), there was an introduction of civil liability legislation throughout Australia through the Civil Liability Acts. As part of tort law reform, each state in Australia enacted different laws that have impacted on medical negligence claims. The Civil Liability Acts of the state legislatures aimed at a redistribution between members of society of the losses that flow from accidents.

The Civil Liability Act 2002 (NSW), which is substantially replicated in all other Australian states and the Australian Capital Territory, provides as follows:

A determination that negligence caused particular harm comprises the following elements:

*(a) that the negligence was a necessary condition of the occurrence of the harm (*factual causation*), and*

*(b) that it is appropriate for the scope of the negligent person's liability to extend to the harm so caused (*scope of liability*).*

Section 50 of the Civil Liability Act 2002 (NSW) defines the standard of care to be applied in circumstances of professional negligence in New South Wales. A professional is not liable in negligence if it is established that the professional acted in a manner that was widely accepted in Australia by peer professional opinion as competent professional practice. A court, however, is not bound by peer professional opinion if the court considers the opinion to be irrational.

In the 2002 legislative recommendations, there were specific recommended legislative codification of medical professionals' duties to inform. Recommendations 5, 6 and 7 proposed that medical practitioners' duties to inform should be expressed as a duty to take reasonable care to give the patient such information as the reasonable person in that patient's position would want to be given before making a decision on treatment, and a duty to take reasonable care to give the patient such information as the reasonable practitioner knows or ought to know the patient wants to be given before making the decision.

Queensland reacted to the recommendations in s21 of the Civil Liability Act 2003 (Qld). This provides that a doctor does not breach the duty owed to a patient to warn of a risk before the patient undergoes any medical treatment (or at the time of being given medical advice) that will involve a risk of personal injury to the patient, unless the doctor at that time fails to give or arrange to be given to the patient the following information about the risk:

- information that a reasonable person in the patient's position would in the circumstances require to enable the person to make a reasonably informed decision about whether to undergo the treatment or follow the advice;

- information that the doctor knows or ought reasonably to know the patient wants to be given before making the decision about whether to undergo the treatment or follow the advice.

When *Rogers v Whitaker* and *Chappel v Hart* were decided, the Civil Liability Acts did not exist and it was the common law that applied to such cases. The principles contained within the Acts should be read in conjunction with common-law principles on foreseeability, remoteness of damage and proximity. When considering consent cases, the various Acts do effectively restate the principles found in *Rogers v Whitaker*.

In Australian information disclosure cases, determination of the scope and duty of a medical practitioner in giving a patient adequate advice and information is a matter for the court. However, the current state of medical knowledge will often be relevant in determining the nature of the risk which attracts the duty in question, including the foreseeability of that risk (*Rosenberg v Percival* (2001) 205 CLR 434; 178 ALR 577).

The duty of a doctor to warn is seen as a both a "proactive" and "reactive" duty. The proactive duty requires the doctor to volunteer information that he or she considers is material to the reasonable patient (an objective test). The reactive duty requires the doctor to provide information in response to a patient's particular circumstances, or their specific concerns or questions (a subjective test).

The standard of disclosure is not dictated by what is judged acceptable by the medical profession. In information disclosure cases the courts have adopted a patient-centred approach with the stated aim of empowering patients to make their own decisions about important procedures on the basis of information about material risks relevant to them.

Whether a risk is material may depend upon the following factors: the likelihood and seriousness of the risk to be disclosed; the nature and/or necessity of the treatment being provided; the patient's desire for information; the patient's health and temperament; and general matters, such as alternative sources of advice or treatment.

The type of evidence thought to assist the court in determining the nature of any warning that ought to be given to a patient about proposed medical treatment includes the:

- extent and severity of the potential injury;

- likelihood of the injury actually occurring;

- need for the operation/other treatment;

- existence of satisfactory and available alternative treatments; and

- fears and concerns of the patient that are known or should have been known to the practitioner.

This section considers the Australian approach to consent, and the Australian approach to causation is considered in Chapter 6.

b.   Reasonable patient test

Since 1992 Australia has adopted a "reasonable patient" test and rejected an approach to information disclosure based upon professional practice. In *Rogers v Whitaker* ((1992) 109 A.L.R. 625; [1993] 4 Med.L.R. 79 (H.C. of Aust.)) the High Court disapproved *Bolam* and *Sidaway* and adopted a "reasonable patient" standard. In *Rogers v Whitaker* the court went further and endorsed the "particular patient" test rejected by Lord

Scarman in *Sidaway*. It is suggested that the test also goes further than the test formulated by Lord Woolf in *Pearce*.

The decision in *Rogers v Whitaker* followed the approach favoured by the full Court of the Supreme Court of Australia in the South Australian case of *F v R* ((1983) 33 SASR 189 (FC)), decided two years before *Sidaway*. In this case a woman who had become pregnant after an unsuccessful tubal ligation brought an action in negligence alleging failure by the medical practitioner to warn her of the failure rate of the procedure. The failure rate was assessed at less than 1% for this particular form of sterilisation.

The court refused to apply the *Bolam* test. King CJ, at para 194, explained:

> *The ultimate question, however, is not whether the defendant's conduct accords with the practices of his profession or some part of it, but whether it conforms to the standard of reasonable care demanded by the law. That is a question for the court and the duty of deciding it cannot be delegated to any profession or group in the community.*

In *F v R*, King CJ considered what factors would be useful in determining whether a reasonable patient, or the particular patient, would be likely to attach significance to a risk. The factors he considered relevant were:

- the nature of the matter to be disclosed;

- the nature of the proposed treatment;

- the patient's desire for information;

- the temperament and health of the patient;

- the general surrounding circumstances.

These five factors were approved of in *Rogers v Whitaker*, in which the claimant was almost totally blind in her right eye following an accident at the age of nine. She was advised that an operation could improve the sight in the right eye. The claimant did ask about the possible consequences of the surgery on the right eye but she did not ask about any dangers to the left eye. There was a 1 in 14,000 chance of sympathetic ophthalmia in the left eye, but this was never mentioned. Following surgery on the right eye, the claimant developed sympathetic ophthalmia and ultimately lost the sight in the left eye. There was evidence from a body of reputable medical practitioners that they would not have warned the claimant of the risk of sympathetic ophthalmia.

The New South Wales Court of Appeal held that the defendant doctor had been negligent in failing to mention this risk, despite the fact there was evidence that he was not negligent within the meaning of the *Bolam* test. There was focus on the fact the claimant had asked questions about the possible complications. The High Court of Australia upheld the decision and specifically disapproved of *Bolam* and *Sidaway*.

It was recognised that there was a fundamental difference between diagnosis and treatment and the provision of advice and information to a patient. In diagnosis and treatment, the patient's contribution is limited to the narration of symptoms and relevant history. In this scenario, the medical practitioner provides the diagnosis and treatment according to their level of skill. However, it was said that, with the exception of cases of emergency and necessity, all medical treatment is preceded by the patient's choice to undergo it.

Choice is meaningless unless it is made on the basis of relevant information and advice. Because the choice to be made calls for a decision by the patient on information known to the medical practitioner but not to the patient, it would be illogical to hold that the amount of information provided can be determined from the perspective of the practitioner alone, or for that matter the medical profession. It was concluded that whether a patient has been given all the relevant information is not a question that can be answered by reference to medical standards or practices.

In *Chappel v Hart* ([1998] HCA 55), Gummow J said:

The nature and purpose of a duty with the content established in Rogers v Whitaker … *concerned the right of the patient to know of material risks which are involved in undergoing or forgoing certain treatment. This, in turn, arises from the patient's right to decide for himself or herself whether or not to submit to the treatment in question … that choice is in reality, meaningless unless it is made on the basis of relevant information and advice.* (para 65)

Kirby J added:

However, the requirement to warn patients about the risks of medical procedures is an important one conductive to respect for the integrity of the patient and better health care…. It must be accepted that, by establishing the requirement to warn patients of the risks to which they would be likely to attach significance, or of which they should be reasonably aware, the law intends that its obligations be carefully observed. Breaches must be treated seriously.

In *Breen v Williams* ((1995) 186 CLR 71) it was said that *Rogers* took away from the medical profession the right to determine, in proceedings for negligence, what amounts to acceptable medical standards.

The High Court in *Rogers v Whitaker* rejected what the court described as the oft-used and "somewhat amorphous phrase 'informed consent'", as had Lord Scarman in *Sidaway*. It was noted that the Supreme Court of Canada was cautious in its use of the term "informed consent". The medical practitioner should consider the nature of the matter to be disclosed, the nature of the treatment, the desire of the patient for information, the temperament and health of the patient and the general surrounding circumstances in deciding whether to disclose a risk.

In *Rosenberg v Percival* ([2001] H.C.A. 18; (2001) 178 A.L.R. 577) the claimant alleged that the defendant dentist had failed to warn her of the risk of complications of jaw surgery. The court considered that she had been provided with information on the potential complications. In any event, it was held that had she been warned she would still have gone ahead. The High Court of Australia upheld the decision of the trial judge. Gummow J said that, in deciding whether a patient was likely to attach significance to a particular risk, the extent and severity of the injury was relevant, as was the probability of it occurring. Consideration should also be given to the patient's circumstances including the patient's need for the operation and the existence of alternative treatments. Kirby J explained:

(1) Fundamentally, the rule is a recognition of individual autonomy that is to be viewed in the wider context of an emerging appreciation of basic human rights and human dignity. There is no reason to diminish the law's insistence, to the greatest extent possible, upon prior, informed agreement to invasive treatment, save for that which is required in an emergency or otherwise out of necessity.

Gummow J said that the structure and sequence of the reasoning in *Rogers* could be understood from the following six passages from the decision:

(i) "In Australia, it has been accepted that the standard of care to be observed by a person with some special skill or competence is that of the ordinary skilled person exercising and professing to have that special skill. But, that standard is not determined solely or even primarily by reference to the practice followed or supported by a responsible body of opinion in the relevant profession or trade."

(ii) "[I]t is for the courts to adjudicate on what is the appropriate standard of care after giving weight to 'the paramount consideration that a person is entitled to make his own decisions about his life'".

(iii) "The duty of the medical practitioner to exercise reasonable care and skill in the provision of professional advice and treatment is a single comprehensive duty. However, the factors according to which a court determines whether a medical practitioner is in breach of the requisite standard of care will vary according to whether it is a case involving diagnosis, treatment or the provision of information or advice; the different cases raise varying difficulties which require consideration of different factors."

(iv) "There is a fundamental difference between, on the one hand, diagnosis and treatment and, on the other hand, the provision of advice and information to a patient. In diagnosis and treatment, the patient's contribution is limited to the narration of symptoms and relevant history; the medical practitioner provides diagnosis and treatment according to his or her level of skill. However, except in cases of emergency or necessity, all medical treatment is preceded by the patient's choice to undergo it. In legal terms, the patient's consent to the treatment may be valid once he or she is informed in broad terms of the nature of the procedure which is intended. But the choice is, in reality, meaningless unless it is made on the basis of relevant information and advice."

*(v) "**Whether** a medical practitioner carries out a particular form of treatment in accordance with the appropriate standard of care is a question in the resolution of which responsible professional opinion will have an influential, often a decisive role to play; **whether** the patient has been given all the relevant information to choose between undergoing and not undergoing the treatment is a question of a different order. Generally speaking, it is not a question the answer to which depends upon medical standards or practices." (Original emphasis)*

(vi) "We agree that the facts referred to in F v R *(1983) 33 SASR 189 at 192–193 by King J must all be considered by a medical practitioner in deciding whether to disclose or advise of some risk in a proposed procedure. The law should recognise that a doctor has a duty to warn a patient of a material risk inherent in the proposed treatment; a risk is material if, in the circumstances of the particular case, a reasonable person in the patient's position, if warned of the risk, would be likely to attach significance to it or if the medical practitioner is or should reasonably be aware that the particular patient, if warned of the risk, would be likely to attach significance to it. This duty is subject to the therapeutic privilege."*

In *Haylock v Morris and Lawrence* ([2006] ACTSC 86), the practice at the hospital was to not disclose the risk of paraplegia from epidural anaesthesia. There was also expert medical evidence that it was not the practice to disclose the risk. The court held that the patient should have been advised of the competing risks for epidural and general anaesthesia to enable the patient to make an informed decision (see also *Arkinstall v Jenkins* [2001] QSC 421, Sup Ct (Qld)).

In *Waller v James* ([2015] NSWCA 232), while referring to *Montgomery* and *Rogers v Whitaker*, it was said that the doctor's duty of care takes its precise content from the needs, concerns and circumstances of the individual patient to the extent they are or ought to be known to the doctor.

c.   When is a risk material?

In Australia, whether a risk is material is essentially a question of fact to be addressed by the court. All relevant facts should be considered and taken into account and weighed in the balance (*Tai v Saxon* (WA FC, 8 February 1996, unreported, BC9600521)).

In *Rogers v Whitaker* the High Court rejected the application of the *Bolam* principle as determinative of whether a risk was material. However, since *Rogers v Whitaker* Australian courts have on occasion said that medical practice may be used as a useful guide in determining whether risks are material. In *Rosenberg v Percival*, Gleeson CJ stated that in *Rogers v Whitaker* the relevance of professional practice was not denied. What was denied was its conclusiveness. It is for the court to adjudicate on the appropriate standard of care.

In *Rogers v Whitaker* the court concluded that there was a duty to warn of a material risk inherent in the proposed treatment. A risk is material if, in the circumstances of the particular case, a reasonable person in the patient's position, if warned of the risk, would be likely to attach significance to it (the objective limb), or if the medical practitioner is or should reasonably be aware that the particular patient, if warned of the risk, would be likely to attach significance to it (the subjective limb).

The first limb of the test applies objective criteria and focuses on the requirements of a reasonable or ordinary person in the patient's position. The second subjective limb recognises that a patient may not be reasonable and allows the courts to consider the particular patient and their requirements or fears (reasonable and unreasonable). This is subject to the caveat that the medical practitioner is or ought to be aware of those considerations. If a patient had special needs or concerns and this was known to the doctor, this would indicate that special or additional information is required.

In *KL v Farnsworth* ([2002] NSWSC 382) the claimant had no choice but to undergo surgery but there were two alternative forms of surgery she could have undergone. She underwent a urinary procedure and the question for the court was whether the doctor had provided her with adequate information about the risks and possible consequences of the procedures to enable her to make an informed choice. The court said in answering the question it is not an assessment of what would have been in the claimant's best interests but an assessment of what decision she would have made in the circumstances. The court focused on the duty of the doctor to ensure that the claimant had an understanding of the relative risks that were reasonably foreseeable. The outcome for the claimant was significantly worse than could have been anticipated. It was not the duty of the doctor to anticipate a complication of the magnitude that befell the claimant. It was found on causation that had she been warned of the reasonably foreseeable complications she would have gone ahead with the surgery.

In *Henderson v Low* ([2001] QSC 496) the claimant had a fixation with his sexual performance and placed a heavy store on physical fitness and strength which related to abuse as a child. The doctor was unaware of this fact. The claimant had back problems and he underwent laminectomy under the care of Dr Low, following which he suffered urinary problems and sexual dysfunction. It was accepted that damage to the cauda equina, or the part of it controlling the bladder and sexual function, was a potential risk of the surgery, although it was a rare complication.

In considering the question of materiality, the court first asked whether Dr Low was aware of the fact that the claimant placed particular importance on sexual function and the answer to that was no. The court then said that the question to be addressed is whether a reasonable person in their position would have attached significance to the risk. The court found that the claimant should have been advised of the risk, particularly so when surgery was not the only option. In this case the doctor suggested that the appropriate warnings were given after a decision was made to proceed with surgery. The court also held that a warning given after a firm decision had been made to proceed with surgery was unlikely to be effective in the same way as one given in the course of the decision-making process.

In *Rosenberg v Percival* the court considered the test of materiality. Gummow J said that the phrase "likely to attach significance to" requires that a patient is likely to "seriously" consider and weigh up the risk before deciding whether to proceed with the treatment. This approach differs from the approach in *F v R* and *Rogers v Whitaker*, where the focus was on information relevant to a course or action or matters that might influence a decision. However, it appears from their decisions that the Australian courts have continued to focus on the tests found in *F v R* and *Rogers v Whitaker*.

In Australia, the likelihood of the risk occurring is seen as a distinct concept from the gravity of the risk. The courts consider the likely occurrence of the risk against the consequences of the risk should it occur. The requirement for disclosure is reduced where the risk is remote. However, greater disclosure is required where the consequences of the risk are significant.

The courts in Australia have in some cases classified risks to be material, even where the likely occurrence of the risk is statistically low (see *Bloodworth v Health Authority* ([2000] NSWSC 1234)). In *Hribar v Wells* ((1995) 64 SASR 129) the likelihood of the risk was less than 1 in 1000. The court held that applying a mathematical formula to assess the magnitude of the risk is not likely to be helpful.

In *Rosenberg v Percival* Gummow J considered that a slight risk of serious harm might satisfy the test of materiality, while a greater risk of less harm might not. In *Rogers v Whitaker* the gravity of the loss of sight in the patient's eye was increased because the claimant was blind in the other eye.

In *Causer v Stafford-Bell* (14 November 1997, unreported, BC9706029) the claimant suffered a vesico-vaginal fistula and urinary incontinence following a hysterectomy. The risk was said to be 1 in 1000–10,000. The fistula resolved without treatment and the court found that a more probable risk of less harm was not material. In *Chappel v Hart* the risk was held to be material, although the risk was very rare.

In *Rogers v Whitaker* it was noted that the "nature of the treatment" is a factor relevant to the question of materiality. The court approved the judgment in *F v R*, where it was said that the more drastic or complex the intervention to the patient's physical make-up, the greater the need to keep the patient informed as to the risks of the treatment. The suggestion appears to be that the courts are less likely to find risks material in routine or common procedures than in more complex procedures.

In *Mazurkiewicz v Scott* ((1996) 16 SR (WA) 162) the court found that the risk of damage to the lingual nerve during an anaesthetic for dental surgery was not a material risk. The court placed significance on the fact that the anaesthetic was routine and commonplace.

In *Bustos v Hair Transplant Pty Ltd* (NSW C.A., 15 April 1997) the New South Wales Court of Appeal accepted the finding at trial that the risk of neuromas was not material as the possibility of neuromas arose from the cutting of the skin and therefore arose with virtually all surgery.

In *Towns v Cross* ([2001] NSWCA 129 (4 May 2001, unreported, BC 200102097)) the risk of perforation of the ear drum while syringing the ear was not a material risk as this was a routine common procedure.

d.   Circumstances where a risk need not be disclosed

In Australia, as in other jurisdictions, it has been recognised that there will be circumstances where a risk or risks need not be disclosed to a patient.

In *Battersby v Tottman* ((1985) 37 S.A.S.R. 524 (S.C. of Aus.)), when referring to *F v R*, the Supreme Court of South Australia considered the circumstances in which a doctor could not disclose a risk if he felt it would be harmful to the patient. In this case the defendant doctor had not failed in his duty in not disclosing the risk of blindness associated with the use of a particular drug in high doses. The claimant had a mental illness and it was held that she would have been likely to react hysterically and irrationally if the information had been given.

In *Lowns v Woods and Procopis v Woods* ((1996) Aust. Torts Rep 81-376 (N.S.W.C.A.)) the court considered the duty of a medical professional to provide emergency medical care even though there was no pre-existing patient–doctor relationship. A young boy suffered severe brain damage following an epileptic seizure. There was a claim against a GP for failing to assist but also a consent case against Dr Procopis, a paediatric neuro-logist, on the basis that he had failed to advise the parents of the benefits of the rectal use of Valium. At first instance the court found against the doctor, however on appeal the decision was reversed by the NSW Court of Appeal.

Dr Procopis sought to distinguish *Rogers v Whitaker* on the basis that this was a case of medical treatment, not one of a warning or advice to a patient of the risks of a particular procedure. The court rejected that argument and said that the principle in *Rogers v Whitaker* was one of general application, governing the relevant communications between a medical practitioner and a patient. The doctor would not have been actually administering the rectal Valium but would have been advising and discussing with the parents the management of his medical condi-tion. It was held that what was required, as in *Rogers v Whitaker*, was the sharing of as much of the medical expertise of the medical specialist with the patient or his carers as was necessary to discharge the duty of care imposed by the law.

The court referred to the unreported decision in *Ainsworth v Levi* (Court of Appeal (NSW) unreported, 30 August 1995), where Handley JA (with the concurrence of Meagher JA) appeared to have endorsed a rule that where the medical practitioner is proved to have followed standard medical practice then, unless the court is satisfied that the medical evidence is "manifestly wrong", it should reject the contention that the practitioner was in breach of their duty of care. In *Lowns* and *Procopis v Woods* it was said that it would be wrong to qualify the very clear decision of the High Court in *Rogers v Whitaker* and restore the *Bolam* principle. The court held that *Ainsworth* should be read to indicate nothing more than, if the medical practitioner sued establishes that they have conformed to ordinary medical practice within the speciality in question, the forensic burden shifts to the patient to satisfy the court that notwithstanding this fact ordinary practice did not conform to the reasonable care demanded by the law in those circumstances.

In *Elbourne v Gibbs* ([2006] NSWCA 127), the patient claimed that the defendant surgeon had failed to warn him of a number of material risks of surgery to repair bilateral inguinal hernias which, in fact, materialised. The risks included: gross swelling of the scrotum, chronic pain resulting from nerve entrapment, and embolism. Evidence was given in relation to each risk that the patient "would not have undergone the operation if he had been properly warned" (at [34]–[37] (Basten JA), [1] (Beazley JA agreeing). See also at [97], [105] (Basten JA) (see also *Ellis v Wallsend District Hospital* ((1989) 17 NSWLR 553, 578–9, 582–90).

e.   Where a patient asks questions

The Australian courts have considered risks to be material in terms of the subjective limb of the test formulated in *Rogers v Whitaker* if a doctor knows or ought to know that the particular patient would attach significance to the risk. Where a patient asks questions and the nature of the questioning reveals their concerns or personal fears, this can be said to satisfy the test. Provided it can be demonstrated that the risk was foreseeable, the Australian courts have attached little significance to the fact it may be very unlikely to occur (*Rogers v Whitaker* and *Chappel v Hart*).

In *F v R* it was said that if a claimant asked questions the duty of the doctor would be to give full and frank advice. However, the court did recognise that there may be circumstances where reasonable care for the patient would justify or even require a less than fully candid answer. A doctor may also reasonably judge that a patient is merely seeking reassurance.

In *Rogers v Whitaker* the claimant incessantly questioned the doctor about possible complications and was noted to be keenly interested in the danger to her good eye. There was no specific question about whether the operation on the right eye could affect the good eye. It was held that such a specific question was not necessary in this situation as the claimant had made it very clear to the doctor that she was greatly concerned that no injury should befall the one good eye. In that situation, the very slight risk of sympathetic ophthalmia was a material risk under the subjective limb of the test.

The High Court explained:

> *Even if a court were satisfied that a reasonable person in the patient's position would be unlikely to attach significance to a particular risk, the fact that the patient asked questions revealing concern about the risk would make the doctor aware that **this patient** did in fact attach significance to the risk. Subject to the therapeutic privilege, the question would therefore require a truthful answer.*

In *Chappel v Hart* there was a failure to warn of the slight risk of damage to the claimant's voice. She had however expressed concerns to Dr Chappel about the fact that the operation could affect her voice, and notwithstanding the remoteness of the risk the risk was held to be material under the subjective limb of the test in *Rogers v Whitaker*.

In *Johnson v Briggs* ([2000] NSWCA 338) significance was attached to a written note the claimant took with her to the preoperative consultation with the neurosurgeon. In the written note, she listed 13 questions about the possible surgery. The questions included "Any further complications after op? from op?" "Very concerned that after op the pain will still be there?" and "Can op cause problems elsewhere?". It was said that the test was that a risk is material either if in the circumstances a reasonable person, if warned of it, would be likely to attach significance to it, or if the doctor was or should reasonably be aware that the claimant, if warned of it, would be likely to attach significance to it. The court found that the claimant's questions were clearly directed to the risk that eventuated which was post-operative pain and therefore the risk was material under the subjective limb of *Rogers v Whitaker*.

In *B v Marinovich* ([1999] NTSC 127) a psychiatrist prescribed Xanax to a patient for treatment of panic attacks. The patient asked whether the drug was addictive and it was found that the question was itself a sufficient basis to find that the risk of addiction was material.

In *Caruso v Beard* ((1997) 196 LSJS 42) the subjective limb of *Rogers v Whitaker* did not apply because the doctor had no way of knowing the patient would have an adverse reaction to injection.

f.   The mental and physical health of the patient

Following *Rogers v Whitaker* the mental and physical health of the patient is a factor that the Australian courts have attached significance to when addressing issues of materiality of risk. Where a patient is at increased risk of a complication as a result of a pre-existing condition or something in the medical history, the courts have been more inclined to find a risk material.

In addressing the issue of materiality, the case law in Australia does support the conclusion that the fact that a risk is higher for a particular patient is highly relevant in whether the risk if found to be material.

One caveat is that the clinician must have known or ought to have known of the underlying condition.

In *Rogers v Whitaker* the evidence of the earlier penetrating injury to the eye increased the risk to the patient. In *Rosenberg v Percival* it was held that the risk of minor temporomandibular joint dysfunction was not a material risk despite the patient's prior history of temporomandibular joint problems.

In *Ibrahim v Arkell* ([1999] NSWCA 95) the Court of Appeal said that where there is an increased likelihood of a risk occurring for the particular patient the duty to warn is very high. In this case the claimant had prolapsed haemorrhoids and underwent a radical haemorrhoidectomy. The claimant also suffered from long-standing ulcerative colitis. This is a condition it was said could affect the blood supply to the rectum. Following surgery, the claimant suffered a post-operative secondary haemorrhage and scar tissue, which caused anal stenosis. She claimed that she had not been warned of the increased risk of anal stenosis prior to surgery. The court found that the risk was material in this situation and therefore the claimant should have been warned of the risk.

In *Uebel v Wechsler* (NSW S.C., Hume J, 2 July 1998, unreported, BC9803398) the claimant suffered from herpetic keratitis, which is an inflammation of the cornea due to the herpes virus. As a result, the risks of corneal rejection and glaucoma were held to be material. In *Melchior v Cattanach* ([2001] QCA 246) the risk of pregnancy following sterilisation was a material risk in circumstances where the existence of one of the claimant's fallopian tubes was uncertain.

In *Tai v Saxon* (WA FC, 8 February 1996, unreported, BC9600521) the court found that the claimant was a more than ordinarily anxious person and this was a factor which rendered the risk material under the subjective limb of the test formulated in *Rogers v Whitaker*. The doctor had attempted to argue that because of her underlying anxiety and depression he was justified in not warning her of the risk as this would cause her more anxiety. The court did not accept this and simply took this statement as evidence that he was well aware she would attach significance to the risk. The claimant underwent an elective vaginal hysterectomy and repair, following which she developed a recto-vaginal fistula that leaked faecal material into the vagina. Because of her pre-existing anxiety and depression it was found that she was less likely to cope should the risk materialise.

g.   The need for treatment and alternatives available

Where the claimant requires treatment urgently and there is no opportunity for reflection of the risks involved, the Australian courts have generally been slow to find that the risks are material. However, in cases of elective surgery (particularly plastic surgery), where there is a choice and time to consider whether to proceed, the Australian courts have considered risks material. They have found even unlikely risks and risks involving minor harm to be material in the elective situation.

In *O'Brien v Wheeler* (NSW C.A., 23 May 1997) it was found that the risk of unsightly scarring following tattoo removal was a risk that a reasonable person in the claimant's position would attach significance to. In *Tan v Benkovic* ((2000) 51 NSWLR 292) there was a held to be a failure to inform the claimant of the full range of risks in the cosmetic facelift procedure. In *Bridges v Pelly* ([2001] NSWCA 31 (2 March 2001, unreported, BC200100620)) the patient underwent elective rhinoplasty and genioplasty and the risk of nerve damage was held to be material despite the fact the risk of it occurring being fairly minor.

A patient should be advised of alternative treatments where alternative treatments are available. The Australian courts have also considered materiality in the context of whether there were alternative treatments available.

In *Henderson v Low* ([2001] QSC 496) the court found that the possibility of the operation failing was a material risk, particularly in a situation where surgery was the only option discussed with the patient.

In *KL v Farnsworth* ([2002] NSWSC 382), where there were two surgical options but one had a higher risk of diarrhoea, the court said that there was a strong duty to provide the patient with information about the relative benefits and risks of the two forms of surgery.

h.   Warning of risks where one risk materialised

In *Wallace v Kam* ((2013) HCA 19; 250 CLR 375) there was no argument on appeal of what risks were material and should have been disclosed to the patient. The case was the first High Court decision on non-disclosure following the civil liability legislation's causation provisions.

The facts on the issue of material risks are straightforward. Mr Wallace sought medical assistance from Dr Kam, a neurosurgeon, because of problems with his spine. There were inherent risks involved in surgery. One risk was of temporary local damage to nerves within his thighs, described as "bilateral femoral neurapraxia", resulting from lying face-down on the operating table for an extended period. Another distinct risk was a 1 in 20 chance of permanent and catastrophic paralysis resulting from damage to his spinal nerves. During the course of the surgical procedure the first risk materialised. Mr Wallace sustained neurapraxia, which left him in severe pain for some time. The second risk did not materialise.

Mr Wallace claimed damages in the Supreme Court of New South Wales on the basis that Dr Kam negligently failed to warn him of risks including the risk of neurapraxia and the risk of paralysis and that, had he been warned of either risk, he would have chosen not to undergo the surgical procedure and would therefore not have sustained the neurapraxia.

The claim was dismissed at trial. Harrison J found that Dr Kam negligently failed to warn Mr Wallace of the risk of neurapraxia. But he also found that Mr Wallace would have chosen to undergo the surgical procedure even if warned of the risk of neurapraxia. He concluded, for that reason, that Dr Kam's negligent failure to warn Mr Wallace of the risk of neurapraxia was not a necessary condition of the occurrence of the neurapraxia. He declined to make any finding on whether Dr Kam negligently failed to warn Mr Wallace of the risk of paralysis, and what Mr Wallace would have done if he had been warned of the risk, on the basis that the "legal cause" of the neurapraxia "could never be the failure to warn of some other risk that did not materialise".

Mr Wallace appealed to the Court of Appeal of New South Wales (Allsop P, Beazley and Basten JJA). He argued that Harrison J erred in holding that the legal cause of the neurapraxia could not be the failure to warn of the risk of paralysis. The Court of Appeal tested that argument by assuming that Dr Kam negligently failed to warn Mr Wallace of the risk of paralysis and that, if warned of that risk, Mr Wallace would not have undergone the surgical procedure. Was Dr Kam, on that assumption, liable for the neurapraxia?

The Court of Appeal was divided in answering that question. The majority, Allsop P and Basten JA, answered it in the negative. The appeal was therefore dismissed. Beazley JA answered it in the affirmative and would have ordered a new trial. The negative answer of the majority of the Court of Appeal was preferred by the High Court and the appeal was dismissed.

The case was considered against the background of the Civil Liability Act 2002 (NSW) and is of interest principally as a causation case; it is considered in detail in Chapter 6. The High Court emphasised that the common-law duty of a medical practitioner to a patient is a single comprehensive duty to exercise reasonable care and skill in the provision of professional advice and treatment. A component of that single comprehensive duty was ordinarily to warn the patient of "material risks" of physical injury inherent in a proposed treatment. A risk of physical injury inherent in a proposed treatment was said to be material if it were a risk to which a reasonable person in the position of the patient would be likely to attach significance, or if it were a risk to which the medical practitioner knows or ought reasonably to know the particular patient would be likely to attach significance in choosing whether or not to undergo a proposed treatment. The component of the duty of a medical practitioner that ordinarily requires the medical practitioner to inform the patient of material risks of physical injury inherent in proposed treatment was said to be founded on the under-lying common-law right of the patient to choose whether or not to undergo that treatment.

In imposing that component of the duty, the court noted that the common law recognised not only the right of the patient to choose but also the need for the patient to be adequately informed in order to be able to make that choice rationally. The policy underlying the imposi-tion of that component of the duty was said to equip the patient with information relevant to the choice, which was the patient's. The duty to inform the patient of inherent material risks was said to be imposed to enable the patient to choose whether or not to run those inherent risks and thereby to avoid the occurrence of the particular physical injury the risk of which the patient was not prepared to accept.

i.   Non-theapeutic treatment and assault

In Australia, in *X v The Sidney Children's Hospitals Network* ([2013] NSWCA 320) the court held that the general principle of the common law was that non-consensual medical treatment involves an assault, thus constituting both a criminal offence and a tort.

However, with reference to *Rogers v Whitaker*, defects in obtaining consent tend to go to negligence rather than establishing assault and battery:

> *Anglo-Australian law has rightly taken the view that an allegation that the risks inherent in a medical procedure have not been disclosed to the patient can only found an action in negligence and not tres-pass; the consent necessary to negative the offence of battery is satisfied by the patient being advised in broad terms of the nature of the procedure to be performed.*

This passage from *Rogers v Whitaker* was an endorsement of what was said in the UK case of *Chatterton v Gearson*, which had followed the Ontario Court of Appeal in *Reibl v Hughes* (see also *Rosenberg v Percival*).

Australian law distinguishes between the negligent failure to warn a patient who consents to treatment, and the fraudulent procurement of consent for non-therapeutic purposes.

In *White v Johnston* ([2015] NSWCA 18) the allegation was that the dental treatment the claimant received amounted to an assault as he was aware that the treatment was unnecessary and ineffective and there was no therapeutic purpose in the treatment given. When a medical practitioner is solely motivated by an unrevealed non-therapeutic purpose, the patient's consent is not valid. Where the question is whether a medical practitioner has fraudulently procured a patient's consent, the onus lies on the patient to establish fraud. The court said that there were some situations where a patient's *prima facie* consent will not be an answer to assault and battery. Reference was made to *Rogers v Whitaker*, *Reibl v Hughes* and *Chatterton v Gearson*, where it was said that if information is withheld in bad faith the consent is vitiated by fraud (see also *Dean v Phung*).

3. Canada

a. Introduction

As far back as 1931, in *Kenny v Lockwood* ([1931] O.R. 438 at 446 (S.C.); [1932] 1 DLR 507), the Ontario Court of Appeal attempted to analyse the doctor–patient relationship as fiduciary in nature, requiring honesty on the part of the surgeon. On appeal the court overturned the trial judge's finding of liability on the basis that there had been proper disclosure of risk. The case was cited with approval in *Hopp v Lepp* ((1980) 112 D.L.R. (3d) 67 (S.C.C)).

In three major decisions (*Reibl v Hughes* (1980) 114 D.L.R. (3D) 1 (S.C.C); *Hopp v Lepp* (1980) 112 D.L.R. (3d) 67 (S.C.C); and *Arndt v Smith* [1997] 2 S.C.R 539), the Supreme Court of Canada set the standard for disclosure of information by medical professionals in Canada. *Reibl v Hughes* was described as representing a dramatic change in direction, and as having significantly reformulated the law.

In Canada, the test to be applied when considering questions of professional negligence is similar to the test applied in the UK. A medical practitioner is obliged to exercise the degree of care and skill which could be reasonably expected of a normal, prudent practitioner of the same experience and standing. If he holds himself out as a specialist, a higher degree of skill is required of him than of a doctor who does not profess to be so qualified by special training and ability (*Sylvester v Crits* (1956) 5 D.L.R. (2d 601 (S.C.C.) affi'g (1956) 1 D.L.R. (2d) 502 (C.A.) at 508; *Smith v Auckland Hospital Board* [1964] N.Z.L.R. 191; *Male v Hopmans et al.* [1966] 1 O.R. 647, 52 D.L.R. (2d) 592 (Ont.H.C.)). An error of judgement is not necessarily negligent (*Ehler v Smith* ((1979) 29 N.S.R. (2d) 309; *Wilson v Swanson* (5 D.L.R. (2d) 113 (S.C.C.)).

Since *Reibl v Hughes* in 1980 the Canadian courts have rejected the professional standard test as a means of deciding whether a patient has been given sufficient information to enable them to make an informed decision on how to proceed.

Arndt v Smith was a British Columbia case which went to trial in 1994. It was heard on appeal in 1995 and reached the Supreme Court of Canada in 1997. The Supreme Court explained that the decision in *Reibl v Hughes* marked the rejection of the paternalistic approach to determining how much information should be given to patients.

In Canada, since the 1980s the patient has had the right to make their own decisions as to which medical interventions to accept or refuse. In *Ciarlariello Estate v Schacter* ([1993] 2 S.C.R. 119, 100 D.L.R. (4th) 609 at 618), Cory J said:

It should not be forgotten that every patient has a right to bodily integrity. This encompasses the right to determine what medical procedures will be accepted and the extent to which they will be accepted.... This concept of individual autonomy is fundamental to the common law and is the basis for the requirement that disclosure be made to a patient.

The doctor does not have to disclose all of the known risks and benefits of a procedure. Under the Canadian test a doctor must disclose all material risks. A risk is material "when a reasonable person, in what the physician knows or should know to be the patient's position, would be likely to attach significance to the risk or cluster of risks in deciding whether or not to forgo the proposed therapy".

When advising a patient about risks, the advice must relate to the condition and circumstances of the particular patient (*Cupido v Sargeant* ([1989] O.J. No. 331 (Ont. S.C.J.)). A general discussion of the risks of a particular procedure or treatment is not sufficient if there are risks peculiar to that patient of which the doctor knew or ought to have known. The requirements relate to surgery, tests and medications.

In *Dickson v Pinder* (2010 489 AR 54; 2010 ABQB 269) Yamauchi J identified five components required for consent:

(a) the medical practitioner's diagnosis of the patient's condition;

(b) the prognosis of that condition with or without medical treatment;

(c) the nature of the proposed medical treatment;

(d) the risks associated with the proposed medical treatment;

(e) the alternatives to the proposed medical treatment, and the advantages and risks of those alternatives.

In Canada, every province has passed legislation to regulate consent to care and treatment. However, there have been a number of useful common-law cases since the introduction of a patient-focused test in the 1980s that have interpreted the nature and extent of the test and these are useful combined with the Australian cases in assisting UK lawyers to apply the test formulated in *Montgomery*.

In this chapter, consideration is given to the application of the test. However, it is notable in many of the decisions that, whilst successful on negligence, the claimant failed on causation. Causation questions are dealt with in more detail in Chapter 6.

b.   Alternative treatment options

There is a requirement to advise the patient of alternative methods of treatment and their risks, including the risks of the alternatives. In *Zimmer v Ringrose* ((1981) 124 D.L.R. (3d) 215 (Alta. C.A.)) it was held that the physician or surgeon should discuss the benefits to be gained from the recommended treatment or operation, the advantages and disadvantages associated with alternative procedures, and the consequences of forgoing treatment (see also *Brito v Wooley* ([2001] B.C.J. No. 1692 (B.C.S.C))). To discharge their duty of care the doctor must give the patient some yardstick against which he can assess the options available to him.

In *Dickson v Pinder* (2010 489 AR 54; 2010 ABQB 269) Yamauchi J said:

> *this is a fact dependent threat assessment process. A patient cannot make a meaningful and informed choice to consent to therapy unless that patient knows the consequences of other reasonable alternatives or inaction, and can balance the risks and benefits of the proposed therapy against those alternatives.*

Failure to advise the patient of options or alternative treatment/s denies them the right to make a fully informed choice (*Van Mol (Guardian ad Litem of) v Ashmore* (1999) 168 D.L.R. (4th) 637 (B.C.C.A.); see also *Walker (Litigation Guardian of) v Region 2 Hospital Corp* 1993 116 D.L.R. (4th) 477, where a 15-year-old was entitled to refuse consent to blood transfusions).

A reasonable alternative may be to delay the procedure, either to obtain more information or to try alternative or conservative measures (*Semeniuk v Cox* (2000) 76 Alta. L.R. (3d) 30 (Q.B.)). Similarly, if non-treatment is a reasonable alternative then that too ought to be disclosed (*Haughian v Paine* (1987) 37 D.L.R. (4ᵗʰ) 624; *Sicard v Sendziak*, 2008 ABQB 690; *Guay v Wong*, 2008 ABQB 638). If inaction involves a risk, then logically this is something a patient would want to know.

Advice should include any other reasonable forms of diagnostic testing, medical or surgical management. What is reasonable depends on the risks and benefits of the options, the availability of the option, and whether it is reasonable in the context of the management of the particular patient (*Rayner v Knickle* (1988) 47 C.C.L.T. 141 72 Nfld).

In *Rayner v Knickle* ((1988) 47 C.C.L.T. 141 72 Nfld.) the doctor failed to disclose the 1 in 1000 risk of serious injury when performing an amniocentesis at 35 weeks to determine the level of lung maturity. The doctor punctured the umbilical cord when performing the procedure, causing a haematoma and hypoxic-ischaemic injury to the fetus. The Prince Edward Island Supreme Court found that there was a failure to discuss with the mother the material risks involved in the amniocentesis test and the alternatives open and available to her in the circumstances. The court held that the correct summary of a doctor's duty of disclosure was that they must describe to their patient:

(a) how the procedure is carried out;

(b) the benefits of having the procedure done;

(c) the material or special or unusual risks of having the procedure done or forgoing the procedure;

(d) any alternatives to the procedure; and

(e) the risks associated with the alternatives.

The patient does not require to raise the issue of alternatives and only reasonable alternatives need to be disclosed.

In *Seney v Crooks* ((1998) 166 D.L.R. (4th) 337 (Alta.C.A.)) the Alberta Court of Appeal held that the scope of the duty to inform must be approached carefully and might not include a "fringe alternative" or "alternative medicine practices". In this case the claimant broke her wrist and it was placed in a cast. She was referred to Mr Crooks for further treatment. The wrist did not heal in alignment and surgery was needed or a special fixation device. She was not advised of the options for treatment. Instead the wrist was recast and she was ultimately left with a deformity. The trial judge found that the doctor had breached his duty by failing to disclose the risks associated with this course of treatment and the existence of available alternatives. Mr Crooks appealed and the court held that the mere fact that a doctor preferred one treatment over another did not relieve them of the obligation to advise of other acceptable and known procedures because "[t]hat is what the duty to inform is all about".

Mr Crooks argued in the appeal that the claimant was contributory negligent by failing to inform him that she wanted to have the wrist restored to its pre-fracture condition as far as medically possible. That argument was rejected and the court found that the claimant should have been advised of the existence of alternative treatments and Mr Crooks should have explained his reasoning for preferring his course of treatment and the risks of that course.

Reasonable alternatives also include those procedures which other physicians may recommend but the treating doctor may not, or may disapprove of. If the option is a reasonable option, the patient must be informed of it.

In *Bucknam v Kostuik* ((1983) 3 D.L.R. (4th) 99 (Ont. H.C.) it was doubted whether a surgeon was under a duty to inform a patient of a less serious alternative procedure which in their own mind was an entirely unreasonable procedure to undertake. That would be so even if there were another school of thought that believed that the alternative procedure was appropriate for the patient's condition. In *Bucknam* an orthopaedic surgeon performed surgery on a woman with scoliosis. She was not informed of a possible procedure which was less invasive because, in the treating doctor's opinion it would not have the potential to alleviate the claimant's primary concern, which was to straighten the curve in her spin (this case was distinguished in *Seney v Crooks*).

In *Martins v Barsoum* ([1998] O.J. No. 441 (Q.L.) a doctor performed surgery to remove a kidney stone without informing the patient that there was an alternative that did not involve surgery. The surgical treatment provided the possibility of avoiding a recurrence of the pain, which was a desire expressed by the patient. The non-surgical treatment was not a real alternative if this aim were to be achieved. The court did not reject the principle of the duty to inform of alternative treatment generally but found that the alternative was not really appropriate. On appeal, it was clear that if there was a realistic alternative this should be included in the discussion.

In *Haughian v Paine* ((1987) 37 DLR (4th) 624 (Sask C.A.) the court held that the doctor's duty extends in principle to disclose alternative forms of treatment. A failure to advise a patient that a more conservative treatment than that advocated by the doctor was available was a breach of the doctor's duty to the patient. In this case the doctor did not take a proper history or consider the extreme weight loss fluctuations of the young patient to determine whether weight loss by itself was an alternative (see also *Sicard v Sendziak* (2008 ABQB 690); *Gallant v Patten* (2010 NLTD 1; 2012 321 Nfld & PEIR 77)).

In *Zaiffdeen v Chua* (2005 ABCA 290) the claimant suffered a stroke while undergoing a hysterectomy. The trial judge had found that there had been a failure to properly discuss the various treatment options open to the claimant for symptoms of heavy bleeding and urinary frequency. The doctor had advised the claimant that the treatment options would be drug therapy or surgery but he presented these as equal options and did not advise the claimant that the treatments fell within a progressive scale, with hysterectomy being the most severe and drug treatment being the conservative option.

The patient should be informed of a known treatment which other doctors in the same speciality consider to be superior, even if the doctor does not agree with that view.

In *Van Mol (Guardian ad Litem of) v Ashmore* ((1999) 168 D.L.R. (4th) 637 (B.C.C.A.)) it was held by the British Columbia Court of Appeal that a patient should have been informed about the three surgical alternatives that were available to repair a narrowing of her aorta. She should have been advised of the risks and advantages of each, and also that she could have a second opinion before deciding whether to proceed with surgery.

In *Brito (Guardian ad litem of) v Woolley* ((2001) BCSC 1178 (CanLII), aff'd 2003 BCCA 397 (Can LII), 16 B.C.L.R. (4th) 2220), a case involving a twin birth, it was said that a patient cannot be taken to have consented to a particular treatment or procedure unless they have been fully informed as to the material risks of that treatment or procedure, and informed of alternative treatments or procedures (see also *Bauer (Litigation Guardian of) v Seager* 2000 MBQB 113 (CantL II), [2000] 11 W.W.W.621, 2000 MBQB 113 (Man. Q.B.); *Mangalji (Next Friend of) v Graham* (1997) CanLII 14728 (AB QB), 47 Alta. L.R. (3d) 19 (Q.B.); *Rhine v Millan* 2000 ABQB 212 (CanLII), [2007] 7 W.W.R. 136, 2000 ABQB 212 (Alta.Q.B.)).

In *Malinowski v Schneider* ([2010] ABQB 734; 2012 ABCA 125), one of the grounds of alleged fault against a chiropractor who had treated the claimant for back pain was that he had failed to warn the claimant of the symptoms of cauda equina syndrome (CES) and the need to seek immediate medical attention if they appeared. The symptoms and consequences of CES were a special and unusual risk that ought to have been disclosed to the claimant. There was an alternative treatment for the claimant's presentation that involved bed rest and analgesics. There had been a failure to inform the patient to allow him to choose an appropriate response to his injury.

In *Brodeur v Provincial Health Services Authority* (2016 BSCSC 986 (CanLII) the claimant failed on the information aspect of the case as the court accepted the doctor's version of what information had been given to the parents.

The case concerned vaginal birth following previous delivery by caesarean section. Amanda Brodeur gave birth to a baby by emergency caesarean section following a rupture of her uterus in the course of delivery. The baby now has life-long cognitive and physical disabilities. Ms Brodeur had undergone a caesarean section during the course of a previous delivery. Uterine rupture was said to be a rare complication of vaginal birth following caesarean section (VBAC). However, if it did occur it was recognised as an obstetric emergency which can result in the death of the mother and baby, or, even without death, catastrophic consequences.

One of the arguments advanced was that there was no informed consent to permit a vaginal delivery instead of an elective caesarean section. From the 1980s it has been said that the medical profession had embraced a trial of vaginal birth after caesarean section. This course of action was said to reduce the risks associated with caesarean section deliveries. Vaginal delivery was viewed by the medical profession as less risky for the mother.

It is noted that the Supreme Court of Canada in *Reibl* had specifically rejected the professional standard of disclosure, finding that it was not for the physician to decide what should and should not be disclosed to a particular patient. The standard of disclosure will often be more than that which the medical profession might consider appropriate to divulge. It was noted that the standard requires presenting the patient with alternative treatments, including the options of forgoing treatment.

In making its decision, the court considered the state of medical knowledge about VBAC in 1999. In doing so, a policy statement issued by the Society of Obstetricians and Gynaecologists of Canada was held to be relevant. Parties were agreed that the guidance was important, although not determinative, in the determination of the applicable standard of care. The incidence of scan dehiscence without maternal or fetal consequence was 0.5%. The risk of uterine rupture with haemorrhage and fetal compromise or even death was 0.1%. The guidance recommended that women with one previous caesarean section (with a transverse low segment scar) undergo a trial of labour. The guidance also stated that the doctor needed to respect the woman's autonomy. Her participation and that of her partner in the decision were noted to be paramount.

It was held that there was no dispute that VBAC carried a statistically small, but sufficiently serious risk so as to be considered a material risk. Although the prevalent medical practice at the time was to encourage VBAC, it was incumbent upon physicians to discuss all material risks and alternatives. Parties were agreed that in 1999 patients required to be advised of the specific risks of uterine rupture and its potential consequences when VBAC was being considered.

In *Cojocaru (Guardian Ad Litem) v British Columbia Women's Hospital* (2009 BCSC 494 (Can LII)) the information questions related to the use of Syntocinon to induce a labour following a previous birth by caesarean section, and the risks involved in vaginal birth after caesarean section. Mrs Cojacaru was from Romania, where her first son had been born by caesarean section. By the time of the birth of her second child, she was in Canada. She had understood from information given to her in Romania that she would have an elective caesarean section in any future pregnancy. The doctor accepted that she had not discussed risks attendant upon induction of labour and it was concluded this was a failure in care. In this case the court again looked at guidance issued and warnings from the drug manufacturer in determining the issue. On the issue of vaginal birth after caesarean section, the court was of the view that the risks should have been, and were not, discussed (note that this case was considered by the Supreme Court of Canada ([2013] 2 SCR 357)).

c.   What is a material risk?

In *Reibl v Hughes* the court explicitly rejected a professional medical standard for determining the material risks and whether there had been a breach of the duty of disclosure. The court did not consider that it was acceptable to hand over to the medical profession the entire scope of the duty of disclosure. Professional standards were only one factor to be considered.

The court held that the right should not be at the disposal of the medical community (*Zeleznik v Jewish Chronic Disease Hospital* ((1975) 366 N.Y.S. 2d 163)).

In *Arndt v Smith*, the Supreme Court of Canada, per Cory J for the majority, said of the decision in *Reibl Hughes*:

> Reibl *is a very significant and leading authority. It marks the rejection of the paternalistic approach to determining how much information should be given to patients. It emphasises the patient's right to know and ensures that patients will have the benefit of a high standard of disclosure.*

The claimant in *Reibl v Hughes* was an intelligent, 44-year-old man whose command of English was limited. He complained of severe headaches and tests demonstrated an arterial occlusion that was reducing blood flow to the brain. He was therefore vulnerable to a stroke or even death. These were also risks that could materialise if the claimant underwent surgery. Hughes was the neurosurgeon who performed the operation. During surgery or immediately following surgery the claimant suffered a massive stroke. The issue was whether the claimant had been properly warned of the risks of surgery. It was alleged that the claimant was told only that he would be better off having the operation and he was left with the erroneous impression that surgery would relieve the headaches.

Chief Justice Laskin rejected the professional disclosure standard:

To allow expert medical evidence to determine what risks are material and, hence, should be disclosed and, correlatively, what risks are not material is to hand over to the medical profession the entire question of the scope if the duty of disclosure, including the question whether there has been a breach of that duty.

The duty of disclosure embraces what the surgeon knows, or ought to know, what the patient deems relevant to the decision to undergo treatment. The question of whether a particular risk is material and whether there has been a breach of duty is a question for the trier of fact. It was explained:

Expert medical evidence is, of course, relevant to findings as to the risks that reside in or are as a result of recommended surgery or other treatment. It will also have a bearing on their materiality but this is not a question that is to be concluded on the basis of the expert medical evidence alone. The issue under consideration is a different issue from that involved where the question is whether the doctor carried out his professional activities by applicable professional standards. What is under consideration here is the patient's right to know what risks are involved in undergoing or foregoing certain surgery or other treatment.

The full disclosure standard described by the Chief Justice in *Reibl v Hughes* had two components. The first relates to the patient and what the patient deemed relevant to their decision, and the second was medical knowledge and the material risks recognised therein:

What the doctor knows or should know that the particular patients deems relevant to a decision whether to undergo prescribed treatment goes equally to his duty of disclosure as do the material risks recognised as a matter of required medical knowledge. (para 822)

On the question of the relevance of expert evidence, it was still considered that such evidence could be of assistance to the court in a restricted sense:

Expert medical evidence was, of course, relevant to findings as to the risks that reside in or are a result of recommended surgery or other treatment. (para 894)

In *Reibl v Hughes*, Chief Justice Laskin stated that the relationship between the doctor and their patient gives rise to a duty to disclose all material risks of a procedure. He then referred to *Hopp v Lepp* for a description of the type of information that should be conveyed to a patient. In summary, the doctor should:

- answer specific questions about risks; and
- disclose voluntarily in relation to the operation:
  - ○ the nature,
  - ○ the gravity,
  - ○ any material risks (which includes risks that are a mere possibility but that carry serious consequences), and
  - ○ any special or unusual risks.

The disclosure standard has reference to two sources. The first is the patient and what they deem to be relevant to their decision, and the second is medical knowledge of material risks recognised therein. Laskin CJC said that:

What the doctor knows or should know that the particular patient deems relevant to a decision whether to undergo prescribed treatment goes equally to his duty of disclosure as do the material risks recognised as a matter of required medical knowledge.

Chief Justice Laskin appeared to use a subjective evaluation, referring to the particular patient in terms of the scope of disclosure.

In Canada, the test is not simply restricted to the objective or reasonable standard. The question is considered in the context of the facts of the particular case.

In *Hopp v Lepp* the Supreme Court said that the surgeon need not go into every conceivable detail of the recommended treatment but:

generally, should answer any specific questions posed by the patient as to the risks involved and should, without being questioned, disclose to him the nature of the proposed operation, its gravity, any material risks and any special or unusual risks attendant upon the performance of the operation.

The court in *Hopp v Lepp* also pointed out that, even if a certain risk is a mere possibility which ordinarily need not be disclosed, it should be regarded as a material risk requiring disclosure if its occurrence carries serious consequences, as for example paralysis or even death (see also *Rocha v Harris* (1987) 187 Can II 2698 (BC CA), 36 D.L.R. (4th 410 (B.C.C.A.))).

Material risks are significant risks that pose a real threat to the patient's life, health or comfort (*White v Turner* (1981) 31 O.R. (2d) 773 (Ont. H.C.J.)). In assessing materiality, a court will balance the severity of the potential result with the likelihood that it will occur. The risk of stroke, paralysis or death have been considered to be material.

In *Haughian v Paine* ((1987) 55 Sask. R. 99 (C.A.)) the Saskatchewan Court of Appeal rejected a physician's argument that a less than 1 in 500 risk of paralysis was too insignificant to be material. However, in *Zimmer v Ringrose* ((1981) 124 D.L.R. (3d) 215 (Alta. C.A.) the Alberta Court of Appeal held that if a risk is "quite remote" the mere fact that its consequences are serious does not make it a material risk.

In *Dickson v Pinder*, at para 74, Yamauchi J summarised the categories of risks that must be disclosed:

A medical practitioner must disclose a risk, where the patient would not know of the risk and either:

(a) The risk is a likely consequence, and the injury that would result is at least a slight injury, or

(b)   The risk has serious consequences, such as paralysis or death, even where that risk in uncommon but not unknown.

In *Martin v Finlay; Martin v Capital Health Authority* (2008 ABCA 161, 432 A.R. 165) the Alberta Court of Appeal commented on the manner in which risks should be disclosed. The terminology used to inform the patient is of less consequence but an explanation of the potential deleterious result is crucial.

In assessing how significant a risk must be in order to be considered material, some courts have focused solely on statistics (*Frerotte v Irwin* (1986) 51 Sask. R. 108 (Q.B.)), while others have placed less emphasis on them.

In *Haughian v Paine* the Saskatchewan Court of Appeal held that the issue of materiality cannot be reduced to numbers for all cases. Statistics are but one factor to be taken into account.

A significant chance of slight injury has been held to be material. In *Rawlings v Lindsey* ((1982) 20 C.C.L.T. 301) a 5–10% risk of nerve damage and resultant numbness following extraction of a wisdom tooth was held to be a material risk. Madam Justice McLachlin dealt with the terminology of risks in the following way:

> *The terminology of "material", "special", and "unusual" risks has in the past given rise to confusion. However, a fair summary of the effect of those decisions, in my view, is that a medical person must disclose those risks to which a reasonable patient would be likely to attach significance in deciding whether or not to undergo the proposed treatment. In making this determination, the degree of probability of the risk and its seriousness are relevant factors. Conversely, a minor result should be disclosed if it is inherent in or a probable result of the process.*

In Canada, special or unusual risks have been defined as risks that are not ordinary, common, everyday matters but ones that are known to occur occasionally. The category of special risks can also be interpreted to include risks that may not be significant to the hypothetical reasonable person but would constitute a significant risk to the particular patient.

The Canadian courts do not impose a duty on the doctor to discover every detail about a patient's particular position. Instead there is onus placed on the patient to inform the doctor that the patient's position, interests or values are unusual in some potentially significant way.

It is recognised that what is material may differ from patient to patient. What is material for one patient may not be material for another because of the medical history of each (*Joshi (Guardian ad Litem of) v Woolley* ((1995) 4 B.C.L.R. (3rd) 208 (S.C.))).

The scope of the duty covers a requirement to explain the nature of the proposed treatment and its purposes, benefits and seriousness and whether the procedure is essential or elective.

In *Poole v Morgan* ([1987] 3 W.W.R. 217 at 262 (Alta. Q.B.) it was held that in elective procedures even minimal risks must be disclosed. The duty to disclose available alternative treatments is especially important where there are more conservative options that present fewer risks to the patient, and where the recommended procedure is elective.

In *Arndt v Smith* ([1997] 3 LRC 198; 1997 2 SCR 539) the claimant contracted chickenpox when 12 weeks pregnant. She telephoned her doctor and asked if the virus posed any risk to her unborn child. Dr Smith admitted a lack of knowledge in the area but told the claimant that she would look into it and they should meet when she had fully recovered. Dr Smith researched the issue and also discussed it with a colleague. When they met, Dr Smith advised the claimant that, as with any viral infection, there was an unpredictable but small risk that chickenpox could result in her child having limb and skin abnormalities.

There was no recommendation that women who have contracted chickenpox should consider a termination of pregnancy. There was no mention in the discussion of the more severe, but less probable, risk of serious fetal injury such as cord atrophy and brain damage, which could cause mental retardation. Dr Smith chose not to warn the claimant of these risks as she thought it inappropriate to unduly worry an expectant mother about an improbable risk and one for which she would not advice a therapeutic termination of pregnancy.

The child was born suffering from congenital varicella syndrome. Her disabilities were caused by the chickenpox suffered by her mother. A claim for wrongful life was brought on behalf of the child and this was rejected by the court. The sole focus of the case was the duty owed to the Mrs Arndt. The court held that to be successful she had to demonstrate that she had been inadequately warned by the doctor of all the risks entailed, and, secondly, that had she been so warned she would have terminated the pregnancy.

The court found that, although she was informed of some of the risks associated with chickenpox, she had not been advised of the more significant and serious risks associated with the virus. Dr Smith had failed to inform her of all material risks faced by the fetus. This factual issue was not questioned by either of the higher courts. The causation issue was the determinative issue and this is dealt with in Chapter 6 (this case was applied in *Huisman v MacDonald* (280 DLR (4th) 1); *Van Dyke v Grey Bruce Regional Health Centre* (255 DLR (4th) 397); *Van Mol (Guardian ad Litem of) Ashmore* (168 DLR (4th) 637)).

In *Martin v Inglis* ([2002] S.J. No.251 (Sask. Q.B.)) the Court of Queen's Bench of Saskatchewan defined material risks as the risks which a reasonable person in the patient's position would want to know. The adequacy of information disclosed to a patient, although based on the so-called "objective" or reasonable person standard, is assessed in the context of the facts of a particular case. The objective test is refined.

In *Rayner v Knickle* ((1998) 47 C.C.L.T. 141) the court concluded that during the procedure there could be complications that could increase the risk that added risk must be disclosed to the patient:

even though the risk of paralysis or death is quite remote (approximately 1 in 1000), yet complications during the administration of amniocentesis can substantially change odds by increasing the risk. In the present circumstances Dr. Kingston decided to pass the needle through the placenta because of its anterior position. In doing so, the risks of injury were thereby increased. That surely constitutes an added risk which ought to have been disclosed to Heather Rayner.

In *Videto v Kennedy* ((1981) 125 D.L.R. (3d) 127 (Ont.C.A.)) the Ontario Court of Appeal set out the principles that could be derived from the decision in *Hopp v Lepp* and *Reibl v Hughes*. In this case the claimant underwent a sterilisation procedure during which her bowel was perforated, bringing her close to death. The trial judge had concluded that, while the danger was not great, the risk of perforating the bowel was a real risk beyond the danger inherent in the operation. If the bowel was perforated, peritonitis and a laparotomy would follow. The appeal was argued on the basis there was a duty to disclose the risk of a larger scar, rather than there was a duty to disclose the risk of peritonitis should there be a perforation. It appeared to have been accepted that if a perforation occurred and it was dealt with expeditiously it would not normally result in death. The Court of Appeal did not consider the possibility that a large scar should be treated as a material risk and the appeal was refused.

However, on the issue of the law to be applied in such cases, the following principles were said to apply:

- The question of whether a risk is material and whether there has been a breach of the duty of disclosure should not be determined solely by the standards of the profession, although that could be a factor to be considered.

- The duty of disclosure embraces what the surgeon knows or ought to know what the patient deems relevant to their decision whether or not to undergo the treatment.

- If a patient asks specific questions he is entitled to be given reasonable answers.

- A risk which is a mere possibility does not ordinarily have to be disclosed, but if its occurrence would have serious consequences it should be treated as a material risk.

- The patient is entitled to be given an explanation of the nature of the operation and its gravity. Subject to this, other inherent dangers such as dangers of anaesthetic or the risks of infection do not have to be disclosed.

- The scope of the duty and whether it has been breached must be decided in the circumstances of each case.

- The emotional condition of the patient may in certain cases justify the surgeon in withholding or generalising information which otherwise should be more specific.

- The question of whether a particular risk is a material risk and whether there has been a breach of duty is a matter for the trier of fact.

In *White v Turner* ((1981) 120 D.L.R. (3d) 269 (Ont.H.C.); affirmed (1982) 12 D.L.R. (4th) 319 (Ont. C.A.)) the Ontario High Court of Justice explained that it was clear that Canadian doctors were obligated to disclose to their patients the nature of the proposed operation, its gravity, any material risks and any special or unusual risks attendant upon performance of the operation. It noted that the court now had a voice in deciding the appropriate level of information that must be conveyed to a patient in the circumstances as a question of fact.

In *White v Turner*, the claimant underwent breast reduction surgery and one argument was that she had not been properly advised of the risks of breast reduction surgery. It was held that a court in deciding the matter would certainly expect to hear expert medical evidence on the question of the risks that were inherent in a particular operation and how serious these risks were and how frequently they occurred. The court would also be interested in what information medical practitioners usually transmit to patients in relation to those risks. But the court would also have regard to the evidence of the patient and their family as to the general situation. The court will be interested in the information they would want to know in the circumstances.

"Material risks" were defined as significant risks that pose a real threat to the patient's life, health or comfort. The court should balance the severity of the potential harm against the likelihood of it occurring. Even if there was a small chance of serious injury or death the risk may be considered material. What is a material risk will always depend on the specific facts and circumstances of each case.

Consideration was also given in *White v Turner* to what could be classified as "unusual or special risks". These are not ordinary, common, everyday matters. They are risks that are somewhat extraordinary, uncommon and not encountered every day, but are known to occur occasionally. Although rare occurrences, they should be described to the patient even though they are not material.

In cases where the procedure is purely aesthetic and elective rather than necessary for medical reasons, the Canadian courts have held that the duty to advise of rare complications is increased (*Bohus v Williams* ((1996) 39 Alta. L.R. (3d) 112 (Q.B.)). In *White v Turner* Linden J held that a physician had a duty to disclose even minimal risks where a procedure is elective. The decision was upheld on appeal. However, in *Dunn v North York General Hospital* ([1989] O.J. No. 402 (H.C.J.)) it was observed that the comment was *obiter* and that the endorsement of the Court of Appeal referred to the failure to disclose material risks (see also *Puranan v Thomson* (1987) 46 Man. R. (2d) 55 (Q.B.)).

d. Examples of cases where the issue of "material risk" is considered

In Canada, there have been a number of cases where the courts have considered what is a "material risk". They have interpreted the duty to disclose very liberally. The courts have in their decisions routinely characterised statistically remote risks as material, especially where they involve death or serious injury.

In *Meyer Estate v Rogers* ((1991) 78 D.L.R. (4th) 307 (Ont.H.C.)) it was held, applying the principles in *Reibl v Hughes*, that the risks of an allergic reaction to contrast medium used during an IV pyelogram should be disclosed. A risk of death of between 1 in 40,000 and 1 in 100,000 was held to be a material risk. In this case the doctors were aware of the possible side effects of the dye, ranging from mild reactions through moderate and severe reactions to death. One of the doctors admitted that he intentionally withheld the information that contrast media injections can cause death. His decision to do so was grounded in the position taken by the Canadian Association of Radiologists. It was said by the court that the position recommended by the Canadian Association of Radiologists directly contravened the standard required from the Supreme Court in *Reibl v Hughes*. It was noted that *Reibl v Hughes* explicitly stated that the risk of death was a material risk.

In *Lachambre v Nair* ([1989] 2 W.W.R. 749) the claimant suffered quadriplegia following a head scan and angiogram with contrast. He had attended hospital suffering from headaches after playing sport and the attending physician suspected that he may have suffered from a subarachnoid haemorrhage. Information was given about risks but the allegation was that incomplete information had been given. There was a risk of serious reactions and paralysis, although it was recognised that the risk was rare. In the circumstances, it was found that they were material risks that ought to have been disclosed.

In *Boschman v Azad* ([2002] BCSC 887; (2002) 2 B.C.L.R. (4th) 342) the claimant was advised of the risk of the risk of phrenic nerve injury but she was not advised of the consequences of such an injury. Boschman's phrenic nerve was damaged by the surgery, as a result of which the claimant's right hemi diaphragm was paralysed. The surgery carried a 3–5% risk of damage to the phrenic nerve. It was found that there was a failure to advise the claimant of the consequences of damage to the nerve. It was held that to mention a risk of harm to a nerve without at the same time advising the patient of the potential consequences of such harm is not generally sufficient.

In *Forgie v Mason* ((1986) 30 D.L.R. (4th) 548 (N.B.C.A.)) the risk of stroke, however minimal, was considered to be a material risk. It was said that there was no distinction between surgical and non-surgical treatment where material risks are concerned. The risk of stroke was between 1 in 100,000 and 1 in 300,000. The risk was well known. It was considered that a reasonable person in the position of the claimant would not have consented to taking such a small risk of a serious possibility, especially since the patient had a deep fear of having a stroke and there were alternative treatments available for the condition, which was debilitating but not life-threatening (see *Zaiffdeen v Chua* [2005] ABCA 290; (2005) 380 A.R. 200 Alta A.C.).

In *Casey v Provan* ((1984) 11 D.L.R. (4th) 708) the risk of permanent loss or serious impairment to the voice was held to be a material risk in carotid endarterectomy. In this case the claimant was a civil servant who earned his living conducting interviews, and this was a fact known to the doctor. The claimant did not ask any questions about the surgery, nor did he express any concerns. The court was satisfied that, given the risk to the vocal cord in the operation (whilst its occurrence may only have been a mere possibility), the nature of the risk was such that it should be treated as a material risk.

In *Huisman v MacDonald* ([2007] 280 D.L.R. (4th) 1, Ont C.A.) following successful elective hip surgery (Ganz procedure) the claimant developed severe left sciatic nerve palsy, which resulted in amputation of the leg below the knee. At first instance the trial judge found in favour of the claimant and the decision was upheld on appeal. The risk of permanent sciatic nerve damage was a material, special or unusual risk that a reas-onable person would wish to be informed of if considering whether to undergo the procedure.

In *Videto v Kennedy* ((1981) 125 D.L.R. (3rd) 127 Ont C.A.) a small risk of bowel perforation during the course of laparoscopic sterilisation was not material

In *Berezowski-Aitken v McGregor* ([1998] 8 W.W.R. 322, Man Q.B.) the claimant underwent a D&C operation following the death of her fetus. There was no discussion of the risks of the procedure, nor was she advised the fetus might have been expelled naturally. During the procedure, the surgeon damaged the uterus and the bowel, as a result of which the claimant required several surgeries and became infertile. Perforation of the uterus was said to be a common risk of D&C procedures, but damage to the bowel was more unusual. The risk of damage to the bowel was said to be "quite remote" but should it occur it could result in infertility. In those circumstances the court concluded that it was a material risk that should have been explained to the claimant.

In *Painter v Rae* ([1998] 8 W.W.R 717, Q.B. (Man)) it was held that the claimant should have been advised of the risk of bowel injury as a complication of tubal ligation despite the fact that the doctor who took her consent had never encountered this in his practice. He stated that he was unaware of any significant risks associated with tubal ligation beyond the common risks of infection, haemorrhage and failure. The expert led for the defendant stated that the risk was less than 1%. This was accepted by the court but it was said that the gravity of the consequences if the risk materialised were such that the risk could be classified as either a material risk or a special or unusual risk which needed to be disclosed.

In this case the defendant's counsel referred to *Gonda v Kerbel* ((1982) 24 C.C.L.T. 222 (Ont.H.C.)), where bowel perforation during the course of sigmoidoscopy was not thought to be a material risk in that perforation did not carry the risk of death or paralysis. He also referred to *Krunik v Wahba* ([1992] 5 W.W.R. 519 (Sask. Q.B.)), where it was held that the risk of experiencing long-term pain was not material.

In *Baksh-White v Cochen* ((2001) 7 C.C.L.T. (3d) 138, Ont S.C.) the claimant's small bowel was perforated during the course of an abdominal hysterectomy. It was argued that the claimant should have been advised of conservative options for managing her condition. She should also have been advised of the risk of bowel perforation, which in her case was increased because she had had three previous surgeries. The risk of bowel perforation was held to be material.

In *Krangle v Brisco* ((1997) 154 D.L.R. (4th) 707 BCSC) a GP was held liable for failing to discuss the possibility of performing an amniocentesis with parents. The GP was involved in most of the early care and the mother did not appear to have been reviewed at hospital by an obstetrician until it was too late to undergo the test. The couple claimed they had no religious or moral opposition to termination of pregnancy. Had they been informed the child might have Down's syndrome they would have terminated the pregnancy.

In *Rawlings v Lindsey* ((1982) 20 C.C.L.T. 301) a 5–10% risk of nerve damage and numbness to the face following extraction of a wisdom tooth was held to be a material risk. It was considered that a fair summary of the terminology "material" "special" and "unusual" risks would be that a medical person should disclose those risks to which a reasonable person would be likely to attach significance to in deciding whether or not to undergo the proposed treatment. The degree of probability of risk and its seriousness were the relevant factors. It was suggested that an unusual or improbable risk should be disclosed if its effects are serious. A minor result should be disclosed if it is inherent or probable in the proposed procedure.

In *Diak v Bardsley* ((1983) 25 C.C.L.T. 159 BCSC), partial paraesthesia of the lower side of the face caused by a needle entering the nerve during the administration of local anaesthetic prior to root canal work was held not to be a material risk.

In *Carter v Higashi* ([1994] 3 W.W.R. 319 Alta Q.B.) the claimant suffered a fractured jaw in the course of having her wisdom teeth extracted by a dentist. He did not advise her of the risk of fracturing the jaw prior to obtaining consent. It was held that the risk of fracturing the jaw was a remote risk (1 in 100,000) and this was not a material risk, therefore there was no duty to inform the patient of it.

In *Kitchen v McMullen* ((1989) 62 D.L.R. (4th) 481 (N.B.C.A.)) it was said that certain risks of infection such as contracting hepatitis from blood products might be an "unusual or special risk" which should be disclosed.

In *Felde v Vein and Laser Medical Centre* ([2002] O.J. No. 3686) the claimant underwent cosmetic surgery to correct a small blemish on her eyelid. She was not advised of the risks of ectropion, lid retraction, scleral show or the possibility of revisionary surgery. It was held that the possibility of those risks were material risks and were risks that she should have been advised of.

Where something is recognised as a complication of a procedure the courts are likely to find it a material risk that needed to be disclosed. In *Shaw v Roy* ((1994) 136 N.S.R. (2d) 1, 388 A.P.R. 1 (S.C.)) the patient was not advised of the 5% risk of collapsed lung, which occurred as a result of an intercostal nerve block injection. This was a recognised complication and considered a material risk. The procedure was elective and the risks that arose came about because of the particular circumstances of the pursuer.

e.   **Duty to answer questions**

In Canada, the test has always been a strict test in terms of a patient asking questions. In *Hopp v Lepp* the court considered that the duty of the surgeon was to answer any specific questions posed by the patient. It was provided that without being questioned the doctor should disclose the nature of the operation, its proposed gravity, any material risks and any special or unusual risks. If a risk were small, or a mere possibility, it could still need to be disclosed if there were serious consequences should it occur.

f.   Clarity of explanation of risks

In Canada, the duty of disclosure includes a duty to take reasonable steps to ensure that a patient actually understands the information (*Ciarlariello Estate v Schacter* ([1993] 2 S.C.R. 119)). The key to consent is communication and therefore the language used must achieve that object (*Schanczl v Santokh Singh* [1987] A.J. No. 1126, 56 Alta. L.R. (2d) 303 (Q.B.), affd [1988] 2 W.W.R.465 (Q.B.)).

In *Ferguson v Hamilton Civic Hospitals et al.* ((1983) 144 D.L.R. (3d) 214) it was said that a patient is entitled to have enough time and an environment to enable them to carefully consider their position. Consent entails the opportunity to evaluate knowledgeably the options available and the risks of each option.

In *Lue v St. Michael's Hospital* ([1997] O.J. No 255 (Gen. Div.) (QL); 1999 122 OAC 46) it was said that where functions of the brain are in issue the court should apply objective standards to assess patient comprehension. A standard based primarily upon an assertion by the doctor is inappropriate. There should be an objective analysis of the assertion by the doctor of the patient's understanding.

Issues of communication of risk arise where the patient's first language is not English (*Adan v Davis* [1998] O.J. No.3030 (Gen. Div.) (QL)). In *Reibl v Hughes* Laskin CJC said that it must have been obvious to the doctor that the claimant had some difficulty with the English language and in that situation he should have made certain that he was understood. The question is whether the patient's linguistic ability is at a level which allows them to understand the information upon which the consent is to be based (see also *Schanczi v Singh* ([1988] 2 W.W.R. 465, 56 Alta L.R. (2d) 303 (Q.B.)) and *Kellet v Griesdale* ([1985] B.C.J. No.1414), which dealt with elderly patients resistant to discussing risks).

In *Smith v Tweedale* ((1995) 4 B.C.L.R. (3d) 325 (C.A.)) the discussion about tubal ligation took place when the patient had been in labour for 13 hours and was contemplating the birth of her child by caesarean section. The issue at trial was whether the doctor had explained that the tubal ligation which he was about to perform on her at her request was a permanent and irreversible procedure. The claimant understood that the procedure was reversible, with a 50% chance of a successful pregnancy. It was held that the gynaecologist was under a legal duty to advise her that the procedure was not reversible, with a 50% chance of a successful pregnancy.

In *Felde v Vein and Laser Medical Centre* ([2002] O.J. No. 3686 (Sup.Ct. Jus.) (QL)) disclosure was held to be inadequate where the discussion about risks took place immediately prior to surgery when the patient was on the operating table (see also *Brown v Degani* ([1996] O.J. No 126)).

Where a doctor uses terminology which is highly technical or difficult to understand, the Canadian courts have found this to be an inadequate communication of information. In *Paradis v Labow* ([1996] O.J. No. 1326 (Gen. Div.) (QL)) the court accepted the patient's evidence that the surgeon used "big words" to explain breast reduction surgery. In *Finch v Carpenter* ([1993] B.C.J. No.1918 (S.C) (QL)) a written explanation of the risks of oral surgery were found to be too technical and not understandable.

In *Bryan v Hicks* ([1995] 10 W.W.R. 145 (B.C.C.A)) the court looked closely at the way information was communicated to the patient in obtaining consent. The surgeon warned the patient undergoing an operation for a ganglion in the wrist that there was a 1–2% risk of "sympathetic pain" following surgery. This was his normal way of advising of the risk of reflex sympathetic dystrophy. The court held that this was not the same as advising a patient that there was a risk that his arm could be useless. Only three cases in 2000 developed a severe and permanent form of this condition. The risk was such that medical opinion did not require it to be disclosed. Nonetheless, the British Columbia Court of Appeal held that this was a material risk. A reasonable patient would wish to know of this risk, particularly given the fact that there were alternative forms of treatment available.

g.   Right to refuse treatment

In Canada, the patient has the right to refuse to have treatment even where a doctor considers that it is in the best interest of the patient to have treatment. In *Reibl v Hughes* the court emphasised the right to refuse treatment based on full information on the consequences of the refusal.

Where a patient waives the right to be given information, the doctor does not have to force the patient to have information.

In *Malette v Shulman* ((1990) 67 D.L.R (4th) 321, Ont C.A.) a surgeon administered blood to an unconscious patient admitted to hospital when the surgeon was aware that the patient carried a card declaring that she was a Jehovah's Witness and would not accept blood in any circumstances. It was held that the principles of self-determination and individual autonomy mean that the patient may reject blood transfusions even if the decision were regarded as foolhardy. The doctor was required to comply with the instructions even although she was unconscious and there was no opportunity to discuss with the patient the effect of this decision. This case also suggested that where the reasonable patient test applies there can never be a situation of therapeutic privilege. It is likely that this view was simply a response to what was seen as attempts to extend the doctrine in the USA.

h.   Where a patient knows risks from previous operation

In Canada, it has been considered relevant that a patient knew of the risks from a previous operation. In *Goguen v Crowe* ((1987) 40 C.C.L.T. 212) it was held that the mother had previously experienced a forceps delivery and it could be assumed that she knew that such a delivery was a possibility.

In *Semeniuk v Cox* ([2000] ABQB 18; [2000] 4 W.W.R. 310) it was held that, where the patient is aware of a risk from a previous operation, and where a revision operation carries a threefold increase in the risks of complications, then the increased risk is material and should be disclosed to the patient.

i.   Acceptable non-communication of risks

In Canada, the courts do recognise that there may be instances in which a doctor is not required to fully inform a patient (*Reibl v Hughes*; *Hopp v Lepp*).

It had been thought that the exception had its foundation in thera-peutic privilege. However, in *Meyer Estate v Rogers* it was said that there was no defence of therapeutic privilege in Canada. Therapeutic privilege is an American exception to the rule that doctors are required to inform their patients of the risks associated with a proposed procedure follow-ing the decision in *Canterbury v Spence* (464 F 2d 772 (1972) at paras 788 and 789). The therapeutic privilege exception was raised and dismissed in *Haughian v Paine*.

It is recognised that doctor need not disclose information to a patient if by doing so he may do more harm to the patient than any benefit to be gained from the treatment. Where there is an emergency situation treat-ment can proceed without consent.

Further, where the emotional condition of the patient is such that a detailed disclosure would cause the patient extreme anxiety the doctor may be justified in withholding information. It has been suggested in Canada that so-called therapeutic privilege should be construed very narrowly and applied in only the most exceptional circumstances.

In *Layton v Wescott* ((1992) 6 Alta. L.R. (3d) 91 at 102 (Q.B) it was held that even though the patient was a very anxious and distraught person there were special risks of which she should have been made aware and time for reflection should have been provided. It was desirable that any patient, especially a visibly anxious one, be given time to consider the information disclosed and formulate questions.

In *Hajgato v London Health Association* ((1982) 36 O.R. (2d) 669); affirmed (1983) 44 O.R. (2d) 264 (Ont. C.A.)) the claimant underwent a Chiari osteotomy and she alleged that she had not been advised of the risks and damagers associated with the procedure and, in particular that there was a risk of infection. The defendant doctor had concluded that the claimant was very anxious and distressed throughout his meeting with her prior to surgery. He did advise her there was a risk of infection but conceded that he did not advise her that should an infection occur it might result in destruction of the hip, as the risk of such an infection was minimal. He thought that advising her of this fact would result in undue distress.

The court held that the risk of infection was disclosed to the claimant but the possibility of destruction of the hip was not disclosed. This was not a risk the court considered required disclosure. The emotional condition of the patient and her apprehension when weighed against the possibility of damage from infection justified the generalisation.

In *Pitman Estate v Bain* ((1994) 112 D.L.R. (4th) 257) the claimant underwent cardiac surgery in 1984 and was transfused with cryoprecipitate. Unfortunately, this was contaminated with the HIV virus. In 1989 the hospital was aware of this and advised the family GP, who thereafter decided not to advise the claimant as he was concerned about his cardiac condition and mental health. He made an assumption that the claimant was not engaged in sexual relations with his wife. The claimant died in 1990 and was HIV+. Shortly thereafter his wife also learned that she was HIV+.

It was accepted that there could be cases where a patient is unable or unwilling to accept bad news from a doctor. In those circumstances a physician is obliged to take reasonable precautions to ensure that the patient has communicated their desire not to be told, or that the patient's health is so precarious that such news will undoubtedly trigger an adverse reaction that will cause further unnecessary harm to the patient.

Where a professional body advises that there should be no communication of risks to the patient this may not be a defence. In *Meyer Estate v Rogers* ((1991) 78 D.L.R. (4ᵗʰ) 307, Ont C.A.) the Canadian Association of Radiologists had specifically recommended that patients should not be informed of the risks of an allergic reaction to contrast media during an IV pyelogram. The court held that this risk was material and that the Association's recommendation directly contravened the standard required in *Reibl v Hughes*.

j.   Withdrawal of consent

In Canada, the patient is able to withdraw consent to treatment, except where there is legislation that requires the treatment.

In *Ciarlariello v Schacter* ((1993) 100 D.L.R (4ᵗʰ) 609, Sup Ct (Can)) the court considered the issue of withdrawal of consent and the duty of the doctor where a patient has language difficulties. The claimant was an Italian living in Canada and had suffered a grade-one subarachnoid haemorrhage which required treatment. During the course of a second angiogram to treat her condition the claimant withdrew her consent to the procedure and it was stopped but then restarted when she had calmed down. When the procedure was restarted, she suffered an immediate reaction to the dye and was rendered quadriplegic.

It was held that withdrawal of consent would always be a question of fact for the trial judge to resolve. Reference was made to *Nightingale v Kaplovitch* ([1989] O.J. No. 585 (QL)) and *Fleming v Reid* ((1991) 4 O.R. (3d) 74 (C.A.)). An individual's right to determine what medical procedures will be accepted must include the right to stop a procedure.

The patient's right to bodily integrity provides the basis for the withdrawal of consent to a medical procedure even while it is under way. If it is found that the consent is effectively withdrawn during the course of the procedure, then it must be terminated. This must be the result except in those circumstances where the medical evidence suggests that

to terminate the process would be either life-threatening or pose immediate and serious problems to the health of the patient:

> *If during the course of a medical procedure a patient withdraws the*
> *consent to that procedure, then doctors must halt the process.*

In *Ciarlariello v Schacter* the court also considered whether a full explanation of risks needed to be given again if the procedure was to be
restarted. It was concluded that the appropriate approach is to focus on
what the patient would like to know concerning the continuation of the
process. Looking at it objectively, it was held that a patient would want
to know whether there had been any significant change in the risks
involved or in the need for the continuation of this process which had
become apparent during the course of the procedure.

In addition, the patient will want to know if there has been a material
change in circumstances which could alter their assessment of the costs
or benefits of continuing the procedure. For example, have the circumstances changed in such a way that the procedure is no longer as
important to making a diagnosis as it was earlier? The court emphasised
that each case will have to be determined on its own facts. Changes may
arise during the course of the procedure which are not at all relevant to
the issue of consent. Yet, the critical question will always be whether the
patient would want to have the information pertaining to those changes
in order to decide whether to continue.

k. Particular surgeon

In Canada, the person who obtains consent and who is in charge of
caring for the patient should advise who will be participating in a
procedure. In *Marcoux v Bouchard* ([2001] SCC 50; 204 D.L.R. (4th) 1)
the claimant alleged that she had not consented to a particular surgeon
assisting in the procedure. The Supreme Court of Canada considered
that the patient was entitled to know who the main surgeons were but
not the secondary players.

In *Halkyard v Mathew* (2001 ABCA 67) the Alberta Court of Appeal held that a doctor did not have a duty to disclose their own medical condition, where there was no causal link between the medical condition and the harm to the patient. One argument made was that the doctor had a duty to disclose to the patient that he suffered from epilepsy. He had been cleared to work, took medication to control his epilepsy and had never suffered a seizure in theatre.

It was argued by the claimant that the non-disclosure amounted to battery, vitiating the consent given for surgery, or alternatively that it was a negligent non-disclosure. The battery argument was rejected on the basis that the surgery performed was one for which the patient had given consent. Lewis J concluded that the defendant was not obliged to disclose his own personal medical history to his patient. He had made disclosure of all the material risks attending the surgery and the risks and potential complications of the procedure and had obtained consent. The Court of Appeal not only reaffirmed the need for the causal link between the non-disclosure and the actual harm suffered but also determined that doctors need not disclose their medical problems, where the problems do not cause harm to their patients.

I.   Where there is a signed consent form with risks detailed

In Canada, the fact that the patient has signed a document that purports to demonstrate that he or she has consented to a particular treatment may be evidence of consent but it is not conclusive. The fact that the form is signed does not demonstrate that the patient has been given full information of the alternatives and risks and benefits of each option.

In *Casey v Provan* (1984) 11 D.L.R. (4th) 708) the court stated that, while the claimant in this case had signed a consent form prior to the operation in which he acknowledged that the nature of the operation had been explained to him, the existence of the consent form did not protect the surgeon from liability unless the patient had been informed to the satisfaction of the court.

In *Coughlin v Kuntz* ([1990] 2 W.W.R. 737 (B.C.C.A.)) the court concluded that a consent form does not discharge the duty of the surgeon to consult with a patient. The existence of the form signed by the claimant cannot protect a doctor if the court concludes that there was a failure to explain and fully disclose all relevant information. For the consent form to have any legal effect there must be an adequate knowledge base on the part of the patient before the exempting language of the form will provide its intended protection for the surgeon or the hospital from the adverse effects of the operation (see also *Archibald v Kuntz* ([1994] B.C.J. No. 199 (QL) (B.C.S.C.)); *Bycluk v Hollingsworth* (2004 ABQB 370); *Martin v Finlay* (2008 ABCA 161 432); *Tremblay v McLauchlan* (2001 BCCA 444)).

In *Dickson v Pinder* it was concluded that the consent form did not document consent as the patient did not understand the meaning and implications of the statements contained in the form.

In *Ken v Forest* (2010 BCSC 938) Kelleher J rejected defence arguments that a consent form had been adequate on the basis that there was nothing on the form about alternative treatments and therapies or the risks associated with the treatment.

However, in *Loffler v Cosman* (2010 ABQB 177) the court concluded that a standard consent form provided by a chiropractic professional organisation was sufficient.

In *Olsen v Jones* (2009 ABQB 371) a signed consent form was found to be adequate, though in this case the patient had an extensive history of treatment and the manner in which the form had been co-signed indicated that both the patient and the chiropractor had discussed its contents.

The consent must also be specific to the procedure being performed. Although in a surgical emergency the procedure may be extended beyond the procedure authorised by the patient (*Marshall v Curry* ([1993] 3 D.L.R. 260)). In Canada, the courts have suggested that the consent form must include the consequence of the treatment being undergone.

It was considered that this is the critical information (*Martin v Finlay*, 2008 ABCA 161).

m.   Experience of the surgeon

Canada has considered and rejected the argument that there is a requirement for a physician to disclose their experience with a procedure to a patient as part of the consent process (*Hopp v Lepp*; *Turner v Bederman* [1996] O.J. No 1712 (G.D.); *Kita v Braig* (1992) 17 B.C.A.C. 55).

In *Huisman v MacDonald* ([2007] ONCA 391; 280 D.L.R. (4th) 1, Ont C.A.) the trial judge did not consider that the doctor needed to advise the patient that he had only performed 8–10 osteotomies prior to her surgery. The medical evidence did not consider this to be material and the court agreed with the submission that in *Hopp v Lepp*, at least inferentially, the Supreme Court of Canada concluded that a physician failing to inform a patient of the extent of their experience is not in and of itself a breach of the duty of disclosure.

However, patients are not without remedy where a doctor's personal health actually causes harm to the patient, on the traditional principles of negligence.

n.   Manufacturers and information

In Canada, in product liability cases manufacturers have a duty to warn consumers about dangers inherent in the use of their products of which the manufacturer has knowledge or ought to have knowledge (*Lambert v Lastoplex Chemicals Co*. [1972] S.C.R. 569).

The duty to warn is a continuing duty, requiring manufacturers to warn not only of dangers known at the time of sale but also of dangers discovered after the product has been sold and delivered. It was recognised that the rationale for the manufacturer's duty to warn can be traced back to the "neighbour principle" set down by Lord Atkin in *Donoghue v Stevenson* ([1932] A.C. 562 (H.L.)).

In exceptional circumstances the manufacturer may satisfy its informational duty to the consumer by providing a warning to what is termed a "learned intermediary". This rule was first elaborated in *Sterling Drug, Inc. v Cornish* (370 F.2d 82 (8th Cir. 1996)), which was an action brought by a patient blinded by taking the drug chloroquine phosphate. The rationale for the rule was outlined in *Reyes v Wyeth Laboratories* (198 F.2d 1264 (5th Cir.1974)). The rule was reaffirmed and developed in a series of American cases during the 1970s and 1980s.

In Canada, the rule was first discussed in *Davidson v Connaught Laboratories* ((1980) 14 C.C.L.T. (2d) 251 (Ont. H.C.)), where a patient alleged that he had not been properly warned about the risks of paralysis or death prior to receiving a vaccine for rabies. The court held that the drug company had an obligation to provide doctors with adequate information about side effects and risks known to them. Thereafter, the doctor should assess the information and advise the patient of the risks. The manufacturer had no duty to directly warn the patient.

The rule was later applied by a five-member panel of the Ontario Court of Appeal in *Buchan v Ortho Pharmaceutical (Canada) Ltd* ((1986) 12 O.A.C. 361)). In *Buchan*, the claimant suffered a stroke after taking oral contraceptives prescribed by her doctor and manufactured by Ortho Pharmaceutical. The Ontario Court of Appeal accepted the learned intermediary rule as an exception to manufacturers' general common-law duty to warn consumers directly. It was said that the prescribing doctor was in a position to take into account the propensities of the drug and susceptibilities of his patient. In taking the drug the patient places primary reliance on the doctor's judgement.

In *Hollis v Birch* ((1996) 27 C.C.L.T. (2d) 1 (S.C.C.)) the Supreme Court of Canada considered the issue. The claimant underwent breast implant surgery on the advice of her surgeon to correct a congenital deformity. She was not warned by him of the risks of post-surgical complications or of the possibility that the implants might rupture inside her body.

Some years later it was found the right-hand implant had ruptured. As early as 1979 the manufacturers Dow were aware that implant ruptures could cause adverse reactions.

In *Hollis*, it was said that in the case of medicinal products such as breast implants the standard of care to be met by the manufacturer in ensuring that consumers are properly warned is high. It was recognised that manufacturers of products that are ingested, consumed or otherwise placed in the body are subject to a high standard of care under the law of negligence.

4.   New Zealand

In *Smith v Auckland Hospital Board* ([1965] N.Z.L.R. 191 (N.Z.C.A.)) the *Bolam* standard was applied to disclosure. However, in this case the patient asked a specific question and the answer given was judged to fall below the appropriate standard. The patient asked whether there were any risks involved in aortography and he was given a reassuring answer and not advised of the risks.

New Zealand has a no-fault compensation scheme. In 1996 New Zealand developed a Code of Health and Disability Services Consumer Rights. The Code became law on 1 July 1996 as a regulation under the Health and Disability Commissioner Act 1994 (the HDC Act). The Office of the Health and Disability Commissioner administers and receives complaints under the Code. The first commissioner, Robyn Stent, provided that the Act and the Code are tools to ensure that health and disability consumer protection in New Zealand did not depend on the changeable priorities of individual providers but is subject to a consistent and fair standard.

The Code followed the 1988 Cervical Cancer Inquiry, known as the Cartwright Inquiry, which was credited with leading to a major overhaul of medical practices and health care ethics in Aotearoa, New Zealand. The Code covers all registered health professionals, such as doctors, nurses and dentists, and applies to all health care providers and disability services providers (whether those providers are registered or not). The Code has been reviewed but has only had one amendment to it since it was introduced.

This code places a heavy emphasis on information disclosure and rights. The code refers to "consumers" rather than "patients" as the intention is to include disability consumers in addition to health care consumers. There is a right to be fully informed and also a right to make informed choices and give what they describe as informed consent.

The test used in the Code is similar to the test in the Australian case of *Rogers v Whitaker*. The test applied is what the reasonable consumer in the consumer's circumstances would want to know. The duty advanced by the Code is to provide fair and balanced information and there is also a separate duty to answer questions honestly and truthfully.

The Code also recognises the dangers of attaching statistical probability to the definition of expected risks. The probability of a risk transpiring must be weighed against the magnitude of the potential harm and the availability of other options. If the potential harm is serious the reasonable consumer should be warned of this harm regardless of the statistical probability of the risk. If a risk is too unusual to require a warning it may still require to be disclosed if the risk is elevated in the circumstances of the individual patient.

Since the enactment of the HDC legislation, there have been many cases where the HDC has found breaches as a result of a failure to meet the appropriate standard of care in relation to consent. The commissioner does not have any powers following their investigations into any complaint, other than to make recommendations following findings. These recommendations can include referring their findings to the director of proceedings for consideration of whether any other proceedings (disciplinary or in the Human Rights Review Tribunal (HRRT)) should follow. These are taken by the director on behalf of the patient (or, where the director declines to, they can be taken by the patients themselves). Disciplinary findings in the Health Practitioners Disciplinary Tribunal can ultimately result in restrictions on doctor's practices (as indeed can be imposed by the Medical Council of New Zealand) and findings against a practitioner in the HRRT can include awards of damages.

5.   Ireland

In 2004, in *A Guide to Ethical Conduct and Behaviour* (6th Edition), the Irish Medical Council provided that:

> *In obtaining consent the doctor must satisfy himself/herself that the patient understands what is involved by explaining in appropriate terminology. A record of this discussion should be made in the patient's notes. A competent adult patient has the right to refuse treatment.*

Whilst there was an early recognition of this ethical principle in Ireland it took some time for the courts to set this as a legal standard.

In Ireland, legal principles to be applied in cases of alleged medical negligence have been settled by the decision of the Supreme Court in *Dunne (an infant) v National Maternity Hospital* ([1989] IR 91 (Ir Sup Ct)). The test laid down by the Supreme Court is similar to the tests applied in the UK in *Bolam* and *Hunter v Hanley*.

Prior to *Dunne*, in *Roche v Peilow* ([1985] IR 232; [1986] ILRM 189) Judge Griffin had defined the standard of care to include the ordinary level of degree of skill and competence generally exercised by "reason-ably careful colleagues" in the doctor's profession. The term "reasonably careful colleagues" referred to medical experts in the same or similar specialism. In *Roche v Peilow* it was recognised that there was an exception to this rule. Where a practice carries a defect which is obvious to a clinician, the clinician can be found liable even if professional practice would support it.

In *O'Donovan v Cork County Council* ([1967] IR 173 (Ir Sup Court)) it was said that doctors can deviate from general and approved practices (in limited circumstances) without having acted negligently.

In *Dunne (an infant)*, as a matter of policy and practice a hospital in the case of twin labour only monitored one fetal heart. This had been a practice at the hospital for 15–20 years. Evidence was led that the attempt to monitor two fetal hearts was so misleading as it could be dangerous. The practice was to identify the fetal heart of the first twin only. The hospital was a large maternity hospital and had outcomes for twin pregnancies comparable to hospitals who adopted a different approach. In this case the first twin was born severely brain damaged and his twin brother was stillborn.

The case was heard by a jury, which awarded IR£1,039,334. One of the principal grounds of appeal related to whether the jury had been properly directed. The Supreme Court, consisting of Finlay CJ and Griffin and Hedermann JJ, set out six principles they said were to be applied to all medical negligence cases.

However, *Dunne (an infant)* also provides that, even where a practice is approved by colleagues of similar specialisation, a doctor cannot escape liability if the claimant can establish that the practice has inherent defects which ought to be obvious to any person giving the matter due consideration (see also *Collins v Mid-Western Health Board* ([2000] 2 IR 154)).

In *Daniels and Another v Heskin* ([1954] IR 73 (S.C.)) the Irish Supreme Court considered the question of a doctor's duty to inform. This was an obstetric case. A needle broke when the doctor was stitching the mother's perineum following labour. The doctor decided not to advise the mother and decided to wait and see if the needle worked its way out of the anatomy naturally.

In *Daniels*, the court held that doctors were free to disclose or withhold information in light of their impression of the patient's character, education, social position and intelligence. Kingsmill-Moore J said that any attempt to substitute a rule of law for the individual judgement of a qualified doctor doing what they consider best for the particular patient would be disastrous (this was applied in *O'Donovan v Cork County Council and Others* ([1967] IR 173)).

Some 40 years after *Daniels v Heskin*, in *Walsh v Family Planning Services Ltd* ([1992] 1 IR 496) the Supreme Court of Ireland again considered the question of information disclosure and the sentiments expressed in *Daniels v Heskin*.

In *Walsh*, the court provided that there was a clear obligation to inform the patient of any possible harmful consequence arising from the operation, so as to permit the patient to give an informed consent. In this case the claimant was considering having a vasectomy and had seen an advert produced by the Family Planning Services saying it was painless and safe. He was counselled and told that it could improve his sex life. He was told that in about one in 40 cases there may be some discomfort in the immediate aftermath of the operation and in about 1 in 40 cases there could be more severe swelling, which could result in time off work.

Following the surgery, the claimant had significant pain and underwent various treatments. He brought an action for negligence in the performance of the operation but also for negligence, assault and battery in failing to advise him as to the consequences of the operation. The expert evidence confirmed he was suffering from orchidalgia, a known but exceptionally rare and not properly accounted for consequence of vasectomy operations. It was not the general professional practice to warn of this occurrence.

The claimant recovered damages in the High Court and the defendants appealed to the Supreme Court. All five judges of the Supreme Court agreed that in elective surgery if there is a risk, however exceptional or remote, which carried the possibility of grave consequences for the patient, this risk must be disclosed. Applying this principle, the Supreme Court considered that the claimant should have been warned about the possibility of orchidalgia notwithstanding the rarity of its incidence, particularly since the operation was elective. It was however found that a warning was given and it was sufficient.

The majority arrived at their conclusions by reference to different legal principles. The contrasting approaches caused considerable difficulty for those seeking to apply the principles formulated in the case. In *Medical Negligence Actions* by John White (p190) the author states that it was not unfair to observe that *Walsh* was bewildering both in the alternative criteria of the decision adopted by its adjudicators and in the application of it to the facts of the case.

Finlay CJ applied the principles and test set out in *Dunne (an infant) v National Maternity Hospital* as indicating the appropriate standard of care. Applying this test, if a medical practitioner followed general medical practice that would be sufficient to exonerate them from responsibility. This was subject to an exception if a general and approved practice might contain inherent defects which should have been obvious to any person giving the matter due consideration. If the latter position was accepted, then the fact that a medical practitioner followed general medical practice would not be sufficient to exonerate them from responsibility.

McCarthy J, in referring to the principles identified by Finlay CJ relating to medical negligence, appeared, at least to some, to adopt the same approach as Finlay CJ but differed in his final conclusion.

O'Flaherty J, with whose judgment Hederman J concurred, took a different approach from the chief justice and did not accept that the question of whether a warning should be given should be determined by the criteria as set out in *Dunne (an infant)*, as regards general and approved practice. He stated that the question of whether there has been a breach of the duty of care should be resolved on the established principles of negligence and referred to the decision of the Supreme Court of Canada in *Reibl v Hughes* ((1980) 114 D.L.R. (3d) 1). This approach concentrates on the patient's right to determine what is to be done to their body. It requires full disclosure of all material risks incident to the proposed treatment, so that the patient, thus informed, rather than the doctor, makes the real choice as to whether treatment is to be carried out.

The fourth judge in *Walsh*, Hederman J, agreed with O'Flaherty J. The fifth judge, Egan J, also did not appear to come down on the doctor-centred test proposed by O'Flaherty J.

In *Walsh*, all five judges of the Supreme Court agreed that in elective surgery any risk which carries the possibility of grave consequences for the patient must be disclosed. O'Flanerty J stated (para 545):

I have no hesitation in saying that where there is a question of elective surgery which is not essential to healthy or bodily well being, if there is a risk-however exceptional or remote- of grave consequences involving severe pain stretching for an appreciable time into the future and involving the possibility of future operative procedures, the exercise of the duty of care owed by the defendants requires that such possible consequences should be explained in the clearest language to the plaintiff.

Finlay CJ in his judgment stated (para 510):

I am satisfied that there is, of course, where it is possible to do so, a clear obligation on a medical practitioner carrying out or arranging for the carrying out of an operation, to inform the patient of any possible harmful consequence arising from the operation, so as to permit the patient to give an informed consent to subjecting himself to the operation concerned. I am also satisfied the extent of this obligation must, as a matter of common sense, vary with what might be described as the elective nature of the surgery concerned. Quite obviously, and even apart from cases of emergency surgery which has to be carried out to persons who are unconscious or incapable of giving or refusing consent, or to young children, there may be instances where as a matter of medical knowledge, notwithstanding substantial risks of harmful consequence, the carrying out of a particular surgical procedure is so necessary to maintain the life or health of the patient and the consequences of failing to carry it out are so clearly disad-

vantageous that limited discussion or warning concerning possible harmful side effects may be appropriate and proper. On the other hand, the obligation to give warning of possible harmful consequences of a surgical procedure which could be said to be at the other end of the scale to the extent to which it is elective, such as would undoubtedly be the operation of vasectomy, may be more stringent and more onerous.

Following the decision in *Walsh* there was uncertainty in Ireland. It was not clear whether the standard of disclosure was to be assessed by reference to the prevailing medical view or the patient-centred approach found in *Reibl v Hughes*. All judges were united in the view that the elective nature of surgery gave rise to a heightened duty to disclose information.

The decision in *Walsh* was subsequently applied by the Supreme Court in *Bolton v Blackrock Clinic & Ors* (unreported decision of the Supreme Court, Hamilton CJ 23 January, 1997), where the operation being performed was described as elective surgery. It was said that there was a clear duty on that situation to inform the claimant of any possible consequences arising from the operation.

In *Peter Geoghegan v David Harris* ([2000] 3 I.R. 536) the court had a further opportunity to analyse the duty of disclosure. This case was described at the time as the most sophisticated and closely reasoned decision on the subject by an Irish court.

In *Geoghegan* the claimant had decided to have dental implants and this required a bone graft from his chin. The claimant suffered damage to the incisive nerve at the front of his chin, which from the time of the procedure left him with a condition of pain at the midline of his chin known as chronic neuropathic pain. It was argued that it was the bone graft rather than the insertion of the dental implants which caused the symptoms.

The claimant brought an action based on negligence and a failure of the defendant to disclose to him in advance of the procedure that there was a risk of chronic neuropathic pain. The question was whether the claimant should have been warned about the risk of neuropathic pain, which was statistically a very remote possibility (less than 1%).

Kearns J considered whether a "reasonable patient" test was a preferable option to the doctor-centred approach favoured by Finlay CJ in *Walsh*:

> *The application of the reasonable patient test seems more logical in respect of disclosure. This would establish the proposition that, as a general principle, the patient has the right to know and the practitioner a duty to advise of all material risks associated with the proposed form of treatment.*

In *Geoghegan* it was held that that the defendant was obliged to give a warning of any material risk which was a known or foreseeable complication of an operation. Despite the fact that the nature of the risk in this case was extremely remote, neuropathic pain was a known complication and a warning of the risk was required. The test to be adopted by the court as to what risks ought to be disclosed to a patient before an operation was the test of the reasonable patient. By adopting that test it was the patient, thus informed, rather than the doctor, who made the real choice as to whether the treatment was to be carried out.

It was submitted on behalf of the claimant that, quite apart from a medical practitioner's obligation to offer information concerning proposed treatment, a patient is entitled to full and comprehensive information when he specifically asks for advice. The court concluded that no category of inquisitive patient existed in Irish law because of the onerous obligations imposed on the medical profession to warn patients of all risks with severe consequences, regardless of their infrequency.

On the issue of "materiality", Mr Justice Kearns said this included consideration of both (a) the severity of the consequences and (b) the statistical frequency of the risk. Kearns J said:

> *The reasonable man, entitled as he must be to full information of material risks, does not have impossible expectations nor does he seek*

to impose impossible standards ... he must be taken as needing medical practitioners to deliver on their medical expertise without excessive restraint or gross limitation on their ability to do so ... at times a risk may become so remote, in relation at any rate to the less than most serious consequences, that a reasonable man may not regard it as material or significant ... an absolute requirement of disclosure in every case is unduly onerous, and perhaps in the end counter-productive if it needlessly deters patients from undergoing operations which are in their best interest to have.

It was observed that "materiality" is not a static concept, and that any absolute requirement which ignored frequency would not be consistent with the rule of reason:

Each case ... should be considered in the light of its own particular facts, evidence and circumstances to see if the reasonable patient in the plaintiff's position required a warning of the particular risk.

In *Fitzpatrick v White* ([2007] IESC 51; [2008] 3 IR 551), the Supreme Court approved the judgment in *Geoghegan*. Kearns J (now elevated) reviewed the recent international case law and found that the common-law world was moving towards a more patient-centred test in the area of consent law. He noted that a "patient centered" approach had been adopted in "virtually every major common law jurisdiction" including Australia, Canada and the United States.

He was of the view that more recently courts in England had moved from the *Bolam* test to a version of the "reasonable patient" test, as evidenced in the decision of Lord Woolf MR in *Pearce v United Bristol Healthcare NHS Trust* ([1999] 48 BMLR 118).

He felt more "fortified to express, in rather more vigorous terms" than he did in *Geoghegan* the view that the patient-centred test was preferable and ultimately more satisfactory from the point of view of the doctor and patient alike.

In *Fitzpatrick v White* the patient underwent elective eye surgery to remove a squint. He developed double vision and headaches attributable to a rare but recognised complication of the procedure. The incidence was less than 1%. At trial, it was found that the appropriate warning was given. On appeal, it was argued that the lateness of the warning was such as to render it ineffective in law because it was given on the day of the operation at the last minute, when the claimant had committed himself to the operation. The court held that that this claimant was not affected by the lateness of the warning but recognised that there may be cases where it could be said that the warning was given too late in the day.

In the Supreme Court of Ireland Kearns J gave the judgment of the court and indicated a preference for a "prudent patient" standard. He applied a test similar to the test applied in *Rogers v Whitaker* as endorsed in *Rosenberg v Percival*. Kearns J said:

> *The analysis undertaken by both Kirby J and other members of the High Court of Australia in Rosenberg v Percival supports the argument that the giving of adequate warning, far from being a source of nuisance for doctors, should be seen as an opportunity to ensure that they are protected from subsequent litigation at the suit of disappointed parties. I am thus fortified to express in rather more vigorous terms than I did in* Geoghegan v Harris *my view that the patient centered test is preferable, and ultimately more satisfactory from the point of view of both doctor and patient alike, than any "doctor centered" approach favoured by this Court in* Walsh v Family Planning Services.

> *[I]f there is a significant risk which would affect the judgement of a reasonable patient, then in the normal course it is the responsibility of the doctor to inform the patient of that significant risk. This is still an onerous test and not dissimilar from the requirement enunciated in* Rogers v Whitaker, *and in this context if would regard the words "significant risk" and "material risk" as interchangeable. In* Geoghegan v Harris *I suggested that any consideration of "materiality" would involve consideration of both (a) the severity of the*

consequences and (b) the statistical frequency of the risk. Putting it another way, a risk may be seen as material if, in the circumstances of the particular case, a reasonable person in the patient's position, if warned of the risk, would be likely to attach significance to it where another patient might not."

In *Fitzpatrick & Anor v K & Anor* ([2008] IEHC104) consideration was given to the question of how capacity to refuse consent to medical treatment on the part of an adult should be tested. In this case the claimant was a Jehovah's Witness who suffered a massive post-partum haemorrhage and refused a blood transfusion. The court considered whether the mother had given a legally valid refusal of treatment. For a refusal of treatment to be valid it must be based on appropriate treatment information, be made by a person with the necessary capacity and be voluntary. The test applied was whether the patient's cognitive ability had been impaired to the extent that they do not sufficiently understand the nature, purpose and effect of the proffered treatment. The patient must understand the consequences of accepting or rejecting that in the context of the choices available (including any alternative treatment) at the time the decision was made.

In *Buckley v O'Herlihy & Another* ([2010] IEHC 5; [2010] 2 JIC 2604) the claimant argued that she was not warned of the risk of inadvertent injury to a blood vessel during the course of a sterilisation procedure.

In *Healy v Buckley & Others* ([2010] IEHC 191; [2015] IECA 251; [2015] 11JIC 1701) there was consideration of whether the claimant's acceptance of drug treatment for a tumour was vitiated by lack of sufficient information or misrepresentation concerning her condition and the appropriateness of the treatment. The trial judge concluded that the consent was not vitiated by a lack of sufficient information concerning her condition and the appropriateness of the drug.

On appeal, it was argued that Dr Buckley failed to tell the claimant that the tumour was stable and had not changed for 18 years, and that the radiation treatment she had previously received would become operative over a future period of years and on that basis she could adopt a wait and see approach. The claimant argued that he had conveyed to the patient the impression that she was deteriorating and as a result she agreed to the treatment. It was also argued that he had failed to convey to her the prospects of success using the drug and the full side effects.

The appeal was unsuccessful. On the issue of conservative treatment or no treatment, the court found that when the patient presented herself with a view to receive treatment to alleviate her condition it was difficult to see how the doctor could held to be negligent for not debating the merit of doing nothing. It was also said that the doctor was not obliged to discover that Ms Healy was under a misapprehension about her condition and then persuade her of the true situation.

On appeal, consideration was given to the decision of the Supreme Court in *Montgomery*, however it was said that no reliance would be placed on this case since it was given in March 2015 and the issues in this case related to care given in 2000:

> *Any such changed standard cannot be imposed on Dr. Buckley in Cork in 2000. The law on consent in this jurisdiction may require to be re-considered in the light of developments, especially in regard to the patient's capacity to choose between treatment and no treatment. However any expansion of patient power will require careful delineation. Having said that, it would be quite unjust to apply a new standard to Dr. Buckley's treatment 15 years ago.*

In *Hill v Health Service Executive* ([2016] IEHC 746) the claimant suffered a tear in his ureter on removal of a stone. The claimant alleged that his consent had not been adequately taken. He said that before the procedure an anaesthetist came to see him and said that he was "going down for a test". He was asked a couple of questions and then asked to sign a consent form. It was contended by the defendant that adequate information had been given to the claimant and in any event a tear would not be mentioned as it was a highly unusual complication. The court considered that this was a rare complication and it was concluded that there was no requirement to advise a patient of a possible though highly unlikely complication.

There is clinical guidance on consent in Ireland emanating from the Medical Council (Medical Council, *Guide to Professional Conduct and Ethics for Registered Medical Practitioners*, 7th Edition (Dublin: Medical Council, 2009)). There is also the comprehensive HSE Consent Policy of 2013 (Health Service Executive, *National Consent Policy* (Dublin: HSE, 2013)). Both note that patient consent is an ethical and a legal requirement whose purpose is to respect the autonomy of the patient and his/her right to self-determination.

Consent is seen as more than simply a formality or a signature on a page (p56, Medical Council guide). It is described as a process of communication that begins at the initial contact and continues through to the end of the service user's involvement in the treatment process. It is recognised that the manner in which the health care options are discussed is as important as the information itself, and that the treatment options should be discussed in a place and at a time when the service user is best able to understand and retain the information. The requirement is to disclose all significant risks or substantial risks of grave adverse consequences in a way that the service user can understand.

It is not sufficient for the doctor to impart a lot of unfamiliar and technical information without attempting to ensure the patient understands that information. Every adult with capacity has the right to refuse treatment or service and this decision must be respected, even where the service user's decision may result in their death.

6.   South Africa

In South African law, consent by a patient to medical treatment is regarded as falling under the defence of *volenti non fit injuria*, which would justify an otherwise wrongful delictual act.

In *Esterhuizen v Administrator, Transvaal* (1957 (3) SA 710 (T) at 719 C/D, 719H) Bekker J stated the following:

> *Generally speaking … to establish the defence of volenti non fit injuria the plaintiff must be shown not only to have perceived the danger, for this alone would not be sufficient, but also that he fully appreciated it and consented to incur it.*

In 1994, with the decision in *Castell v De Greef* (1994 (4) SA 408 (C)) the South African Supreme Court established the "reasonable patient" standard for disclosure in providing informed consent. Prior to that there was not a great deal of case law on the subject. In *Castell* there was reference to two previous cases – *Richter v Estate Hamman* (1976 (3) SA 226 (C) at 232H) and *SA Medical & Dental Council v McLoughlin* (1948 (2) SA 355 (A) at 366).

In *Castell*, the claimant underwent a subcutaneous mastectomy, a simultaneous breast reconstruction using silicone implants and a transpositional flap procedure performed by the defendant, who was a plastic surgeon. The operation had a 50% rate of complication, which in this case involved necrosis and infection. The claimant had a family history of breast cancer, and her mother and probably her grandmother had died of breast cancer. Following the surgery, she suffered necrosis and needed to undergo a number of procedures. There were a number of issues raised in relation to the information she had been given about the way the procedure would be performed and risks

The court held that a doctor was under a legal duty of obtain the patient's consent and for consent to be informed the patient must fully appreciate the nature and extent of the harm or risk to which he is consenting. "Material risks" needed to be disclosed and a risk is "material" if a reasonable person in the claimant's position would have considered the risk to be material. Alternatively, it may be material if the doctor ought reasonably to have known the patient would consider it significant enough to require disclosure. The court noted that medical paternalism "stems largely from a bygone era predominantly marked by presently outmoded patriarchal attitudes".

The court defined a risk as being material if:

in the circumstances of the particular case: (a) a reasonable person in the patient's position, if warned of the risk, would be likely to attach significance to it; or (b) the medical practitioner is or should reasonably be aware that the particular patient, if warned of the risk, would be likely to attach significance to it.

In determining the standard of care, the court blended the "reasonable patient" test with the individual patient's "additional needs test". It followed *Rogers v Whitaker* and rejected the approach in *Sidaway*. The South African Court viewed the standard as being in accordance with the fundamental right of self-determination and individual autonomy.

In *Broude v McIntosh and others* (1998 (3) SA 60 (SCA) at 68) the court appears to have accepted the test, although in *Louwrens v Oldwage* (2006 (2) SA 161 (SCA)) the Supreme Court of Appeal did not apply the test formulated in *Castell* but referred to the "reasonable doctor" test set out in the 1976 case of *Richter and another*. In *Louwrens* the lower court was reversed. In the lower court, there was reference to the UK case of *Chester v Afshar* and it was recognised that the objective of informing a patient about risks and dangers was to enable the patient to decide whether or not to run the risk. One of the requirements for valid consent was that available alternatives to the proposed treatment also had to be disclosed. On appeal, it was concluded that the risk was remote and a remote risk did not require to be disclosed, although there was no definition of what is a remote risk.

7.   Comment

It is of note how many jurisdictions rejected the *Bolam* test and its application to the law on consent to medical treatment at around the same time *Sidaway* was being decided in the UK.

In some other common-law jurisdictions, there was an early recognition that in the area of information disclosure the view of the patient was relevant. It was also recognised that patient autonomy and the right to self-determination were the effective starting point in assessing the duty of information disclosure required by law. The area of information disclosure could and should be separated from the duties of the doctor in diagnosis and treatment. As a direct result, it was also recognised that the professional practice test could not be an appropriate test to determine what information patients are entitled to receive from their doctors. This rejection occurred in Canada in the 1980s and in Australia in the 1990s. New Zealand, Canada and Australia have now all moved on to statutory provisions to supplement the common law.

In *Montgomery*, the Supreme Court made specific reference to the fact that the court had been referred to a number of cases of other major common-law jurisdictions. The court's attention was specifically drawn to the major decisions on information disclosure in Australia, Canada, New Zealand and Ireland. The UK Supreme Court noted that the Supreme Court of Canada had adhered to the approach adopted in *Reibl v Hughes*, and that the approach had been followed by the High Court in Australia in *Rogers v Whitaker* and *Rosenberg v Percival*. They developed a test on information disclosure based on the tests which had been applied in Canada and Australia for many years.

On the test of "materiality", in *Montgomery* the Supreme Court said:

> *The test of materiality is whether, in the circumstances of the partic- ular case, a **reasonable person in the patient's position** would be likely to attach significance to the risk, **or the doctor is or should reasonably be aware that the particular patient would be likely to attach significance to it**.*

This statement is taken directly from the Australian case of *Rogers v Whitaker*. The test applied in Australia is not the test found on *Sidaway*. It is also not the test found in *Pearce*, which was seen in the UK to innovate on *Sidaway* prior to *Montgomery*. The court provided that the correct test:

> *can now be seen to be substantially that adopted in* Sidaway *by Lord Scarman, and by Lord Woolf MR in* Pearce, *subject to the refine- ment made by the High Court of Australia in* Rogers v Whitaker....

An adult person of sound mind is entitled to decide which, if any, of the available forms of treatment to undergo, and her consent must be obtained before treatment interfering with her bodily integrity is undertaken. The doctor is therefore under a duty to take reasonable care to ensure that the patient is aware of any material risks involved in any recommended treatment, and of any reasonable alternative or variant treatments. (para 87)

The Supreme Court pointed out that the approach they describe in Montgomery has long been operated in other jurisdictions, where healthcare practice adjusted to the requirements of the test (para 93).

In *Rogers v Whitaker* the High Court did adopt the "reasonable patient" standard seen in *Pearce* but went further and qualified that with a "particular patient" test. A risk is material if a reasonable person in the patient's position if warned of the risk would be likely to attach significance to it, or the doctor is or should reasonably be aware that the particular patient would be likely to attach significance to it. In Canada, there is also an emphasis on considering the circumstances of the particular patient, and the duty is not restricted to the "reasonable" hypothetical patient.

The test formulated in *Montgomery* by the Supreme Court has two limbs. The first is the objective limb. This is what a reasonable person in the patient's position would have done. This limb of the test focuses on the requirements of the reasonable person in the position of the patient. It should be noted that this is not analogous to the man on the Clapham omnibus approach.

The second subjective limb recognises that a patient may not be reasonable and allows the courts to consider the particular patient and their requirements or fears (reasonable and unreasonable). The second limb of the test, allowing a patient to make what may be considered to be an irrational or unreasonable decision, is an important aspect if recognition is to be given to the rights of the individual. This is subject to the caveat that the medical practitioner is or ought to be aware of those considerations. If a patient had special needs or concerns and this was known to the doctor, this would indicate that special or additional information is required. In the second limb of the test, only foreseeable risks can be material.

The Supreme Court specifically referred to the comment in *Rosenberg v Percival* that courts should not be too quick to discard the second limb of the test and it is suggested that in making this specific reference this would suggest that they wished the UK test to be extended to encompass this aspect.

Whilst recognising that the paramount consideration is the principle of self-determination, the principles emanating from *Rogers v Whitaker* do not permit the court to impose on doctors excessively onerous obligations of foresight and care. If a risk is not foreseeable it cannot be material. If a patient had special needs or concerns, and this was known to the doctor, this would indicate that special or additional information is required.

Where a patient asks questions, the Australian courts have tended to consider that this would suggest that the risk/s was material within the subjective limb of the test. In *Rogers v Whitaker* it was said that, even if a court were satisfied that a reasonable person in the patient's position would be unlikely to attach significance to a particular risk, the fact that the particular patient asked questions revealing concern about the risk would make a doctor aware that this patient did in fact attach significance to the risk. Subject to therapeutic privilege, the question would therefore require a truthful answer.

In the UK, where a patient asks questions the law is settled that a doctor requires to answer those questions truthfully. However, it is now arguable that in the UK where a patient asks questions this is also relevant to the assessment of materiality of risk following *Montgomery*, applying the principles found in *Rogers v Whitaker*.

Rogers v Whitaker also sets out what factors should be taken into account in determining whether a reasonable patient in the particular patient's position would be likely to attach significance to a risk which are helpful for those in the UK attempting to apply the test.

The Australian courts have always recognised that applying a mathematical formula to assess the magnitude of the risk is unlikely to be helpful and this was also the view of the Supreme Court in *Montgomery*. The Australian courts have also recognised that the mental and physical health of the patient is a factor relevant to the assessment of materiality.

What of the use of expert evidence? Australia and Canada continue to accept that expert evidence has a role to play in relation to the risks and their materiality. A useful summary of issues on which medical evidence is considered relevant in Canada is found in *New Trends in Informed Consent?* (1975) (54 Neb. L.Rev 66 pp. 90-91). It was said that even *Canterbury* specifically notes that expert testimony will still be required in all but the clearest instances, to establish (a) risks inherent in a given procedure or treatment, (b) the consequences of leaving the ailment untreated, (c) alternative means of treatment and their risks, and (d) the cause of injury suffered by the claimant. If the defendant-physician claims a privilege, expert evidence is needed to show the existence of (a) an emergency which would eliminate the need for obtaining consent, and (b) the impact upon the patient of risk disclosure where a full disclosure appears medically unwarranted. The expert witness has a role in advising the court of the existence of risks and their significance. The court also needs to know whether there are other reasonable alternatives.

In *White v Turner,* the court said that in deciding the matter they would certainly expect to hear expert medical evidence on the question of what the risks inherent in a particular operation were, how serious these risks were and how frequently they occurred. The court would also be interested in what information medical practitioners usually transmit to patients in relation to those risks. But the court would also have regard to the evidence of the patient and their family as to the general situation. The court will be interested in the information he would want to know in the circumstances. This is not application of the

Bolam test. The courts are engaged in making a decision on the issue based on all relevant factors in the case.

In Australia, the medical profession received the decision of the High Court in *Rogers v Whitaker* with some consternation. It was said that the floodgates of informed consent litigation appeared to be opening. In Canada, it was suggested that the Supreme Court in *Reibl v Hughes* had prescribed some strong medicine to improve the doctor–patient relationship. Doctors would now need to spend more time with their patients and the ultimate effect would be physicians who were even more sensitive, concerned and humane.

In 1982, an empirical study was performed to assess the impact of the decision in *Reibl v Hughes* and it was found that it had no effect on the practice of approximately 85% of surgeons in Canada (G. Roberston, "Informed Consent in Canada: An Empirical Study" (1984) 22 Osgoode Hall L.J. 139). However, in a later study it was said that physicians were now spending more time with their patients discussing the risks and benefits of proposed treatments. It was concluded this effect was due to the fear of legal liability and not because of their understanding of the law (G. Robertson, "Informed Consent Ten Years Later. The Impact of *Reibl v Hughes*" (1991) 70 Can. Bar Rev. 423).

In the UK, there appeared to be a similar response to the decision of the Supreme Court in *Montgomery*. One fear expressed was that there would be a vast increase in litigation costs. The experience of Australia and Canada would suggest that there was no such opening of floodgates. Indeed, the experience in Canada was that increasingly cases failed because the required information had in fact been disclosed to the patient by the doctor.

The duty of disclosure is higher than in the *Bolam* days. Review of the Australian and Canadian cases would suggest that the court's approach to questions of causation is strict. There has been a flurry of litigation in the UK but it does seem likely that a similar pattern will be seen albeit many years later in the UK.

In "The Silent World of Doctor and Patient (1984); M.A. Somerville, Informed Consent: An Introductory Overview, in Law Reform Commission of Victoria", Professor Katz noted:

Doctors and judges will have to learn to live at least with the doctrine's symbolic significance. While it has always been the fate of symbols to be honoured more than in words than in deeds, and informed consent will prove to be no exception, symbols can nag and prod and disturb and ultimately bring about some change.

CHAPTER FOUR
MONTGOMERY V LANARKSHIRE
HEALTH BOARD

1.   The background facts

The claimant in the action was Nadine Montgomery, the mother of Sam `Montgomery, who was born at Bellshill Maternity Hospital on 1 October 1999. Sam was diagnosed with a dyskinetic cerebral palsy affecting all four limbs. He also suffers from Erb's palsy of the upper limb.

The defender (defendant) in the action was Lanarkshire Health Board. This health board has responsibility for Bellshill Maternity Hospital, and for the actions and omissions of staff employed at the hospital at the relevant time. Damages were agreed in the action. The issues in dispute related to whether there was a failure and care in the obstetric management, and whether any loss could be said to related to any failure in care.

This was Mrs Montgomery's first pregnancy, at age 24. She is of small stature (1.55m tall) and suffers from insulin-dependent diabetes mellitus. When she was confirmed to be pregnant with Sam she was referred to a specialist combined obstetric and diabetic antenatal clinic under the care of Dr McLellan, consultant obstetrician and gynaecologist. It was expected that she would be cared for at this specialist clinic throughout the pregnancy.

It was well recognised at that time that diabetic mothers could have larger than average babies, and Mrs Montgomery was aware of this risk during the course of her pregnancy and, because of this risk, she was also at increased risk of mechanical problems in labour, such as cephalopelvic disproportion (where the fetal head fails to descend) or shoulder dystocia (where the head is delivered but the shoulder becomes impacted preventing delivery). She was also at increased risk of fetal abnormalities. She was unaware during the course of the pregnancy of the increased risk of mechanical problems in labour, including shoulder dystocia.

Should shoulder dystocia occur, there was a risk of brain damage to the fetus. The risk of shoulder dystocia occurring in evidence was said to be 9–10%, which in the vast majority of cases would be dealt with by simple procedures. In 1 in 500 cases, shoulder dystocia resulted in a brachial plexus injury. The percentage of those children sustaining a more severe injury, such as cerebral palsy, was small.

Dr McLellan, the clinician in overall charge of her care, was aware of the increased risks, and she said that she had them at the forefront of her mind when caring for Mrs Montgomery. Because the pregnancy was classified as high risk, a greater degree of vigilance was also required in terms of monitoring the pregnancy and the labour.

There were options in relation to managing the birth. The fetus could have been delivered by elective caesarean section prior to the commencement of labour, or Mrs Montgomery could have proceeded to labour with the option of a caesarean section, should difficulties be encountered during the course of the labour. These options were never discussed with her prior to labour commencing.

Mrs Montgomery had undergone repeated ultrasound scan examinations to assess fetal size and growth during the pregnancy. The decision by Dr McLellan on the method of delivery was directly related to fetal size. At the 28th week of the pregnancy the estimated fetal weight was between the 50th and 95th centiles. At the 32nd week it was just below the 95th centile and at the 34th week it was just below the 95th centile. At week 36 the estimated fetal weight was on the 95th centile.

At the clinic visit on 15 September 1999, at 36 weeks' gestation, Mrs Montgomery was reviewed by Dr McLellan. Mrs Montgomery stated that she told Dr McLellan that she was concerned about the size of the baby. Dr McLellan made a note in the medical notes at the clinic to highlight that she had raised concerns, and to record that a discussion had taken place. She noted that Mrs Montgomery was "worried about the size of the baby" and said in evidence that Mrs Montgomery was worried that the baby would be too big to deliver. There was a dispute between the parties as to whether Mrs Montgomery had raised the issue of concerns with delivery of the baby at an earlier stage in the pregnancy. However, it was accepted on this occasion there had been a discussion about the size of the baby.

Dr McLellan cancelled the ultrasound scan to be performed at 38 weeks' gestation as she considered that the scans demonstrating the increasing weight of the fetus were making Mrs Montgomery anxious. Dr McLellan's position was that, having regard to the whole clinical picture, Mrs Montgomery would be able to deliver vaginally, and if there were difficulties she could resort to a caesarean section at any time during the labour.

Dr McLellan was of the view that the risk of mechanical problems in labour was not a risk she needed to consider when deciding if she should warn Mrs Montgomery. Her position was that the risk she required to consider was that of brain damage should shoulder dystocia or mechanical problems in labour arise. If *she* felt that the vaginal delivery was safe, then she would not advise the patient about risks.

She did not consider that the concerns expressed by Mrs Montgomery on 15 September 1999 were sufficient to engage her duty to warn of the risks of mechanical problems in labour/shoulder dystocia or brain damage. She said that she did not need to advise Mrs Montgomery about the risk of mechanical problems in labour, or shoulder dystocia, unless she specifically asked about them. In her opinion she had not specifically asked about them. Had she specifically asked about mechanical problems, Dr McLellan would have told her about risks and would have said the problems were easily overcome.

Dr McLellan plotted the fetal weight increase during the pregnancy on a fetal growth chart. The purpose of the chart was to enable the trends and increase in the weight to be monitored. This also enabled an estimate of fetal weight to be made at the time of delivery. Dr McLellan estimated that the birth weight of the fetus would be 3.9kg, or between

3.9 and 4kg. This was based on the previous weights obtained by ultra-sound scan. She assumed that the fetus would be delivered at 38 weeks when making her calculations.

The guidance in force at the time suggested that it was safe to deliver vaginally up to a weight of 4.5kg. Dr McLellan had modified this general rule in this case as Mrs Montgomery was smaller than average. She said she would have offered a caesarean section if she estimated the fetal weight to be 4kg or over.

Ultrasound scan estimation of birth weight is recognised to be unreli-able, and the margin for error can be 10–15% either way, a fact that Dr McLellan was aware of. In calculating the projected weight of the fetus at 38 weeks, Dr McLellan did not factor in a margin for error. She concluded that Mrs Montgomery was on the borderline for a caesarean section. She did not advise her that the weight she projected at delivery at 38 weeks' gestation was on the borderline of the weight at which she considered that a caesarean section should be discussed. She did not consider that she had a duty to do so.

Dr McLellan considered that at a weight of 4kg the risks in labour would be such that Mrs Montgomery needed to be told of them. It was not disputed that at that weight Mrs Montgomery would have been advised of the risks of mechanical problems in labour and shoulder dystocia. Dr McLellan considered that at that weight the risks were such that she must have a discussion with the patient.

In fact, it was planned that the labour would be induced at 38 weeks + 5 days. Despite this, Dr McLellan did not project the fetal weight to delivery at 38 weeks + 5 days, and accepted that she should have plotted the fetal weight to a point beyond 38 weeks if she wanted to assess the actual birth weight at the time of the planned delivery. Using the growth chart as a foundation, the proper estimate of projected birth weight at 38 weeks + 5 days would have been 4.25kg, and Dr McLellan accepted that, if she had plotted the fetal weight to 38 weeks + 5 days on the growth chart, the projected weight would have been just over 4kg.

Shoulder dystocia, defined by the Royal College of Obstetricians and Gynaecologists as "a delivery that requires additional obstetric manoeuvres to release the shoulders after gentle downward traction has failed", is an obstetric emergency. It occurs when the anterior fetal shoulder impacts on the maternal symphysis or sacral promontory. Less commonly, the problem is caused by the posterior fetal shoulder. The RCOG issued guidance in relation to the management of shoulder dystocia.

During the pregnancy Mrs Montgomery was not offered an elective caesarean section. She said that, had she been properly advised of the risks of mechanical problems in labour (including shoulder dystocia), she would have asked for a caesarean section. It was not disputed that had Mrs Montgomery asked for a caesarean section Dr McLellan would have proceeded with one. Nor was it disputed that had she opted for an elective caesarean section she would not have had to encounter the risks of mechanical problems in labour, or shoulder dystocia. It was not disputed that had there been a caesarean section Sam would not have cerebral palsy. Sam weighed 4.25kg when he was born.

2.   Evidence given to the court by the parties

In the Outer House of the Court of Session in Edinburgh, witness evid-ence in medical cases is traditionally led in full before a judge (Lord Ordinary). The witnesses, including expert witnesses, are led in chief, and then cross-examined by the opposing side. Thereafter there is a re-examination of the witness if it is felt necessary. This approach is different from the approach in England where witness statements form part of the evidence of the witness.

Mrs Montgomery's evidence

Mrs Montgomery said in evidence that the only risk she was informed of was that she was at risk of having a big baby because she was diabetic. She was not given any options for the delivery of her baby. She was not given the option of elective caesarean section. Dr McLellan proceeded on the basis that the baby would be delivered vaginally. She indicated that as the pregnancy progressed she became more anxious as the baby grew larger. She said that she expressed her concerns to Dr McLellan from around the 28th week, when the fetal weight had gone above the 50th centile. She maintained that she had asked what kind of problems could be encountered with a small mother having a large baby. She also said she specifically asked what problems could be encountered during delivery. Her position was that these questions were never answered. She said that Dr McLellan's position was that they were monitoring the baby and if there was a problem she would discuss it with her. It was not for her to worry, as that was Dr McLellan's job. She took her mother, who is a GP, to the 34-week appointment in the hope that she could obtain answers. She stated that had she been properly advised of the risks or the alternatives she would have opted for an elective caesarean section.

Supporting evidence for the claimant

Mrs Montgomery's husband gave evidence and supported her version of events as he had accompanied her to some of the antenatal appointments. He stated that during the last third of the pregnancy Mrs Montgomery had expressed concerns to Dr McLellan about the size of the baby and her ability to deliver it vaginally, and he said that Dr McLellan was dismissive. Her position was that she felt that the size of the baby was not a concern, and if complications arose she would deal with these. Mrs Montgomery's mother also gave a similar story of reassurance by Dr McLellan that there was close monitoring and if a caesarean section were required it would be done.

The evidence of Dr McLellan

Dr McLellan accepted in evidence that at the 36-week appointment Mrs Montgomery had expressed concerns about the size of the baby. She accepted that the concern raised was that the baby would be too big to deliver. She accepted that it was also possible on a number of previous occasions at the clinic concerns were expressed by Mrs Montgomery. She had decided, because of the concerns, not to proceed with the 38-week ultrasound scan as this was making Mrs Montgomery more anxious. She did not accept that Mrs Montgomery had asked her specifically about the risks associated with the pregnancy. Had she asked specifically about risks, she indicated she would have advised her of risks.

She accepted that there were two options for delivery of the baby. She accepted that she did not mention shoulder dystocia to Mrs Montgomery. She did not consider that the risk of serious injury arising from shoulder dystocia, namely cerebral palsy or a brachial plexus injury to the baby, to be of such significance that it was appropriate to advise her of this. She advised Mrs Montgomery that, in her view, she should be able to deliver vaginally, and if there were problems then a caesarean section would be performed. At no time did she suggest that she discussed elective caesarean section with Mrs Montgomery, or the risks and benefits of that option when compared with the risks and benefits of vaginal delivery.

The national guidance issued at the time suggested a consultation with a mother where the projected weight of the baby exceeded 4.5kg. Dr McLellan said she revised this guidance in relation to Mrs Montgomery. She considered that it would be safe to deliver vaginally until the birth weight was thought to be over 4kg. Her position was that if the projected birth weight did exceed 4kg she would have offered Mrs Montgomery a caesarean section. In her view that option only became available at a specific weight. In this case, she estimated the birth weight to be 3.9kg and for that reason she did not offer a caesarean section.

Expert evidence led for the claimant

The claimant led expert evidence from Professor Neilson and Mr Stewart, both consultant obstetricians and gynaecologists. Mr Stewart was of the opinion that Dr McLellan should have offered a caesarean section to Mrs Montgomery at the antenatal stage. In failing to do so he was of the opinion this was a failure in care. He stated that the risk of shoulder dystocia occurring was 10% and as such this was a risk that Mrs Montgomery should have been warned of irrespective of practice.

Professor Neilson stated that if Mrs Montgomery had expressed concerns about the size of the fetus it was Dr McLellan's duty to discuss the potential problems that could arise because of the very large size of the baby. That would require a discussion, which would need to include the possibility of cephalopelvic disproportion and shoulder dystocia. His view was that Dr McLellan should have discussed the different options. He thought that the options would probably include a caesarean section as a planned procedure, or seeing how things progressed during labour. His view was that the conversation would have to include a recognition of a high chance of caesarean section proving necessary during the course of labour. The discussion would also need to include the pros and cons of caesarean section versus vaginal delivery. His position was broadly the same if Mrs Montgomery had specifically asked about risks.

Professor Neilson accepted that 70–90% of cases of shoulder dystocia were easily dealt with. He accepted that the figures for Erb's palsy arising from shoulder dystocia were 1 in 450 and that the figures for cerebral palsy would be 1 in 2000 or 3000. He accepted that the national guidance was that a caesarean section should only be offered if the predicted weight was over 4.5kg. He would not have advised of the risk of cerebral palsy.

Expert evidence led on behalf of the Health Board

The Health Board led evidence from Dr Phil Owen, consultant obstetrician and gynaecologist in Glasgow. His primary position was that most obstetricians would not have offered a planned caesarean section where the predicted weight was under 4.5kg. He stated there was a wide range of opinion among obstetricians and gynaecologists on the question of warning mothers of risks in circumstances such as this. He was of the view that as a matter of practice it was very unlikely that shoulder dystocia would be mentioned in the course of a discussion with a patient such as Mrs Montgomery. He was of the opinion that Dr McLellan's response was an adequate response to a patient raising concerns about the size of her baby and her ability to deliver vaginally.

The Health Board also led evidence from Mr Mason, consultant obstetrician and gynaecologist. He provided evidence about the risks of caesarean section and he felt that the approach taken by Dr McLellan was a reasonable way to proceed in view of the fact that the risks of a serious outcome following shoulder dystocia were so small that they did not need to be discussed. In his opinion, if doctors were to warn of the risk of shoulder dystocia every mother would want a caesarean section and that would not be in the interests of the mother or baby. The vast majority of shoulder dystocia cases are relatively mild and fairly easy to deal with by a midwife, not a doctor. He would not have offered an elective caesarean section and he did not believe that it was a failure in care not to discuss this where the projected weight was under 4.5kg. Only if the predicted birth weight was in excess of 4.5kg would there be a failure of care in not offering a caesarean section.

3.   Montgomery – The first argument

Introduction

The case was first heard in the Outer House of the Court of Session in Scotland by Lord Bannatyne (*Outer House decision [2010] CSOH 104 Lord Bannatyne 2010 G.W.D. 34-707*). This was a full evidential hearing. Lord Bannatyne issued his decision on 30 July 2010.

At first instance in the Outer House of the Court of Session there were a number of grounds of fault advanced. There was criticism of how the labour itself was managed by Dr McLellan. It was alleged that there was a failure in continuing with labour when the fetal heart rate was grossly abnormal. The "failures in the management of the labour" case was based on the interpretation of the CTG trace. This is a method of assessing the fetal heart rate in relation to maternal contractions in labour. It can be used as a means to identify if a fetus is in distress and intervention is required. This case was separate and distinct from the "consent" case. The "failures in management of labour case" was unsuccessful.

There was also a case based on the failure to offer Mrs Montgomery the option of elective caesarean section, and provide her with the risks and benefits of this option compared to the risks and benefits of proceeding with vaginal delivery. Mrs Montgomery was never offered the option of elective caesarean section and there was little evidence in the first hearing of the case dealing with the comparative risks between elective caesarean section and vaginal delivery. This chapter will focus only on the arguments made in information disclosure case.

The information disclosure case was based on the following grounds:

(a) failure to discuss with Mrs Montgomery the options for managing her delivery. The options were delivery by elective caesarean section, or vaginal delivery on the basis that she could have a caesarean section if problems were encountered in the delivery;

(b) failure to advise Mrs Montgomery of the risks of vaginal delivery;

(c) failure to inform her of the risks during vaginal delivery of shoulder dystocia, and the risks of cephalo pelvic disproportion.

Submissions made on behalf of the claimant

The claimant submitted that there was a duty incumbent upon Dr McLellan to provide Mrs Montgomery with adequate information. She failed to advise her that there were options for delivery of the fetus. She failed to advise her of the comparative risks and benefits of the options. In particular, she failed to advise her of the mechanical risks associated with her labour, which included the risk of shoulder dystocia. This was compounded by the fact the claimant had voiced concerns about the size of the baby: since she had raised the question of risks attached to giving birth vaginally this engaged the duty to advise her of the mechanical risks associated with her labour, including shoulder dystocia. As a result of that failure, the claimant did not have the opportunity to make a proper decision on the course of action to take.

Reference was made to the decision in *Sidaway v Board of Governors of the Bethlem Royal Hospital* ([1985] A.C. 871) and the fact the court had to apply the *Hunter v Hanley* or *Bolam* test to the question. It was said that this had been expressly confirmed in Scotland in the case of *Moyes v Lothian Health Board* (1990 S.L.T 444) and followed in *Goorkani v Tayside Health Board* (1991 S.L.T 94).

The claimant also referred the court to the decision of Lord Woolf MR in *Pearce v United Bristol Healthcare NHS Trust* (1999 P.I.Q.R. 53 at 59), who, having looked in some detail at the speech of Lord Bridge, said:

> *In a case where it is being alleged that a plaintiff has been deprived of the opportunity to make a proper decision as to what course he or she should take in relation to treatment, it seems to be the law ... that if there is a significant risk which would affect the judgement of a reasonable patient, then in the normal course it is the responsibility of a doctor to inform that patient of the significant risk, if the information is needed so that the patient can determine for him or herself as to what course he or she should adopt.*

Reference was also made to the case of *Jones v North West Strategic Health Authority* (2010 EWHC 178 (Q.B.)), which had proceeded on similar facts, and to the comments of Lord Justice Nicol (para 24) that whether a risk was "significant" or not was ultimately a matter for the court to decide.

It was argued that, had Mrs Montgomery been properly advised of risks, and options for management of her labour, it was clear that she would have opted for an elective caesarean section. Reference was made to the decision of the House of Lords in *Chester v Afshar* (2002 EWCA Civ 724) and specifically to the speech of Lord Hope of Craighead at paras 85–88 (paras 162–163).

Submissions made on behalf of the Health Board

The Health Board accepted that if a patient "specifically" asked about risks there must be a full response. However, it argued Mrs Montgomery should not be accepted as having asked about specific risks. Taking her evidence as a whole, she was a first-time mother with an understandable anxiety about her diabetic control and, towards the end of her pregnancy, a concern about the likely size of her baby and whether or not she would be able to deliver vaginally. Her mother and sister were GPs and knew that there were two options, namely elective caesarean section or vaginal delivery with recourse to caesarean section.

The Health Board argued that where there is no substantial risk of grave consequence there was no requirement to warn of the risk. In that situation, it is for the doctor to judge what information is given. It was argued that shoulder dystocia could not on the evidence be characterised as giving rise to a grave risk of adverse outcome. In relation to the substantial risk, the Health Board focused its argument on the occurrence of brain damage or permanent disability should shoulder dystocia occur, not the statistical probability of shoulder dystocia occurring. Shoulder dystocia was not an adverse event in terms of the test envisaged in *Sidaway*. In a baby over 4.5kg there was a 1 in 2000 chance of permanent disability and a 1 in 450 risk of a brachial plexus injury. Where the risk of serious injury is over 1–2% then the doctor had a duty to advise of this unilaterally. This was not the case with Mrs Montgomery's baby.

The Health Board's position was that Dr McLellan made a clinical decision to proceed to vaginal delivery based on a reasonable estimate of birth weight, and on all the information available to her that the claimant should be able to deliver vaginally, and if problems were encountered then a caesarean section would be performed. Her approach was supported in evidence by Dr Owen's and Dr Mason's expert evidence. It was not open to the court to prefer the claimant's experts. The claimant's experts were "out on a limb" on this matter when compared to other competent professionals.

On the issue of causation, it was submitted that the claimant had to satisfy the "but-for" test and *Chester v Afshar* had no application to the facts and circumstances of the case. In any event, given the very small risks of any adverse event occurring should shoulder dystocia occur, no intelligent person would have decided to proceed by way of caesarean section. As such the claimant must fail on causation.

The decision of the court

The court considered that the question to be addressed was whether there was "a substantial risk of grave consequences". The focus was not on the incidence of shoulder dystocia at 4kg but on the risk of brain damage or some other consequence should the shoulder dystocia occur. Lord Bannatyne said:

> *Accordingly in my view on the basis of the authorities it is to the risk of adverse outcome to which the court should have regard when considering whether a warning should be given. In my view this must be correct. If there is a substantial risk of a problem arising but not risk of an adverse outcome following therefrom I can identify no reason why a doctor should advise the patient of that risk. To use the words of Lord Woolf in Pearce although there is a substantial risk of that problem arising, given the likelihood of an adverse outcome it would not be a risk which would affect the judgement of a reasonable patient.*

The court then addressed the question based on the traditional approach and the application of the *Hunter v Hanley* or *Bolam* traditional test of negligence. The court was faced with two competing bodies of medical evidence supporting different approaches. The Health Board experts had given evidence that there was a responsible body of obstetricians who would not have advised of the risk of shoulder dystocia in a case such as this. The national guidance from the college did not suggest to clinicians that they should have a discussion with a mother when the projected weight of the fetus was under 4.5kg. Since the experts on behalf of the Health Board could not be said to be illogical or unreasonable (*Bolitho* test), this aspect of the case failed.

On the question of whether the claimant had raised concerns about her ability to deliver the baby, the court found that there was a material difference between expressing concern and specifically raising the question of risks. Lord Bannatyne stated:

> *To merely say that one had concerns about one's ability to deliver vaginally would not in my opinion engage the duty to fully explain all the risks involved in vaginal delivery. It is in my view only where the patient asks questions specifically related to the risks involved in a particular course of treatment i.e. in this case vaginal delivery that the duty would be engaged.*

Lord Bannatyne also did not accept that had the claimant been advised of the risks of shoulder dystocia she would have proceeded to vaginal delivery. This was on the basis that the real risk of grave consequences arising were so small. He decided to engage in an exercise to consider whether there were any factors which could be said to either negate or support the position expressed by the claimant in evidence. One of these factors was the minimal risk of adverse outcomes from shoulder dystocia. The Lord Ordinary also considered that the fact that there were risks with caesarean section would tend to support the view that she would not have selected this option. He also formed the view that the consultant would have continued to recommend a vaginal delivery, and it was likely in that situation that Mrs Montgomery would have followed the advice.

Having conducted this balancing exercise as a means of cross-checking the claimant's evidence, the court considered that this supported the contention that she would not have proceeded with a caesarean section.

Comment

The claimant failed on all grounds of fault at first hearing in the Outer House of the Court of Session. Lord Bannatyne proceeded on the basis that in the first instance the court should look at practice in terms on the *Hunter v Hanley/Bolam* test. The Health Board was able to provide expert evidence from two eminent consultant obstetricians who supported Dr McLellan's decision not to discuss the risks of mechanical problems in labour, including shoulder dystocia, on the basis of professional practice at the relevant time. The court accepted this evidence and came to a decision that fault could not be established on a traditional *Hunter v Hanley* or *Bolam* basis.

The Health Board's expert evidence was that at a weight of 4kg and under there was a responsible body of obstetricians who would not have discussed the risks. If a claimant is to succeed in the face of such expert evidence, they would have to satisfy the court that this expert evidence is illogical and unreasonable in terms of the *Bolitho* test. If the claimant is unable to do this then they must fail.

Applying the *Sidaway* test, it was accepted at first instance by Lord Bannatyne that the question is not simply confined to the question of what professional practice at the time was. In *Sidaway* a number of their Lordships permitted an exception to the use of the professional practice test. This is set out at length in Chapter 2. The difficulty is that they used different language to describe and define this exception. There was however a clear exception.

In its argument in the Outer House before Lord Bannatyne the Health Board appeared to proceed on the basis in the first instance it was acceptable to only offer Mrs Montgomery the option of vaginal delivery. On assessment of risk the defenders only focused on the words of Lord Bridge of Harwich in *Sidaway* and appeared to suggest that this passage defined the exception to the traditional professional practice test. They focused on only one small part of what he said when addressing the question of materiality. It was argued that only where there was a "substantial risk of grave adverse consequences" would the doctor be under a duty to advise the patient, whatever the prevailing medical view. The defenders submitted that the occurrence of mechanical problems in labour/shoulder dystocia could not be described as "grave adverse consequences". It was the occurrence of brain damage or cerebral palsy that satisfied this definition. The court accepted this submission.

The claimant had argued that in fact what should be considered was any "material" or "significant" risk that a patient would wish to know of. The risk of mechanical problems in labour and/or shoulder dystocia was a significant risk and was one that any mother would wish to know of. The court rejected this interpretation.

The claimant also argued that in any event Mrs Montgomery had raised concerns about the size of her baby and her ability to deliver it vaginally, and this engaged Dr McLellan's duty to advise her of the risks of mechanical problems in labour and shoulder dystocia. There was some argument about when and on how many occasions concerns had been raised but it was not in doubt that Mrs Montgomery had raised the issue with Dr McLellan at least once.

In *Sidaway* Lord Diplock indicated that that if a patient's questioning suggested that he did want information it would be the duty of the doctor to tell the patient whatever it was he wanted to know. Lord Bannatyne did not consider that there was enough to engage the duty to advise her of the risks. He considered that there had to be focused and specific questioning to engage the duty of the doctor to advise of risks. Since, according to the court, there was not a specific question, merely a general expression of concern, there was no duty upon Dr McLellan to advise of the risks. If there had been specific questions, the court agreed that this would have engaged the duty to warn of the risk of mechanical problems in labour, which would include shoulder dystocia.

The claimant also failed on the causation argument. Lord Bannatyne concluded that, even if properly advised, the claimant would not have opted for an elective caesarean section. On this question the court considered that the claimant was not lying, and genuinely believed that this is what she would have done, but her view had been tainted by what had happened to her son. The court also engaged in a balancing exercise to cross-check this evidence and came to the conclusion on the factors considered that this supported she would have proceeded to vaginal delivery.

4. Montgomery in the Appeal Court in Scotland

Introduction

Having failed in the Outer House of the Court of Session, the claimant appealed to the Inner House of the Court of Session (Appeal Court). The case was heard by an Extra Division of the Inner House consisting of Lord Eassie (in the chair), Lord Hardie and Lord Emslie ([2013] CSIH 3; 2013 S.C. 245; 2013 G.W.D. 5-136).

In Scotland, there are procedural rules that govern the powers of the Appeal Court to overturn the decision of a Lord Ordinary at first instance. The rules provide that it must be demonstrated by those who bring the appeal that the Lord Ordinary was "plainly wrong" in coming to the decision he did. Where a first-instance judge has made a finding on the credibility of a witness, the Appeal Court will not usually be inclined to interfere with that finding. The Inner House in Scotland is also bound by decisions of the House of Lords, so the claimant could not ask them to overturn or depart from the decision in *Sidaway*.

The argument made on behalf of the claimant

The claimant argued that the Lord Ordinary who had heard the case had failed in two broad areas. The first ground related to the "information case", the second to the "management of labour case". The focus of the argument in the consent or information case was as follows:

- It was accepted that the traditional approach as stated by the House of Lords in *Sidaway* was binding upon the court. In that sense, the first question was whether the claimant could establish a breach on the basis of the traditional professional practice test found in *Hunter v Hanley* and *Bolam*. On the question of whether there was a breach of professional practice the Health Board had been able to provide evidence from two consultant obstetricians, who indicated that in failing to discuss the risk of shoulder dystocia Dr McLellan had not been negligent in applying the *Hunter v Hanley* or *Bolam* tests of negligence. As the claimant was unable to ask the court to reject that evidence as illogical or unreasonable, she could not succeed on the traditional test of negligence.

- It was argued the claimant could and should have succeeded on the basis of what was referred to at that time as "the *Sidaway* exception". Parties did not dispute that there was an exception to the professional practice test in consent cases following *Sidaway*. It was argued that in *Sidaway* there was a recognition of the patient's right to self-determination. On this basis, the claimant had the right to choose between the available options for delivery of the fetus. To enable her to exercise choice, she needed to have information detailing the risks and benefits of the options. If there were a significant risk (in any of the options) the patient should have been warned of that risk, and the court could then set aside the professional practice test. In this case, the risks of mechanical problems in labour/shoulder dystocia were significant and material, and risks that any reasonable patient would wish to know of. The claimant should therefore have been warned of those risks. The court could make a finding of fault on the basis of this failure applying the *Sidaway* principles.

- The risk of shoulder dystocia occurring was significant at around 10%. The claimant argued that the risk of shoulder dystocia occurring was something any reasonable mother would wish to know of. The question of whether it could be easily overcome, and the smaller risks of brain damage or cerebral palsy, were matters that were relevant to the discussion between the doctor and the patient and the decision over how to proceed. The whole picture was relevant to the mother making an "informed decision" or "choice" on whether to proceed with a vaginal delivery or caesarean section.

- It was argued that the dicta emanating from the decision in *Sidaway* was wider than the extract from the speech of Lord Bridge referred to by the defenders. The court was not confined merely to the question of significant adverse consequences, as was suggested by the defenders. If the court wished to follow the speech of Lord Bridge, the whole picture of shoulder dystocia with a potential for Erb's palsy, brain damage and cerebral palsy satisfied the definition of something that required to be discussed with the patient in relation to the option of vaginal delivery.

- There were options for managing the delivery of the fetus, and where there are options the patient should have been advised of the options and the risks and benefits of each option. The options case is separate and distinct from the basic professional practice test and the "*Sidaway* exception" argument. A woman did have to deliver the baby but there were options for the delivery. The options were elective caesarean section, or to proceed to vaginal delivery with the option of a caesarean section should matters not progress.

- The decision on which option to choose was one for Mrs Montgomery, having been fully advised of the risks of each approach by Dr McLellan. The decision was not one for Dr McLellan to make without reference to the patient's wishes. Dr McLellan had a duty to respect Mrs Montgomery's right to choose how to deliver her baby.

- Dr McLellan had made the decision for the patient. She made a decision that Mrs Montgomery would only be provided with one option, that of vaginal delivery. She also made a decision to not inform her of the risk of shoulder dystocia/mechanical problems in labour. She had decided that she would not discuss this until the fetus reached a certain weight. She should not have done so.

- It was for the court to decide what was a significant risk for a patient, not the experts who gave evidence to the court. The experts could provide background evidence on the nature of risks, and the statistical probability of those risks occurring, but they should not decide what was significant to the patient.

- It was also for the court to decide what options should have been discussed. This is a factual question and not a matter of professional practice.

- What was significant must also be linked to the particular patient.

- On her own evidence, Dr McLellan considered that the risks would have been significant in this patient at 4kg and stated that she would have offered an elective caesarean section at this time. Had she properly calculated the weight of the fetus to the correct gestation, and had she applied the margin for error (which was recognised to exist) when estimating weight, she would have had a duty to discuss elective caesarean section.

- There was no dispute that where a patient asks questions the doctor is under a duty to answer truthfully and as fully as the patient requires. The fact that Mrs Montgomery had raised the question of a large baby and whether she could deliver such a large baby was sufficient to engage the duty to advise her of the risks of mechanical problems in labour, including shoulder dystocia. This was sufficient to require Dr McLellan to answer honestly and provide her with the risks and benefits of the options for delivery. Dr McLellan knew what her concern was and she chose to ignore it.

- The decision in *Pearce* should be considered as innovating on *Sidaway*. The duty was to advise of a substantial risk that would affect the judgement of a reasonable patient. Much greater focus was now given in the law to the concept of patient autonomy. Reference was made to decisions in England and Wales in which it was clear that the courts had accepted that *Pearce* had refined the *Sidaway* approach (*Wyatt v Curtis & Central Nottinghamshire Health Authority* [2003] EWCA Civ 1779 and *Jones v North West Strategic Health Authority* 2010 MLR 90). The decision in *Pearce* was also referred to in the opinions delivered by the House of Lords *in Chester v Afshar* ([2002] EWCA Civ 724) and, whilst it was accepted that the references were *obiter*, no criticism had been made of the Master of the Rolls. In the opinions delivered in *Chester v Afshar* there were indications of a greater awareness of patient autonomy.

• In any event, the claimant had expressed concerns about the size of her baby and her ability to deliver the baby vaginally and this expression of concern should have engaged the duty of the doctor to advise her of her options for delivery and of the risks of mechanical problems in labour, including the risk of shoulder dystocia. Reference was made to the well-known observation of Lord Bridge in *Sidaway* (para 898), where he stated that when questioned specifically by a patient of apparently sound mind about the risks involved in a particular treatment proposed, the doctor's duty is to answer truthfully and as fully as the questioner required. This would require her to discuss the options for delivery and the risks and benefits of each option. Dr McLellan was clear what the concerns were. She knew that Mrs Montgomery was worried that her baby would be too big to deliver.

• Lord Bannatyne found that Mrs Montgomery genuinely believed she would have opted for a caesarean section, but had been influenced in this view by what had happened to Sam. The Lord Ordinary's assessment was that she would not have opted for an elective caesarean section. This was not a decision on credibility but reliability. In this situation, the decision of the Lord Ordinary on the issue of causation should be reviewed.

• Had Mrs Montgomery been properly advised of the options for delivery and the risks and benefits of each option, she would have chosen an elective caesarean section. Her evidence was clear on that and Dr McLellan accepted that had she asked for an elective caesarean section she would have agreed to this request. There was no evidence to support the view of Lord Bannatyne that Dr McLellan would have continued to suggest a caesarean section; quite the contrary.

- The Lord Ordinary had embarked on a balancing exercised to test the evidence of Mrs Montgomery, but this balancing exercise was flawed in that he failed to consider all of the relevant information. He had included information which was incorrect, namely that the risk was small, and he had excluded the risk of shoulder dystocia. Had he considered all of the relevant information he could not have concluded that she would not have proceeded with a caesarean section.

- In any event, the court should not apply the normal "but-for" test on causation to a consent case. The relationship between a doctor and patient is a relationship of trust. The causal link was established if the significant risk the patient should have been warned about had materialised. The basis of this argument was the decision of the House of Lords in *Chester v Afshar*.

- Alternatively, there should be an evidential shift of the burden of proof in a consent case. Where it is established that there was a failure to provide a patient with information to enable the patient to make an informed decision, the onus of proof should shift to the defenders/defendants to satisfy the court as to what the claimant would have done. By the very failure to provide information claimants had been placed in a position where they always had to prove causation on a hypothetical basis.

- Further causation should be considered on a mixed subjective/objective basis.

The argument made on behalf of the Health Board

- The law to be applied was found in *Sidaway* and the test to be applied was the *Hunter v Hanley* and *Bolam* test; the claimant had failed to establish fault on the basis of the test.

- The *Sidaway* exception related to a risk of serious adverse consequences, and it was the risk of brain damage or cerebral palsy occurring that was the relevant risk for the court to consider. The risk of each occurring was not significant and therefore there was no duty to warn irrespective of professional practice.

- *Pearce* did not, and could not, advance the law beyond the position in *Sidaway*.

- Mrs Montgomery merely expressed concerns generally, and any expression of concern did not engage the duty to warn her of mechanical problems in labour, including shoulder dystocia. There was a material difference between expressing a concern and specifically raising the question of risks. It was accepted that where a patient asked specific questions a doctor had to answer truthfully.

- The traditional rules should be applied on causation. The findings of the Lord Ordinary at first instance should not be disturbed.

- The decision in *Chester v Afshar* had no relevance to the discussion.

The decision of the court

The claimant failed and the decision was unanimous. It was decided that the test to be applied when assessing whether the duty to advise of risks had been breached was that of ordinarily competent practice, as found in Scotland in *Hunter v Hanley* and in England in *Bolam*.

The judges of the Appeal Court recognised, following Lord Bridge in *Sidaway*, that there may be exceptional cases where the court should override medical practice on what should be communicated to the patient. This could occur in exceptional cases where the risk was obviously substantial. In such a case, the court could say that no doctor acting with ordinary care could reasonably fail to omit to advise the patient, irrespective of professional practice.

They rejected the submission made by the claimant that *Pearce* advanced the law from the position as set out in *Sidaway* by focusing on a patient-centred test:

> *We do not consider that the decision of the Court of Appeal in England and Wales in Pearce does other than follow, and endeavour to apply, the majority view of the House of Lords in Sidaway. Plainly the decision in Sidaway was binding upon the Court of Appeal, as, effectively, it is upon us. Counsel were, moreover, able to confirm that the judgement delivered by Lord Woolf in Pearce was delivered ex tempore and it might be thought unlikely, if it were the intention of the Master of the Rolls or the other members of the Court of Appeal materially to refine or qualify what was decided in Sidaway, that this would be done otherwise than in a reserved judgement.* (para 26)

With reference to paragraph 21, their Lordships concluded as follows:

> *While it may be that taken wholly in isolation the passage might be suggestive of a "reasonable patient" approach, contrary to the approach of the majority in Sidaway, we are persuaded that when the judgement is read as a whole it is evident that the Court of Appeal were not departing from the majority view in Sidaway that the test for liability for failure to warn of risks was essentially the Bolam test.* (para 24)

The court referred to the consideration of *Sidaway* by the Master of the Rolls at paragraph 15. He said of Lord Scarman's speech in *Sidaway*:

> *The views he expresses are a minority view and do not in this juris-diction represent the law, although they do reflect the law in the United States and, to some extent, in Canada. They also reflect the developments which have taken place in the law since the decision was given in Australia.* (para 25)

They also referred to the fact the Master of the Rolls also quoted passages from the speeches of Lord Diplock and Lord Bridge in

Sidaway and in respect of the speech of Lord Templeman they quoted the Master of the Rolls in paragraph 19, where he said:

> *While recognising that Lord Templeman's approach is not precisely that of the majority, it seems to me that the statement of Lord Templeman does reflect the law and does not involve taking a different view from the majority.* (para 25)

It was considered that the Master of the Rolls founded his views on the basis of the judgments in *Sidaway* and *Bolitho*. He concluded that a significant risk might be in the region of 10%, and evidence from an obstetrician that a risk was in that order would give rise to a duty to warn.

They accepted that the judgement in *Pearce* was later quoted by the majority of the House of Lords in *Chester v Afshar*, in which the only issue was one of causation. The court considered there was no recognition in *Chester* that the judgement delivered in *Pearce* had departed from, or advanced, the law after *Sidaway*.

The Inner House rejected the submission that the relevant risk to be considered was the 9–10% risk of shoulder dystocia and not the much lower risk of grave adverse outcome. The judges determined that Lord Bridge in *Sidaway* had held that it was a "substantial risk of grave adverse consequences" that would qualify for consideration. Further, they stated that the opinions delivered by the Judicial Committee of the House of Lords in *Chester v Afshar* all referred to a risk of serious injury, adverse outcome, seriously adverse results or equivalent phrases. They considered that this must be logically correct and that what was of interest to the patient must be outcome, adverse or otherwise, and not some possible complication for the medical practitioner, which, if it arose, could be dealt with by ordinary procedures entailing no adverse consequences for the patient. In these circumstances, they concluded that Dr McLellan was not required to spell out the very small risk of a grave outcome such as that which, unfortunately, materialised.

Applying the traditional *Hunter v Hanley* (*Bolam*) test, their Lordships did not consider that it was negligent to fail to advise the claimant of the risks of shoulder dystocia or mechanical problems in labour.

The court did not accept that argument that this was a case where there were options open to the patient. Their Lordships took the view that this area was not truly one of elective surgery.

On the "expression of concerns" case, they considered that the duty as identified by Lord Bridge was a duty that arose by operation of law, and was not to be measured against any yardstick of medical practice or opinion. On the issue of concerns raised by the claimant as recorded in the clinic notes, it was concluded that this was merely a communication of anxiety by a mother. The Inner House stated that the harbouring or communication of general anxieties or concerns, in a manner which does not clearly call for the full and honest disclosure of factual inform-ation in reply, falls short of qualifying under Lord Bridge's observation. They were of the view that a patient's expression of generalised anxiety in advance of surgery, or any other medical procedure, might appear to warrant only reassurance in reply. In the absence of specific questioning, or its equivalent, they regarded it as very difficult to define the limits of any supposed duty to "answer" on the part of the treating doctor. They considered that much would depend on the individual case and the precise tone of the communication.

Their Lordships made a clear distinction between specific questioning, which they concluded did require a full and truthful answer, and gener-alised anxieties and concerns, which they concluded set no obvious parameters for a required response. They concluded that too much information could alarm the patient and that it was for the experienced practitioner to decide, in accordance with normal and proper practice, where the line should be drawn in any given case. They found that Mrs Montgomery's anxiety about the increasing size of the fetus was a justi-fication for not holding Dr McLellan responsible for the decision to not advise her of risks:

... if the pursuer was sufficiently anxious that a further ultrasound scan at 38 weeks was judged by Dr McL to be better avoided, it would seem incongruous to hold Dr McL nevertheless to have been under a legal duty to cause potentially greater alarm by discussing all the ways in which a vaginal delivery might go wrong. (para 41)

They also concluded that, even on Dr McLellan's own evidence as to the prospective weight of the fetus and the point at which she would offer a caesarean section, she had no duty to offer a caesarean section independent of practice. They held that she did not have a duty to advise the claimant that she was on the borderline for consideration of a caesarean section.

On the question of causation, the Appeal Court applied the traditional "but-for" test to the issue of causation, and concluded that in this case the claimant had failed to satisfy this test. The court upheld the finding of the Lord Ordinary that had Mrs Montgomery been properly advised of her options and the risks she would not have proceeded to elective caesarean section. It also held that the principles in *Chester* did not apply since this case was not truly one in the area of elective surgery. The court did not consider that there was any intention in *Chester* to modify the principles of causation.

Comment

The claimant again failed in every single argument advanced in the Extra Division of the Inner House of the Court of Session. In the Inner House the claimant had accepted that the court was bound to follow the decision of the House of Lords in *Sidaway*. In applying *Sidaway* the court could apply the *Hunter v Hanley* or *Bolam* test to the question of disclosure of risks. However, this was not the end of the matter. The court was urged to accept that there was a clear exception to the use of the *Hunter v Hanley* or *Bolam* tests found in the speeches in *Sidaway* and they did accept there was such an exception.

Applying the *Sidaway* exception to the choices available, the claimant argued that the test was whether there was a significant risk in one of the options that would have affected the judgement of a reasonable patient. It was not disputed by the parties that the risk of shoulder dystocia in Mrs Montgomery's case was significant. What was disputed was whether that risk engaged the duty of the doctor. A major ground of battle between the parties was how the court should define the exception to the professional practice test as found in *Sidaway*. The Health Board's position was always based on one small section from the speech of Lord Bridge of Harwich. They argued that it was the risk of adverse consequences that was relevant, and in the context of this case the "adverse consequences" had to be the risk of brain damage or cerebral palsy. Given that the risk of those occurrences was low, they suggested the duty was not engaged.

The difficulty for the claimant on appeal was that at first instance the Lord Ordinary had accepted the submission that it was the risk of adverse consequences, as described by Lord Bridge in *Sidaway*, that engaged the risk. Both courts had applied a traditional meaning to the words and concluded that the relevant risk to be considered was the risk of cerebral palsy/brain damage. The original view was "adverse consequences" must relate to the potential of brain injury/cerebral palsy not to the occurrence of shoulder dystocia. To overturn this finding, the claimant had to establish that the judge was plainly wrong.

The court did not accept the submission that the test was whether there was a significant risk that a reasonable patient would wish to know of. It did not consider that the mere occurrence of shoulder dystocia, which has been described as a significant and frightening obstetric emergency, was itself relevant to the question. The focus appeared to be on the fact that most occurrences of shoulder dystocia could be overcome with simple manoeuvres. They were advised that it was impossible to predict in advance if shoulder dystocia occurred whether it could be overcome by simple manoeuvres. It was suggested that this would be relevant to a mother who is attempting to make an informed decision on how to proceed.

It was suggested that the area of information disclosure is separate and distinct from the doctor's duty in respect of diagnosis and treatment.

Where the question is one of information disclosure there must be respect for patient autonomy and the right to self-determination. In this area of the law the court should be slow to allow doctors to filter information. When information is filtered, a patient is not in a position to make an informed decision. This is particularly so when the filter that operates is a professional standard that takes no account of the individual patient's position.

The claimant sought to argue yet again that the decision in *Pearce* demonstrated an innovation and departure from traditional principles, and one that was permissible in law on a reading of the various speeches in *Sidaway*. The Appeal Court was urged to follow this and accept that the focus in respect of risk was what the reasonable patient would want to know, and not what the doctor considered the patient needed to know.

If the court were to apply a patient-focused test, it was argued that Mrs Montgomery should have been given two options: (a) elective caesarean section or (b) vaginal delivery with the option for caesarean section if difficulties were encountered, or where she changed her mind. Both were viable options for delivery of the fetus. She should have been provided with the risks and benefits of each viable option.

In the case of the vaginal delivery option she should have been advised of the risk of shoulder dystocia. The occurrence of brain damage should shoulder dystocia occur was also relevant in the context of the overall decision-making process. It was suggested that to enable the claimant to make an informed decision she needed information on the likelihood of shoulder dystocia/mechanical problems in labour, on whether this was something that could be easily overcome should it occur, and on the probability of injury to both her and the fetus should these events occur. She should also have had information on the risks of elective caesarean section.

The Appeal Court did not consider that the Master of the Rolls in *Pearce* had intended to advance the law and refine *Sidaway* by introducing a patient-focused test. They considered that he could not, and indeed did not, intend to depart from the law as stated by the House of Lords.

There are some who have said that the decision in *Montgomery* was not necessary as English law had already departed from the decision in *Sidaway* and introduced a patient-focused test following the decisions in *Pearce and Chester v Afshar*. It may be that in practice some held this view, but the Scottish Appeal Court gave very clear reasons why they considered this could not be so. It is also arguable that there was a clear difference between the test formulated by Lord Woolf in *Pearce* and the test which can now be applied following the Supreme Court decision in *Montgomery*. It was not possible for the decision in *Pearce* to remove the *Bolam* test from the law on information disclosure. Lord Woolf also formulated a test based on the reasonable patient only.

The claimant also argued that, in any event, there were options and these should have been discussed and that was an entirely separate duty. The Appeal Court did not consider that this was an "options case". There was a great deal of argument in court on whether in pregnancy there were options. The view of the court at the hearing was that there were no options as Mrs Montgomery required to deliver the fetus. The claimant argued that, although she did require to deliver the fetus, there were options for delivery. She could elect for a planned caesarean section or she could agree to proceed to vaginal delivery with the option to opt out should problems be encountered. It was also argued that the question of the options for delivery needed to be considered throughout the pregnancy, and the options could change depending on what occurred as the pregnancy developed. The court did not accept this submission.

The claimant also argued that the court should find in her favour on the "expression of concerns" issue, namely whether Mrs Montgomery had asked questions which were sufficient to engage the duty to advise on options and the risks and benefits of each option. In the first hearing of the case, Lord Bannatyne had not accepted that Mrs Montgomery had raised the question of her baby being large on a number of occasions. However, it was agreed that at one visit it was recorded that Mrs Montgomery had raised this issue. This enabled the claimant to focus on this clinic visit for the purposes of the appeal. Dr McLellan recalled that the issue had been raised at one clinic visit. She also accepted that Mrs Montgomery was anxious about the size of the baby and her ability to deliver it, and it was for this reason that she cancelled the last scan.

The claimant argued that there was clear communication on what concerned Mrs Montgomery. Dr McLellan was also aware of what the concern was. There could not be any logic in stating that where a patient had concerns about an issue they had somehow to articulate that concern in a precise way. Mrs Montgomery had communicated to Dr McLellan what she was worried about. The Appeal Court rejected this submission, as the Lord Ordinary had done, and considered that the comments made were mere general expressions of concern which did not require an answer.

In the appeal hearing there was no reference to the GMC guidance on patient consent. The guidance had not been raised in the original court hearing and the original court had not heard evidence on the duties of the doctor as specified in that guidance. On that basis, the guidance could not be used in the appeal.

On causation, the court was not persuaded by any argument that there had been a failure on the part of the Lord Ordinary. In Scotland, where there is an issue of the credibility of any witness, that is traditionally considered a matter for the judge who hears the evidence of the witness. If such a judge forms an adverse view of the credibility of any witness, it is highly unlikely that a Scottish court would interfere with that finding. In this case, the original trial judge, Lord Bannatyne, had not formed an adverse view of Mrs Montgomery's credibility on the issue of whether she would have proceeded to an elective caesarean section had she been warned of the risk of shoulder dystocia. He formed the view that she genuinely believed she would have done so, and this belief was partly reinforced by what had occurred. In this situation, in Scotland it is possible to ask an Appeal Court to review the causation question.

Lord Bannatyne had set himself what he described as a balancing exercise to test the evidence of the claimant that she would have proceeded to caesarean section. In the Appeal Court, it was argued that, whilst a balancing exercise might be appropriate, this balancing exercise was flawed as he had failed to put on the scales all of the evidence, which in fact supported Mrs Montgomery that she would have proceeded to elective caesarean section had she been appropriately warned.

The Appeal Court refused to accept that he had failed in this exercise. The claimant also argued that there should be strict liability if there had been a failure to consent, or a transfer of the onus of proof to the defenders/defendants in a case where it was established there was a failure to provide a patient with information to enable the patient to make an informed decision on how she wished to proceed. The causation arguments advanced are considered in more detail in Chapter 7.

5. Montgomery in the Supreme Court

Introduction

Mrs Montgomery then took her case to the Supreme Court, where the decision was issued on 11 March 2015 ([2015] UKSC11; [2015] A.C. 1430; [2015] 2 W.L.R. 768; [2015] 2 All E.R. 1031; 2015 S.C. (U.K.S.C.) 63; 2015 S.L.T. 189; 2015 S.C.L.R. 315; [2015 P.I.Q.R. P13; [2015] Med.L.R. 149; (2015) 143 B.M.L.R. 47; 2015 G.W.D. 10-179). At that time a claimant in Scotland did not have to seek the leave of the court to bring a Scottish appeal to the Supreme Court. The case was heard by a bench of seven including the president, Lord Neuberger, and the then deputy president, Lady Hale. As this was a Scottish appeal there were two Scottish judges on the bench.

The claimant now had an opportunity to ask the Supreme Court to provide a clear statement of the UK law on patient consent. The claimant wanted to argue that the UK law should be brought into line with the law in Australia and Canada. The claimant intended to use this opportunity to ask the court to recognise that the professional practice test found in *Bolam* and *Hunter v Hanley* had no relevance in this area of the law, which could be (and should be) separated from the question of diagnosis and treatment.

The claimant had previously not been able to argue for a change in the law in either the Outer House of the Court of Session or the Appeal Court in Scotland. Both were bound to follow the House of Lords decision in *Sidaway*. The Supreme Court was aware in advance that the claimant sought to overturn the decision in *Sidaway* and convened a bench of seven judges to consider the question.

<u>The arguments made on behalf of the claimant</u>

The principal submission before the Supreme Court was to invite the court to depart from the decision of the House of Lords in *Sidaway* and remove the professional practice test (*Hunter v Hanley*, *Bolam*) completely from the consent case.

The focus in the argument was on the patient's rights in this area of the law, which is distinct from diagnosis and treatment. Patients have the right to self-determination. A patient's right to information to enable them to make a meaningful choice about treatment options (including the option of no treatment) should not be decided on the basis of the test found in *Hunter v Hanley* and *Bolam*. It is inappropriate to apply a practice test in this area of the law.

Given that the underlying principle is one of self-determination, the focus must be on the particular patient and that patient's needs. The right is frustrated by reference to a body. This is particularly so when the right includes the right to act irrationally for reasons personal to the patient.

Where there is a risk that affects the judgement of a reasonable patient in the patient's position, there should be a duty on the doctor to inform the patient of that risk, irrespective of medical practice. It was submitted the correct approach in information cases was to apply a standard of disclosure based on what a reasonable patient in the patient's position would wish to know. A particular patient test should be applied where a doctor was aware of specific factors relevant to the patient, with reference to the test in *Rogers v Whitaker*. The thrust of the argument advanced was to bring UK law into line with other common law jurisdictions, and in particular Australia and Canada.

The claimant submitted that the starting point is whether there are options for treatment. If there are options, and these are reasonable, they must be discussed with the patient. The question of which options are reasonable is one which can be determined by expert medical evidence as a matter of fact, but should not be determined by the professional practice test as this is an inappropriate filter. The option/s did need to be reasonable. It was not suggested that hypothetical or unreasonable options needed to be considered.

If there was only one option for treatment it was suggested that the question should in the first instance be "Is there a risk?" Thereafter, the question should be "Is that a risk that the reasonable patient in the patient's position would consider significant?" On the question of materiality, the court must also consider what this particular patient would wish to know, taking account of this particular patient's idiosyncrasies. If there are options for treatment, the legal obligation on the doctor should be to advise the patient of the options, and thereafter the risks and benefits of each option.

It was submitted the court should not impose a predetermined threshold of what would constitute a significant risk or what was material. That should be determined by the facts and circumstances of each particular case, and the peculiarities of the individual patient. The test must be patient-centred or -focused.

It was argued the court, not the medical profession, should be the arbiter of what information the patient should have been given. The nature of the issues before the court in consent cases involves questions a judge can assess. Expert evidence may be of assistance to the court in providing evidence on the probability and nature of risks. Expert evidence should not be used to determine what options should be discussed or what any patient would want to know, nor should expert evidence decide what was a "reasonable patient". Experts should not be gate-keepers to what a patient considers to be significant in terms of risks. By relying on expert evidence, the test ceases to be what the reasonable person considers to be significant and becomes what the expert thinks the reasonable person ought to think is significant. This is unacceptable in this area of the law.

In support of these propositions, the argument advanced was as follows:

- Consent is valid only where it is freely given by a patient with the capacity to consent, on the basis of adequate information as to the nature and consequences of the proposed treatment, and its alternatives, including that of non-treatment. These elements are not independent but interdependent and valid legal consent requires all three to be present.

- A conscious adult patient of sound mind is entitled to decide whether or not to submit to a particular course of treatment proposed by a doctor. The patient does not have to accept the advice of a doctor in respect of proposed treatment.

- The underlying philosophy of consent is rights-based. The patient has an overarching right to know as a necessary feature of the overarching right to self-determination. Patient autonomy cannot be divorced from the law on consent. Human rights law reinforces the common law's position through the protection of an individual's physical integrity as part of the right for respect for private life protected by Article 8 of the European Convention on Human Rights.

- Central to the argument is the question of the patient's ability to make a true choice about whether to accept or reject a course of treatment. The notion is best expressed as respect for a person's bodily integrity, stemming from a right of self-determination. Choice is meaningless unless it is made on the basis of relevant information and advice. Where a doctor offers an incomplete picture of the therapy he proposes by withholding information on alternatives, and the risks and benefits of those alternatives, the patient's right of choice is usurped.

- It is not appropriate to apply a professional practice test, such as that found in *Hunter v Hanley* or *Bolam*, to the issue of consent. There is a fundamental difference between, on the one hand, diagnosis and treatment and, on the other, the provision of advice and information to the patient. In a counselling case the doctor provides the information but the choice should be that of the patient.

- In the *Hunter v Hanley* or *Bolam* test the duty is based on what doctors as a profession consider it appropriate for a patient to know. The effect is that the medical profession dictates by practice what information is given. This reflects a philosophy of paternalism, according to which the doctor is the better judge of what a patient needs to know before embarking on a procedure. It is illogical to hold that the amount of information to be provided by the doctor can be determined from the perspective of the doctor alone, or for that matter the medical professional generally.

- The position derived from *Sidaway* – that doctors are entitled to set the standard of legal disclosure by practice, but at some point if there is a significant risk they have to inform the patient – is unsatisfactory and vague. There is an inherent difficulty in knowing when the significant test acts to displace the *Bolam* test.

- The position derived from *Sidaway* does not sufficiently take account of the particular patient, and the peculiarities of the particular patient.

- A patient should be entitled to make a balanced judgement and a patient cannot do so where information is filtered. The current law permits two filters to operate. The first is the application of the *Hunter v Hanley* or *Bolam* test to the question of patient information. The second is that there is only an obligation to advise of risks independent of practice where a risk is considered by a doctor to be significant. Neither filter takes account of the views or wishes of the patient, or takes account of the peculiarities of the particular patient.

- Application of the *Hunter v Hanley* or *Bolam* tests to the question of consent assumes that the doctor has a duty to communicate only that information which other doctors would communicate. This requires a degree of professional agreement which is unlikely to be demonstrated in practice. Indeed, the courts are often faced, as in this case, with a dispute among professionals as to the correct course of action, and what in fact the professional practice standard was at the relevant time. The professional practice approach inevitably means that there is no focus on the peculiarities of the particular patient.

- In *Sidaway* there was some recognition that a doctor also has a duty to act in the "best interests" of the patient. The best interests of a patient must amount to more than simply not treating them negligently. It cannot be said that ignoring the views of the patient, or filtering or withholding information, would be acting in the best interests of the patient.

- The relationship between the doctor and the patient is a therapeutic relationship or alliance. Where doctors share information with patients and allow them to become involved (should they choose to so do) in the decisions about their health this enhances the relationship.

- What risks are significant are questions on which the doctor's and the patient's perspectives may differ. It is recognised that patients make choices about their health care on the basis of non-medical information. Factors related to their lifestyle and family circumstances are relevant to their choice. It is for this reason that the information that should be disclosed cannot be fully determined by a doctor.

- It is the patient, or their family, who would normally bear the consequences should a risk materialise. In this context, it seems illogical to exclude the patient from the decision on whether to accept that risk.

- Should a patient not wish to be given full information, or should the patient wish the doctor to make the decision for them, the application of a patient-focused test would not prevent this approach.

- The current approach in *Sidaway* – where if a patient asks questions full disclosure is made, but where the patient does not the professional practice test dictates what information they receive – is illogical and unsatisfactory.

- Clear guidance has been provided by a professional body, the GMC, and the courts should have regard to the guidance in determining questions relating to information disclosure.

The options for treatment argument

If the Supreme Court were not prepared to depart from *Sidaway*, the claimant contended that she could in fact still be successful in the case. It was argued that there were options for the delivery of the fetus in this case. This argument had first been raised in the Outer House of the Court of Session, and in the Inner House on appeal. Both had rejected this as an option for treatment in this case.

In this case Mrs Montgomery had the option of delivery by elective caesarean section. She could also have proceeded to vaginal delivery, with the option to have a caesarean section should difficulties be encountered during the course of the labour. Where there are options for treatment, it was argued that it was incumbent upon the doctor to advise the patient, firstly, that there were options, and, secondly, the risks and benefits of each option. It was stated that, where one option does not expose the patient to significant risk and the other does, it is particularly incumbent upon the doctor to advise the patient of those options and the risks and benefits of each.

It was submitted the duty was incumbent upon a doctor on the basis of *Sidaway* and the duty existed irrespective of professional practice. Reference was made to *Birch v University College London Hospital NHS Foundation Trust* ([2008] EWCH 2237 (QB)), where it was held there was a duty to disclose alternative treatments. If it was accepted that there were options for treatment and that the options and risks of benefits of each option were not discussed then this amounted to a failure in care.

The definition of what is a significant or material risk

The claimant had to address how the court should look at the question of the risk that engaged the duty of the doctor. There were two aspects to this argument. If the court were not disposed to set aside the decision in *Sidaway*, what was the risk that engaged the duty of the doctor?

Lord Bridge in *Sidaway* indicated that in his view a judge might come to the conclusion that disclosure of a particular risk was so obviously necessary to the informed choice on the part of the patient that no reasonably prudent medical man would fail to make it. He then stated that he had in mind an operation involving a substantial risk of grave adverse consequences, as for example the risk of stroke. In such a case, in the absence of some cogent reason why the patient should not be informed, a doctor recognising and respecting the patient's right of decision could hardly fail to appreciate the necessity for appropriate warning. Lord Templeman's approach in *Sidaway* of general and special damages is an approach that is highly unsatisfactory. The terms "general" and "special" are unclear.

If the court wished to depart from *Sidaway*, it was argued that assistance in what was a significant risk and how that should be interpreted could be found in cases from other jurisdictions. The Australian and Canadian cases provide clear information on how this test should be construed. This is considered in detail in Chapter 3. In *Canterbury v Spence* (464 F.2d 772 (1972) (U.S.C.A., District of Columbia)), a risk was held to be significant if it is material to the reasonable patient's decision. The question is answered hypothetically based on the informational needs of a hypothetical reasonable patient. It is not just a question of incidence of risk but also depends on the severity of the risk should it materialise. In Canada, it was held in *Hopp v Lepp* ((1979) 98 D.L.R. (3d) 464; affirmed (1980) 112 D.L.R. (3d) 67 (S.C.C.)) that a risk, even if it is a mere possibility, should be regarded as material if the occurrence causes serious consequences. In Australia, *Rogers v Whitaker* provides clear guidance on the test to be applied.

In *Pearce*, it was held that a significant risk affecting the judgement of a reasonable patient would place the onus upon the doctor to advise the patient of that risk. In the formulation by Lord Woolf, the question of whether a risk is significant acts as a gateway to the question of whether the information would be material to the reasonable patient's decision. He also said that it was not possible to talk in precise percentages when one talks of significant risk.

On the question of significant risk, the claimant argued:

- Logically, the question of risk must be concerned with both the likelihood of the risk and also the nature of the harm being risked. It is not possible to separate these when consideration is given to whether consent should be given.

- It must be clear that what is significant or grave is a question upon which the doctor's and the patient's perception may differ. It is however the patient who is being exposed to the risk and the patient who must suffer the consequences should the risk materialise. The patient should therefore make the choice.

- In this particular case, the risk that engaged the duty to warn in relation to the vaginal delivery option is the risk of shoulder dystocia/mechanical problems in labour. This was a significant risk and did require to be discussed. It is also an adverse event in the sense that it is defined as an obstetric emergency.

- The discussion should have involved the percentage risk of mechanical problems in labour/shoulder dystocia occurring. Thereafter there can be a discussion on what can be done should this occur. The probability of brain damage, Erbs palsy and cerebral palsy should shoulder dystocia occur should also be part of the consent decision. This discussion could also include information that most cases of shoulder dystocia are overcome easily and quickly without adverse occurrence. The patient should however have been advised that it is not possible to predict accurately in advance which cases will be overcome with no adverse consequences. A patient is not able to make an informed choice without this information.

- There is no logic in ignoring the risk of shoulder dystocia/mech-anical obstruction in labour and simply focusing on the statistical probability of brain damage or brachial plexus injury when considering how to counsel a mother with a large baby. This provides only part of the picture. The occurrence of shoulder dystocia and mechanical problems in labour with the potential of brain damage or cerebral palsy could be described as a relevant conjunction of circumstances. Where the risk of shoulder dystocia occurring is significant at 10% a mother may not wish to take that risk at all irrespective of the fact should shoulder dystocia occur it may be easily overcome. A mother may also not wish to take a 1–2% risk of brain damage to her child. This is particularly so when no useful prediction can be made in relation to which mothers will have an easily overcome shoulder dystocia.

- The significance of the risk should also be considered in the context of the choices a patient has. In this case the claimant had the opportunity to avoid the risk of shoulder dystocia entirely by proceeding with an elective caesarean section. It is true that there are risks associated with delivery by elective caesarean section but these also require to be considered in context.

<u>Arguments for and against a patient-focused test</u>

It has been suggested that the Supreme Court did not give full consider-ation to the arguments for and against the introduction of a patient-focused test. There were submissions on this issue from the Health Board and the GMC. These submissions are set out in detail in Chapter 5, which deals with the GMC guidance.

The claimant set out in the written case for the Supreme Court the arguments that had been advanced over the years for and against the introduction of a patient-focused test. The arguments are as follows:

Proponents for the retention of the duty of disclosure based on the *Hunter v Hanley/Bolam* model would argue:

- Many patients prefer to place themselves unreservedly in the hands of their doctors. They do not want to know about risks and side effects. In fact, to tell them of all the risks would simply frighten them unnecessarily.

- There will be cases where treatment that is necessary is capri-ciously refused by patients frightened by information given to them, and this is not in the best interest of the patient.

- Society, or the "collective patient", has ceded to the doctor the right to make medical and ethical decisions in the patient–doctor interaction.

- Many patients are incapable of understanding a medical assess-ment of risks and benefits. A layperson cannot possibly make a medical judgement. They entrust such judgements to their doctor.

- The function of the doctor is to take such decisions away from patients and make them based on the doctor's knowledge and expertise. To involve the patient in the decision-making process affects the ability of the doctor to make ethical and correct decisions about medical treatment.

- There is a danger of self-serving testimony.

- Patients may take decisions about their own health care that the treating doctor does not agree with.

- The *Sidaway* test does permit the patient who seeks information to obtain information and in that sense the patient's rights are protected.

- Withholding information does not undermine patient autonomy as the patient has decided to go ahead with a procedure, and in that circumstance the patient has autonomously, and voluntarily, conferred on the doctor a right to take decisions for him.

- The doctor has a duty to provide the best health care for the patient. In that situation, even if patient autonomy is derogated from, that derogation is justified. This argument underpins the defence of therapeutic privilege in the USA.

Those who advance a more open, informed and patient-focused duty of disclosure argue as follows:

- A doctor does not require to provide full information about risks if the patient states that they do not wish that information. A patient's decision not to seek full information must equally be respected. The doctor's obligation is not to force-feed the patient. A patient who elects to entrust all the necessary decisions to a doctor would still be entitled to do so.

- There should be a clear signal to the medical profession that a patient's right to know should not be limited to what the medical profession decides by practice that patients generally should be told.

- It is time for the law to be critical of medical expertise claiming that a level of disclosure was acceptable based on standards of the profession and thus also legally acceptable.

- A patient cannot compel a doctor or a hospital to provide treatment that is determined by the doctor's clinical judgement not to be in the patient's best interests, or which cannot be provided because of limited resources.

- A patient's increased vulnerability and dependence induced through illness should not be used as an excuse for eliminating their autonomy.

- If patients fail to comprehend information this may be due to deficiencies in communication. It is for the doctor to use their skills to communicate the information in a way the patient can comprehend. There is no room for the view that disclosure of relevant information to patients is a waste of time because they do not understand it anyway.

- Patients are entitled to take decisions conflicting with the doctor's advice. The right to self-determination and autonomy includes the right to take decisions based on factors other than pure reason, and also embraces the right to make a wrong decision.

- There is no logic in denying a patient their right to self-determination while he is a patient and to restore this when he has ceased being a patient.

- As said by Lord Donaldson MR, the courts should not stand idly by if the profession, by an excess of paternalism, denies its patients a real choice. They must critically consider and scrutinise professional practices to ensure that they accord with the law, which prefers self-determination to paternalism.

- On occasion, medical expertise is misused and overestimated and physicians do not always recognise the limits of their medical experience.

- The courts should remember the warning of King CJ in *F v R* ([1983] 33 S.A.S.R.189 (S.C. of S. Aus.) that practices may develop in professions not because they serve the interests of the patients but because they protect the interests or convenience of members of the profession.

- In *Sidaway* there was a failure to properly take account of the complex nature of the doctor–patient relationship. There was an assumption that patients did not want comprehensive information on treatment options and the risks and benefits of each option. It was assumed that patients might react capriciously to such information. This assumption is not founded on any hard evidence and also this was a different era where the doctor–patient relationship was different.

- There has been a significant change in the delivery of health care and the nature of the doctor–patient relationship since the decision of the House of Lords in *Sidaway*. The GMC provides clear guidance to doctors on the issue of consent and what information should be given to a patient on options for treatment and the risks and benefits of each option. The GMC has clearly given consideration to whether this can operate in practice. The current legal test is at odds with the professional duties incumbent upon a doctor as set out in the GMC guidance. This is incongruous.

- The danger of self-serving testimony exists to some extent whichever test is applied. The courts are well able to test the veracity of witness evidence and also the reliability of the evidence of the witness. This is something that courts are accustomed to doing.

- A patient who expressly seeks information can obtain it. A test that requires the patient to take the initiative cannot ever genuinely promote patient autonomy. The articulate, confident patient may be able to initiate a discussion with a doctor about options for treatment and risks. The less articulate, apprehensive patient may feel intimidated and may be hesitant to ask questions.

How should the test be applied in practice?

The claimant set out for the court a submission on how a patient-centred test could be applied in practice. It was suggested that the starting point should be that a doctor has a duty to consider whether there are options for treatment. This does not require to include every option. This is a factual question for the court to address and should not be based on what doctors normally offer. If there are alternative viable treatments available elsewhere, it is the duty of the doctor to advise the patient of these. The doctor should discuss with a patient a material or significant risk inherent in a proposed treatment or option for treatment.

A risk would be significant or material if a reasonable patient in the patient's position, if warned of the risk, would be likely to attach significance to it, or if the medical practitioner is or should be reasonably aware that the particular patient, if warned of the risk, would be likely to attach significance to it. This is the test in *Rogers v Whitaker*. There was reference to how this test was applied in other jurisdictions. A risk may be material if the incidence of the risk is high. It may also be material if the incidence of the risk is low but the risk is of death, severe damage, or consequences which would be lifelong.

It was argued that it was important that the test found in *Hunter v Hanley* and *Bolam* (the professional practice test) is completely removed from the question of what options were available, whether to discuss a risk, or whether a risk is material.

It was submitted that this approach retained two benefits over the professional standard test. The first is the importance of the emphasis on the patient's right to know. The second is that this test places an onus upon the doctor to consider, at least in general, what the patient would want to know. Such an approach would promote co-operative decision-making in addition to the promotion of individual autonomy.

The current legal approach to consent to medical treatment is at variance with the advice given by the GMC to doctors. The *Sidaway* test is not consistent with good medical practice as defined by the GMC. The test does not promote good health care since there is no incentive to improve practice. If there is a reasonable body of doctors who have decided for whatever reason, whether logical or illogical, not to advise of a risk then a patient can legitimately be denied information. The doctor who withholds the information is protected by the law. The GMC guidance can provide assistance to the court in the determination of the issues.

In the application of a test like this, a patient who has been advised that there were risks in the treatment generally would still be entitled to state that they did not wish to be informed of those risks. They would still be entitled to leave the decision-making process to the doctor. A doctor would still be permitted to withhold information if it was thought that the dissemination of that information would pose a risk of serious psychological harm to the patient. Where any of the aforementioned occurred, this should be recorded within the patient's clinical notes.

A court must take an active role in determining what risks the reasonable patient in the patient's position would wish to know of. The court should not defer to expert witnesses' evidence of what risks they consider a patient would wish to know.

Where there are options for treatment it is particularly important that they are discussed with the patient, and the risks and benefits of each option are discussed. This is separate and distinct from the general duty to warn. A doctor should not select the option they consider the best for the patient. The decision on which option to select is the patient's.

If these principles had been applied to the circumstances of Mrs Montgomery's case, it was submitted that there were clearly options for the delivery of her baby, and she should have been advised of the options. In any event, she should have been advised of the risk of mechanical problems in labour/shoulder dystocia as this was a significant risk. It is a risk that any reasonably patient would wish to know of. There was evidence to support this contention. Dr McLellan said in evidence that no mother would wish to encounter shoulder dystocia in any form. Dr

Mason, the expert for the Health Board, also said in evidence that if mothers were told of the risk of shoulder dystocia the tendency would be to opt for caesarean section.

It was argued that Mrs Montgomery should also have been advised of the risk of brain damage/cerebral palsy. Although the risk was small, the consequences should they occur are significant. In that situation, a reasonable patient would wish to know of this risk. There is however no logic in separating out risks since they are interdependent.

<u>What is the nature and extent of questioning required from a patient to engage the duty of the doctor to warn of risks?</u>

Mrs Montgomery had "raised concerns" about how she would deliver a large baby vaginally and that concern had to be addressed and answered truthfully. The concern is not addressed by withholding information, as was done here (cancelling the last scan).

The submission was that it was not disputed that Mrs Montgomery had conveyed to Dr McLellan at the clinic visit on 15 September 1999 that she was concerned as she was small, and she was worried whether she would be able to deliver her large baby vaginally. The claimant's argument was that this expression was sufficient to require Dr McLellan to answer truthfully and advise her of the risk of shoulder dystocia/mechanical problems in labour. This argument had failed at the initial court hearing in the Outer House of the Court of Session and also in the Appeal Court.

It had previously been held that the harbouring or communication of general anxieties or concerns, in a manner which does not clearly call for the full and honest disclosure of factual information in reply, falls short of qualifying under Lord Bridge's observations in *Sidaway*. The Extra Division concluded that a patient's expression of generalised anxiety in advance of surgery, or any other medical procedure, might appear to warrant only reassurance in reply. In the absence of specific questioning, or its equivalent, they regarded it as very difficult to define the limits of any supposed duty to "answer" on the part of the treating doctor.

They considered that much would depend on the individual case and the precise tone of the communication. They also made a clear distinction between specific questioning, which they concluded did require a full and truthful answer, and generalised anxieties and concerns, which they felt set no obvious parameters for a required response. The felt that too much information could alarm the patient and that it was for the experienced practitioner to decide, in accordance with normal and proper practice, where the line should be drawn in any given case. They felt that the claimant's increasing anxiety about the size of the fetus was a justification for withholding information that could further alarm Mrs Montgomery.

The judgement in *Sidaway* setting the professional standard of disclosure is limited in outlining what degree of information a doctor must volunteer to a patient. In *Sidaway* Lord Scarman implied that a doctor should respond truthfully to any direct questions. He said that the moral ideal would be to disclose what that particular patient subjectively needed to know, but the law was constrained by practical considerations to an objective obligation. If a patient through direct questioning alerts a doctor to their own particular needs, then the doctor would be obliged to meet them.

In the same case, Lord Diplock commented that if the patient in fact manifested an attitude of wanting to be fully informed by direct questioning, the doctor would no doubt tell them what he wanted to know. This was unqualified but was stated as an alternative to the *Bolam* test. This would suggest that direct questioning does create an exception to the *Bolam* test, and in that situation it is the duty of the doctor to answer truthfully.

Lord Bridge added that specific questions must be answered truthfully and fully. The answer must be as full as the questioner requires. This is explicit in relation to precise questions but it does leave unanswered the duty where the question is vague or general.

The limits of the duty were highlighted in the case of *Blyth v Blooms-bury Health Authority*. The trial judge's decision in favour of the plaintiff was reversed on appeal. He was found to be in error in holding that there was an obligation, when asked, to pass on all the information available to the hospital. It was said that the question of what a patient should be told in response to a general inquiry could not be detached from the *Bolam* test, any more than when no such inquiry was made. In this case the argument centred largely on obscure therapeutic notes written in hospital.

In *Pearce* the Court of Appeal restored the *Sidaway* position. Lord Woolf MR held that, if a patient asks a doctor about the risk, the doctor is required to give an honest answer.

In *Chappel v Hart* ([1998] H.C.A. 55), Mrs Hart expressed general concern about the possibility of losing her voice following an operation. She had said she did not want to "wind up like Neville Wran", an Australian politician who suffered voice damage following a similar procedure. This was held to be sufficient to engage the duty to inform.

The claimant made the following submissions in relation to the specific question posed – *What is the nature and extent of questioning required from a patient to engage the duty of a doctor to warn of risks?*

- There is a distinction to be drawn between an affirmative duty to volunteer information, and a duty to respond to questions. They are both aspects of the general duty of care. To classify it as a duty to respond does not define the content of the duty.

- Where a patient asks a doctor questions, it is established law that the duty of the doctor is to answer the patient truthfully, not filter information based on the doctor's own assessment of risk.

- Where a patient asks questions, the issue of medical practice is irrelevant. The doctor cannot decide to advise only of risks the doctor, or the profession generally considers to be relevant.

- There was no dispute that concerns were expressed by Mrs Montgomery at the 36-week clinic visit. The issue was whether those concerns were sufficient to engage the accepted duty of the doctor to answer truthfully.

- There was no dispute that Mrs Montgomery was worried about the size of the baby and her ability to deliver it vaginally. She successfully communicated the concern to Dr McLellan, who accepted in evidence that she knew that Mrs Montgomery was concerned about the size of the baby and her ability to deliver it vaginally. This is not a situation where Dr McLellan failed to advise her of the risks of shoulder dystocia/mechanical problems in labour because she didn't understand what the patient was worried about. In fact, she deliberately withheld the information because she considered that the risk was something that would not materialise. She felt in that situation that she had no duty to discuss this.

Causation

The claimant made detailed arguments on causation. These are dealt with in Chapter 7 on causation.

The argument on behalf of the Health Board

- No change in the law is necessary, reasonable or desirable. The *Bolam/Hunter v Hanley* test has the flexibility to protect both doctors and patients.

- There is no proper basis for a change in the law. The maximum *cessante ratione cessat ipsa lex* does not apply. If a change in the law is required, it ought to be carried out by Parliament.

- Although it is asserted that the law ought to be rights-based, that is not how allegations of negligence are, or ought to be, decided. It ought to remain for a claimant to aver and prove duties owed and how they are said to be breached. The case made by the claimant is fundamentally incoherent and flawed.

- The arguments set out by the claimant for and against the introduction of a patient-focused test do not amount to any good
reason to depart from the decision in *Sidaway*.

- No good reason has been advanced to depart from the decision
in *Sidaway*. The power of the court to depart from its own
precedent should be exercised rarely and sparingly. Where a
development in law is required, it ought to be developed on a
principles basis, rather than one that might distort the development of the law. The proposed test would result in, rather than
cure an anomaly. Duties with a different juridical basis would
be owed to the same patient where consent arises on the one
hand and diagnosis and treatment arise on the other.

- Dr McLellan had a duty to act with the ordinary care of a
consultant obstetrician of ordinary skill and she did so.

- Hypoxic-ischaemic encephalopathy in babies following a
shoulder dystocia is rare, and the majority of incidences of
shoulder dystocia are overcome by the McRoberts manoeuvre
without injury to the baby.

- Dr McLellan did explain to Mrs Montgomery that if a caesarean
section was necessary during labour it would be carried out. She
said that if she felt it fair to allow someone to deliver vaginally
she would tell the patient she would be vigilant in labour and if
there were signs of obstruction a caesarean section would be
performed.

- Caesarean section itself carried certain risks, particularly if
carried out as an emergency close to full dilation.

- The claimant has no basis to import a "patient-focused test" as
this argument was not made before the Inner House. She did
not argue a "patient-centred test" before the Lord Ordinary. She
previously argued that a "reasonable patient" test should be
applied based on the decision in *Pearce*.

- The case of *Rogers v Whitaker*, referred to by the claimant, should be treated with caution. In Australia, even in the sphere of diagnosis and treatment the *Bolam* principle has not always been applied and it has been discarded in the field of disclosure of risk and the provision of advice and information.

- The change in law sought by the claimant lacked any flexibility and would apparently impose an absolute duty. How one defines what patients should be advised of presents very real difficulties. The suggestion that it would be what a reasonable patient would want to know lacks any precision. Does the patient want advice or information? The scope of the duty is likely to be materially different depending on which it is. A removal of any discretion ignores the reality of the doctor–patient relationship.

- There would be a lack of consistency. What one judge may consider a reasonable patient would want to know might differ markedly from what another judge may think. The information given must depend on the circumstances.

- The adherence to the *Bolam* principle does not necessitate handing over to the medical profession the entire question as the court always has the power to override medical evidence.

- There is no need to change the law, which would result in uncertainty and inconsistency and produce a prescriptive approach, and in all probability cause confusion among the medical profession without any real benefit to patients. The law at present demands disclosure of significant risks.

- It is the risk of severe adverse consequences which is the relevant risk and in the present case the risks of adverse consequences were small. There is no pressing public policy reason to suggest that as a matter of law it should be mandatory to advise of such a risk. Nor is there any pressing public policy reason to employ a different approach in the realm of advice and information from the realm of diagnosis and treatment. The distinction the claimant seeks to make between the two is chimaeric. Both involve decisions to be made by the patient on information, given by the doctor but not all of which can be imparted to the patient.

- The claimant was not given the option of elective caesarean section but she was aware this option was open to her. She proceeded to labour on the basis that Dr McLellan thought it was safe to do so. Had there been any discussion about risks it is likely that Dr McLellan would have continued to opine it was safe to proceed with labour and it was most likely she would have accepted that advice.

- Dr McLellan did not remove the claimant's right to choose.

- The claimant expressed a general concern about her ability to deliver vaginally on one isolated occasion and the sole question is whether that comes within the ambit of Lord Bridge's observation in *Sidaway*. The overwhelming problem was how to define the ambit of any answer. It would be of no assistance to the medical profession to impose some sort of prescriptive obligation uniformly to warn of risks. The appropriate response must depend on a number of different factors and vary according to circumstances.

- The absence of warning about risks did not cause any harm since the claimant would have attempted vaginal delivery in any event.

- There is no justification for any departure from the normal rules of causation. The facts of the present case are straightforward and do not warrant a departure from sound and established principle. The Inner House was correct in concluding that in *Chester* the court did not intend that the modification of causation principles should apply generally to all cases where a doctor has failed to warn of risks. The modification of causation principles was peculiar to the facts and circumstances of that case.

- The subjective approach to causation is the correct approach and there are likely to be fundamental and unnecessary difficulties in a combined subjective/objective approach. It is difficult to envisage how a "reasonable patient" and the real patient in question can be amalgamated.

- It is asserted by the claimant that the *Bolam* and *Hunter v Hanley* test involves a form of paternalism. The claimant does not define paternalism. It is assumed that she considers all forms of paternalism to be inimical. Any relationship that involves a degree of care and welfare involves a degree of paternalism. The claimants approach is a form of "coerced choosing".

The decision of the court

The decision of the Supreme Court has been extensively reported and commented upon. A panel of seven Supreme Court Justices unanimously allowed the claimant's appeal. The correct legal approach in consent cases was set out in a joint judgement ([2015] UKSC11; [2015] A.C. 1430; [2015] 2 W.L.R. 768; [2015] 2 All E.R. 1031; 2015 S.C. (U.K.S.C.) 63; 2015 S.L.T. 189; 2015 S.C.L.R. 315; [2015 P.I.Q.R. P13; [2015] Med.L.R. 149; (2015) 143 B.M.L.R. 47; 2015 G.W.D. 10-179).

In determining the test to be applied in consent cases in the UK, the Supreme Court recognised the fundamental importance of patient autonomy and the patient's right to make choices about his/her own life. There has been a clear shift in focus from medical paternalism to respect for patient autonomy.

In *Montgomery* Lords Kerr and Reed held that:

patients are now widely regarded as persons holding rights, rather than as the passive recipients of the care of the medical profession. They are also widely regarded as consumers exercising choices.... It would therefore be a mistake to view patients as uninformed, incapable of understanding medical matters, or wholly dependent upon a flow of information from doctors. (para 75)

The social and legal developments which we have mentioned point away from a model of the relationship between the doctor and the patient based upon medical paternalism.

Lady Hale held that:

It is now well recognised that the interest which the law of negligence protects is a person's interest in their own physical and psychiatric integrity, an important feature of which is their autonomy, their freedom to decide what shall and shall not be done with their body. (para 108)

It is clear that the Supreme Court took account of the view of the General Medical Council in coming to its conclusion:

The submission on behalf of the General Medical Council acknowledged, in relation to these documents, that an approach based upon the informed involvement of patients in their treatment, rather than their being passive and potentially reluctant recipients, can have therapeutic benefits, and is regarded as an integral aspect of professionalism in treatment. (para 78)

In its decision, the Supreme Court accepted that the doctor's duty in relation to information disclosure is separate and distinct from the duty of the doctor in the area of diagnosis and treatment. It recognised as important the fact that patient choice in this context did not depend exclusively on medical considerations.

They recognised an important distinction between the doctor's role and the patients' views. The patient may well have in their mind circumstances, objectives and values that would lead them to a different decision from that suggested by a purely medical opinion:

The relative importance attached by patients to quality as against length of life, or to physical appearance or bodily integrity as against the relief of pain, will vary from one patient to another. Countless other examples could be given on the ways in which the views or circumstances of an individual patient may affect their attitude towards a proposed form of treatment and the reasonable alternatives. The doctor cannot form an objective, "medical" view of these matters, and is therefore not in a position to take the "right" decision as a matter of clinical judgement. (para 46)

They emphasised the fundamental distinction between, on the one hand, the doctor's role when considering treatment options and, on the other, the role of the doctor when discussing with a patient "any recommended treatment and possible alternatives, and the risks of injury which may be involved".

The court held:

… it is a non sequitur to conclude that the question whether a risk of injury, or the availability of an alternative form of treatment, ought to be discussed with the patient is also a matter of purely professional judgement. The doctor's advisory role cannot be regarded as solely an exercise of medical skill without leaving out of account the patient's entitlement to decide on the risks to her health which she is willing to run (a decision which may be influenced by non-medical considerations). Responsibility for determining the nature and extent of a person's rights rests with the courts, not with the medical profession. (para 83)

There was recognition that a patient could decide that they did not wish to be informed of risks, in the same way that a patient can choose not to read an information leaflet. The court emphasised that a doctor would not be obliged to discuss risks inherent in a treatment with a patient who made it clear that they did not wish to discuss those risks. However, even in this area, the court did not consider that the *Bolam* test would apply.

The Supreme Court in *Montgomery*, in departing from the professional standard, expressly acknowledged a role for what the judges called the "therapeutic exception". A doctor would be entitled to withhold information reasonably considered detrimental to the patient's health (para 88) or in circumstances of necessity. However, the court did warn that this exception must not be abused or used to prevent patients from making decisions that the doctor might see as contrary to the patient's best interests (para 91). The scope of this therapeutic exception remains undefined by the Supreme Court. However, it seems clear that any reason given for withholding information must relate to the particular patient in question, and not based on patients generally.

The Supreme Court took the view that it would be wrong to regard the decision in *Sidaway* as an unqualified endorsement of the application of the *Bolam* test to the giving of advice about treatment. It considered that only Lord Diplock adopted that position.

The Supreme Court correctly identified the problem with a professional practice test in the area of information disclosure:

> *Furthermore, because the extent to which a doctor may be inclined to discuss risks with a patient is not determined by medical learning or experience, the application of the* Bolam *test to this question is liable to result in the sanctioning of differences in practice which are attrib-utable not to divergent schools of thought in medical science, but merely to divergent attitudes among doctors as to the decree of respect owed to their patients.* (para 84)

Lady Hale held (para 115):

> *Once the argument departs from purely medical considerations and involves value judgements … it becomes clear … that the* Bolam *test, of conduct supported by a responsible body of medical opinion, becomes quite inapposite.* (para 115)

In correctly identifying and defining the fact that information disclosure to patients can and should be separated from the duty in respect of diagnosis and treatment, and in highlighting the difficulties with the application of a professional practice test in this area of the law, the Supreme Court heralded the death of *Bolam* in this area of the law:

It follows that the analysis of the law by the majority in Sidaway *is unsatisfactory, in so far as it treated the doctor's duty to advise her patient of the risks of proposed treatment as falling within the scope of the* Bolam *test, subject to two qualifications of that general principle, neither of which is fundamentally consistent with that test. It is unsurprising that courts have found difficulty in the subsequent application of* Sidaway, *and that the courts in England and Wales have in reality departed from it; a position which was effectively endorsed, particularly by Lord Steyn, in* Chester v Afshar. *There is no reason to perpetuate the application of the Bolam test in this context any longer.* (para 86)

The Supreme Court then set out the correct test to be applied and pointed clearly to the decision of the High Court of Australia in *Rogers v Whitaker*:

The correct position, in relation to the risks of injury involved in treatment, can now be seen to be substantially that adopted in Sidaway *by Lord Scarman, and by Lord Woolf MR in* Pearce, **subject to the refinement made by the High Court of Australia in Rogers v Whitaker**.

The competent patient is recognised as an autonomous person who has a right to decide which of the available forms of treatment they wish to undergo:

A doctor is therefore under a duty to take reasonable care to ensure that the patient is aware of any material risks involved in any recommended treatment, and if any reasonable alternative or variant treatments.

The court concluded that there was a duty to warn of a material risk inherent in the proposed treatment. The test of materiality is replicated from the decision in *Rogers v Whitaker*. A risk is material if, in the circumstances of the particular case, a reasonable person in the patient's position would be likely, if warned of the risk, to attach significance to it (the objective limb), or if the medical practitioner is or should reasonably be aware that the particular patient would be likely, if warned of the risk, to attach significance to it (the subjective limb).

It is important to recognise that this is a two-limbed test. The first limb of the test applies objective criteria and focuses on the requirements of a reasonable or ordinary person in the patient's position. The second subjective limb recognises that a patient may not be reasonable and allows the courts to consider the particular patient and their require-ments or fears (reasonable and unreasonable). This is subject to the caveat that the medical practitioner is or ought to be aware of those considerations. If a patient had special needs or concerns and this was known to the doctor, this would indicate that special or additional information is required.

Lord Woolf spoke of a "significant risk", whereas Lord Bridge, when describing the case he had in mind, had referred to a "substantial risk". It was considered that "significant" was the more apt adjective. It was said that Lord Bridge accepted that a risk had to be disclosed where it was "obviously necessary to an informed choice". It was recognised that the relevance of a risk to the patient's decision does not depend solely upon its magnitude, or a medical assessment of its significance.

The court recognised that the doctor's advisory role involves dialogue, the aim of which was to ensure that the patient understands the serious-ness of their condition and the anticipated benefits and risks of the proposed treatment and any reasonable alternatives, to enable the patient to make an informed decision.

The court considered that the significance attached in *Sidaway* to a patient's failure to question a doctor is profoundly unsatisfactory. There was reference to the comments of Sedley LJ in *Wyatt v Curtis* ([2003] EWCA Civ 1779), where it was said there is something unreal about placing the onus of asking on a patient who may not know there is something to ask about. It was said:

> It is indeed a reversal of logic: the more a patient knows about the risks she faces, the easier it is for her to ask specific questions about

those risks, so as to impose on her doctor a duty to provide informa-
tion; but it is those who lack such knowledge, and who are in
consequence unable to pose such questions and instead express their
anxiety in more general terms, who are in the greatest need of
information. Ironically, the ignorance which such patients seek to
have dispelled disqualifies them from obtaining the information they
desire. (Montgomery)

The Supreme Court recognised that what was proposed was a significant change and that some health care providers would not welcome
the change. In departing from the *Bolam* test, they noted that this
might reduce the predictability of the outcome of litigation. However,
they pointed out that the approach adopted had in fact been recognised
for some time by the GMC in its professional guidance to lawyers. It
was also an approach that had long been operated in other jurisdictions.
The driving force for changes was seen as the requirement of respect for
individual autonomy and dignity:

It appears to us however that a degree of unpredictability can be
tolerated as the consequence of protecting patients from exposure to
risks of injury which they would otherwise have chosen to avoid. The
more fundamental response to such points, however, is that respect for
the dignity of patients requires no less. (para 93)

6.   Comment

The Supreme Court decision in *Montgomery* now focuses the law on
information disclosure to patients and brings it in line with the guidance produced by the General Medical Council and also with many
other Commonwealth jurisdictions.

It has been said by some that the Health Board did not advance a
strong defence to the action in the Supreme Court, and did not properly advise the Supreme Court of the downside or practical difficulties
of introducing a patient-focused test. This is quite wrong. The Supreme
Court did have submissions from the Health Board on this issue, and

the claimant in her written argument set out in detail all of the arguments for and against the introduction of a patient-focused test over the years. It was considered important that if the court were to consider making such a change it must be fully advised on the change and whether it was workable in practice.

The Supreme Court also considered how the courts were applying the test in other jurisdictions. It specifically endorsed the approach set out in *Reibl v Hughes*, *Rogers v Whitaker* and *Rosenberg v Percival*. In doing so it is arguable that the Supreme Court intentionally extended the patient-centred test in consent beyond the test envisaged by Lord Woolf in *Pearce*. The application of the test found in these case is dealt with in detail in Chapter 3.

The Supreme Court specifically made reference to the approach of Lord Scarman in *Sidaway* and Lord Woolf MR in *Pearce* and then said: "subject to the refinement made by the High Court of Australia in Rogers v Whitaker". On the question of what risks are to be considered to be material, the judges endorsed the approach found in *Rogers v Whitaker* and in doing so advanced the law on information disclosure to the particular patient and embraced the two-limbed test found in *Rogers v Whitaker*.

Further the Supreme Court had detailed submissions from the GMC and had copies to all of the GMC general guidance to doctors since 1995 and specific guidance issued by the GMC on patient consent since 1998. The GMC provided submissions on its view on how patients should be consented. This is dealt with more fully later in Chapter 5.

The GMC current guidance on consent (*Consent: Patients and Doctors Making Decisions Together*) focuses on doctors working in partnership with their patients, discussing their condition and treatment options in a way that they can understand and respecting their right to make decisions about their care. It reinforces the fact that no single approach to discussions about treatment or care will suit every patient or apply in all circumstances. In essence, this guidance is rejecting a one-size-fits-all approach.

The focus is on patients making "informed decisions" and it is suggested that this description of what is to be achieved is preferable to the much-used "informed consent", described by Lord Scarman in *Sidaway* as a misnomer. The focus now is on patients making "informed decisions" about their own health care needs. Where there has been an informed decision the patient has given valid or real consent.

The GMC provides a basic model for obtaining consent which is consistent with the view of the Supreme Court in *Montgomery*. The basic model proposed by the GMC requires the doctor to identify options for treatment and then set out the potential benefits, risks, burdens and side effects of each option, including the option to have no treatment (*Consent: Patients and Doctors Making Decisions Together*, Part 1, para 5). The focus is on the particular patient, and it is the patient who makes the decision on the options given. The patient has the right to refuse an option, even if the doctor considers that it is the best option for them. Further, the GMC guidance provides a list of information that a doctor "must" give to a patient when obtaining consent (*Consent: Patients and Doctors Making Decisions Together*, Part 2, para 9).

What is found within the general guidance, and also the specific guidance of the GMC on consent, is also a useful guide for the court in assessing what the professional standard is for doctors when obtaining consent. Courts however must now take an active role in deciding factually what the options were in any given situation, and whether these options were discussed with the patient. The courts must also decide what the risks and benefits were for that patient with each option.

The courts should have regard to the written record in assessing what information was given to the patient. The GMC makes it clear in its documentation circumstances in which written consent must be obtained (*Consent: Patients and Doctors Making Decisions Together*, Part 2, paras 44–51).

In the Outer House of the Court of Session and on appeal there was focus on the nature of the risk that engaged the duty to warn. The Health Board focused on the words of Lord Bridge of Harwich, which indicated that there may be situations where the *Bolam* test would not be applied, only on this issue. What he actually said was that there were certain situations where a judge might come to the conclusion that disclosure of a particular risk was so obviously necessary to an informed choice on the part of the patient that no reasonably prudent medical man would fail to advise of it. He then gave an example of such a situation and that would be an operation involving a substantial risk of grave adverse consequences, such as the 10% risk of a stroke in the Canadian case of *Reibl v Hughes* (114 DLR (3d)).

The Health Board used these words in isolation to suggest that this would not refer to the risk of shoulder dystocia but to the risk of brain damage/cerebral palsy, as that was an example of "grave adverse consequences", whereas shoulder dystocia was not. In the Supreme Court, it was noted that it was important to note that Lord Bridge was merely giving an example to illustrate the general proposition that disclosure of a particular risk may be so obviously necessary to the informed choice of the patient that no reasonably prudent medical man would fail to make it. The Supreme Court considered that in fact Lord Bridge had arrived at a position not far distant from that of Lord Scarman:

> *The inherent instability of Lord Bridge's qualification of the Bolam test has been reflected in a tendency among some judges to construe it restrictively, as in the present case, by focusing on the particular works used by Lord Bridge when describing the kind of case he had in mind ("a substantial risk of grave adverse consequences"), and even on the particular example he gave (which involved a 10% risk of a stroke), rather than on the principle which the example was intended to illustrate.*

Some have questioned the role of experts in the new post-*Montgomery* era. Expert evidence must still be of use to the court in providing factual information on what the options for treatment were for a patient, and whether the options were reasonable options for the particular patient. This is a factual question and is not determined by the *Hunter v Hanley* or *Bolam* tests. To allow expert witnesses to decide what options should be discussed would frustrate the underlying concept of patient self-determination. Expert evidence would still be required in all but the clearest instances to establish the risks inherent in a given procedure or treatment, and the consequences of leaving the condition untreated.

Expert evidence will still be required on issues of causation. Where a privilege is claimed, expert testimony may be required to demonstrate the existence and nature of the emergency which would eliminate the need for obtaining consent and the impact on the patient.

Expert witnesses should also be able to provide statistical information on the risks and benefits of treatments and options for treatment. What they must not do is resort to any professional practice test. It is important that courts do not permit experts to tell the court which option was the correct option for the patient, since that is simply re-introducing *Hunter v Hanley/Bolam* through the back door.

Further expert evidence on what patients normally do in given situations must be treated with caution. Previous responses of patients may have been influenced by inadequate information on choices, or the nature of risks and benefits. Further, the principle of patient autonomy permits a patient to make an illogical choice.

The GMC guidance on consent also provides an answer to the issue of what happens when a patient asks questions or expresses concerns. When a patient asks a question, the GMC guidance is clear in stating that the doctor must answer the patient's questions honestly and, as far as practicable, as fully as they wish (*Consent: Patients and Doctors Making Decisions Together*, Part 2, para 12). It is not envisaged that a patient must ask a question to obtain information on options and the risks and benefits of treatment since there is an inherent duty to provide that information. Patients are to be given the information they need to make decisions about their care. Courts in Canada have considered guidance issued by manufacturers and professional colleges in making a factual assessment of risks of procedure and this appears worthy of consideration in the UK.

The Supreme Court rightly said "Why should the patient's asking a question make any difference in negligence, if medical opinion determines whether the duty of care requires the risk to be disclosed?" The exception is logically destructive of the supposed rule.

The GMC does permit a doctor to recommend an option for treatment they consider is best for the patient. It does not suggest that the doctor may decide the best option and then fail to tell the patient of other options/alternatives. In such a situation, the doctor has removed the choice of the patient. The primary duty is to advise of all reasonable options for treatment. A doctor should not pressurise a patient to accept their advice on any option (*Consent: Patients and Doctors Making Decisions Together*, Part 1, para 5 (b)).

CHAPTER FIVE
THE ROLE OF THE GENERAL
MEDICAL COUNCIL IN
MONTGOMERY

1.   Introduction

The General Medical Council (GMC) was represented in the Supreme Court by Andrew Smith QC. This section details the guidance produced by the GMC relevant to the issue of patient consent, and the submissions made by Andrew Smith QC to the Supreme Court on behalf of the GMC.

All parties to the case considered that the GMC had an important role in providing information to the court in a situation where the court was being asked to consider a new approach to the law on patient consent.

The GMC had become aware of the claimant's intention to appeal against a decision of an Extra Division of the Inner House of the Court of Session. Standing the content of that appeal, Mr Smith QC indicated that the GMC considered it might usefully contribute to the appeal by way of assistance to the court and the parties by way of intervention.

It was stated that the GMC had an interest in not only assisting the court by way of submissions but also in the outcome of the appeal insofar as it might shape future decisions taken by the GMC in both the content of its guidance and in the application of that guidance to individual cases. It was felt that GMC guidance would be helpful for a correct resolution of the issues in the case.

2.   What is the GMC?

The GMC is a body incorporated by statute (The Medical Act 1983, section 1). The GMC is a registered charity charged with regulating the profession of medical practitioners in the United Kingdom. Its stated role is to "protect, promote and maintain the health and safety of the public by making sure that doctors follow proper standards of medical practice". It seeks to achieve this by keeping up-to-date registers of qualified doctors, fostering good medical practice, promoting high standards of medical education and training, and dealing firmly and fairly with doctors whose fitness to practise is in doubt. The GMC describes its functions on its website at http://www.gmc-uk.org/about/role.asp.

All doctors practising in the United Kingdom have to be registered and licensed by the GMC (http://www.gmc-uk.org/doctors/medical_register.asp). Any doctor whose fitness to practise is in question may be subject to disciplinary proceedings at the instance of the GMC.

If it was considered that particular treatment was undertaken by a medical practitioner without the consent of the patient, or if particular treatment was carried out without the patient being made aware of the reasonable alternatives to that treatment, then this is a matter which would ordinarily lead to investigation and if appropriate disciplinary proceedings being brought against the medical practitioner in question.

2.   GMC guidance over the years – *Good Medical Practice*

Since 1995, the GMC has issued guidance entitled *Good Medical Practice*. This guidance sets out what the GMC considers to be the professional values, standards of competence and conduct expected of all registered doctors at the time of issue. It describes what makes a good doctor and can be seen as the foundation of the doctor–patient relationship.

It has been made available to doctors directly by the GMC, and is made available to doctors by reference via their professional bodies such as the

British Medical Association and the Medical Royal Colleges and by their professional indemnity organisations (the MDDUS and the MPS for example). The guidance (including historical guidance stored on an archive page) is and continues to be available on the GMC's website and is accessible to any party.

GMC guidance is updated on a regular basis. The GMC's aim is to update the general guidance whenever required by changes in the law, or where clarification is thought prudent. Historically this has been every few years. The guidance on good medical practice is supplemented by further explanatory guidance on particular issues. Doctors are expected to be familiar with both the general guidance and also the guidance issued on particular issues (http://www.gmc-uk.org/ guidance/ethical_guidance.asp).

Good Medical Practice 1995

As early as 1995 the GMC stated, in its guidance *Good Medical Practice*:

1. *Providing a good standard of care*

Patients are entitled to good standards of practice and care from their doctors. Essential elements of this are professional competence, good relationships with patients and colleagues and observance of professional and ethical obligations. (p2)

Under the heading "Professional relationship with patients" the guidance provides at p4, para 11:

Professional relationships with patients

11. Successful relationships between doctors and patients depend on trust. To establish and maintain that trust you must:

- *listen to the patients and respect their views;*

- *treat patients politely and considerately;*

- *respect patients' privacy and dignity;*

- *give patients the information they ask for or need about their condition, its treatment and prognosis;*

- *give information to patients in a way they can understand;*

- *respect the right of patients to be fully involved in decisions about their care;*

- *respect the right of patients to refuse treatment or take part in teaching or research; …*

Good Medical Practice 1998

The 1995 *Good Medical Practice* was withdrawn and reissued in 1998. The 1998 guidance was described as "Protecting patients and guiding doctors". The 1998 guidance repeated the instruction that all patients are entitled to a good standard of practice and care from their doctors. It also repeats the instruction on patient information but adds that a doctor should:

> *be satisfied that, wherever possible, the patient has understood what is proposed, and consents to it, before you provide treatment or invest-igate a patient's condition.* (p6, para 12)

Good Medical Practice 2001

In 2001 the GMC reissued *Good Medical Practice*. The 2001 guidance was described as "Regulating doctors, ensuring good medical practice". At the outset in the guidance, under "The duties of a doctor registered with the General Medical Council", there is a list of what professional standards are. Included within the list of professional standards are the following:

- *listen to patients and respect their views;*
- *give patients information in a way they can understand;*

- *respect the rights of patients to be fully involved in decisions about their care; …*

In the 2001 general guidance there is a specific section on obtaining patient consent. It provides:

17. *You must respect the right of patients to be fully involved in decisions about their care. Wherever possible, you must be satisfied, before you provide treatment or investigate a patient's condition, that the patient has understood what is proposed and why, and any significant risks or side effects associated with it, and has given consent. You must follow the guidance in our booklet Seeking Patients' Consent: Ethical Considerations.*

Under the heading of "Good communication" it is stated that good communication involves listening to patients and respecting their views and beliefs. It also requires the doctor to give patients the information they ask for or need about their condition and its treatment and prognosis in a way they can understand.

Good Medical Practice 2006

Good Medical Practice was then further updated in November 2006. This guidance set out the principles and values upon which good medical practice is to be founded. These principles were said to describe "medical professionalism" in action. The guidance is addressed to doctors but is also intended to let the public know what they can expect from doctors.

The 2006 *Good Medical Practice* provides that doctors must be prepared to explain and justify decisions and actions. The terms "you must" and "you should" are introduced to the guidance. For example:

- *"You must" is used for an overriding duty or principle,*

- *"You should" is used when the GMC is providing an explanation of how they would expect the doctor to meet the overriding duty,*

- *"You should"* is also used where the duty or principle will not apply in all situations or circumstances, or where there are factors outside the doctors control that affect whether or how they can comply with the Guidance.

This guidance provides that good clinical practice includes assessing the patient's condition and also taking account of the patient's views (para 2). There is a focus on the nature of the doctor–patient relationship, which the GMC says is based on openness, trust and good communication. This is required to enable doctors to work in partnership with their patients to address their individual needs. There is clear focus on treating the patient as an individual.

In 2006 the GMC set out clearly (para 22) that to communicate effectively a doctor *must*:

(a) *listen to patients, ask for and respect their views about their health, and respond to their concerns and preferences*

(b) *share with patients, in a way they can understand, the information they want or need to know about their condition, its likely progression, and the treatment options available to them, including associated risks and uncertainties*

(c) *respond to patients' questions and keep them informed about the progress of their care.*

On the question of patient consent, the guidance provides that doctors must be satisfied that they have consent before they undertake any examination or investigation, provide treatment or involve patients in teaching or research. The general guidance also referred to the specific guidance in *Seeking Patients' Consent: The Ethical Considerations*.

Good Medical Practice 2013

On 25 March 2013, the GMC again updated *Good Medical Practice*, the new version coming into effect on 22 April 2013. The terms "you must" and "you should" continue to be used. In this guidance, the GMC focuses on the patient as an individual and the fact that the doctor must give patients the information they want or need to know in a way they can understand. This guidance states that a doctor should make sure that arrangements are made, wherever possible, to meet a patient's language and communication needs.

The focus is on establishing and maintaining partnerships with patients. It is suggested to that to achieve such a relationship doctors "must" treat patients as individuals and "must work in partnership with patients, sharing with them the information they will need to make decisions about their care" (para 49). The information that patients need to have is information on their condition, likely progression and the options for treatment, including associated risks and uncertainties.

4. Specific GMC guidance on consent

Seeking Patients' Consent: The Ethical Considerations 1998

In addition to _Good Medical Practice_, specific and more detailed explanatory guidance was issued by the GMC relating to the obtaining of consent for treatment. The first such guidance was issued in November 1998, and this was reissued in 2008 to reflect changes in the law and professional and public expectations about standards of good practice. The 2008 version remains the current standard on consent.

The GMC is currently reviewing its consent guidance. As part of the review it has consulted patients, a process that closed on 19 March 2017. The GMC is expected to launch a public consultation in March 2018.

The 1998 guidance was entitled _Seeking Patients' Consent: The Ethical Considerations_. The introduction to the 1998 guidance provides that doctors must respect patient autonomy and a patient's right to decide whether or not to undergo any medical intervention, even where a refusal may result in harm or even death. Patients must be given sufficient information, in a way that they can understand, to enable them to exercise their right to make informed decisions about their care (para 1).

The guidance goes on to provide as follows:

> *Effective communication is the key to enabling patients to make informed decisions. You must take appropriate steps to find out what patients want to know and ought to know about their condition and treatment. Open, helpful dialogue of this kind with patients leads to clarity of objectives and understanding, and strengthens the quality of the doctor/patient relationship. It provides an agreed framework within which the doctor can respond effectively to the individual needs of the patient. Additionally, patients who have been able to make properly informed decisions are more likely to co-operate fully with the agreed management of their conditions.* (para 3)

The GMC recognises in its 1998 guidance that, whilst patients have a right to information about their condition and the treatment options available to them, the amount of information each patient will be given will vary. Relevant factors are said to be factors such as the nature of the condition, the complexity of the treatment, the risks associated with the treatment or procedure and the patient's own wishes. It is said that patients may need more information to make an informed decision about a procedure which carries a high risk of failure or adverse side effects, or about an investigations for a condition which, if present, could have serious implications for the patient's employment, social or personal life (para 4).

The 1998 guidance explains that the information which patients might want or ought to know, before deciding whether to consent to a treatment or investigation, may include:

- details of the diagnosis, and prognosis, and the likely prognosis if the condition is left untreated;

- uncertainties about the diagnosis including options for further investigation prior to treatment;

- options for treatment or management of the condition, including the option not to treat.

For each option, there should be an explanation of the likely benefits and the probabilities of success. There should be a discussion about any serious or frequently occurring risks, and of any lifestyle changes which may be caused by, or necessitated by, the treatment (para 5). Doctors are advised that when providing information they must do their best to find out about a patient's individual needs and priorities. It points out that a patient's beliefs, culture, occupation or other factors may have a bearing on the information a patient may need in order to reach a decision. Doctors should not make assumptions about a patient's views but discuss matters with them and ask them whether they have any concerns about the treatment or the risks it may involve. Doctors should ask patients if they have understood the information given and whether they would like more before making a decision.

As early as 1998 the explanatory guidance provided:

> You (the doctor) should provide patients with appropriate information, which should include an explanation of any risks **to which they may attach particular significance**.

On the issue of responding to patient questions, the GMC states that a doctor must respond honestly to any questions the patient raises and, as far as possible, answer as fully as the patient wishes. It noted that some patients may want to know whether any of the risks or benefits of treatment are affected by the choice of institution or doctor providing the care.

On the question of withholding information, the GMC directed that a doctor should not withhold information necessary for decision-making unless the doctor considers that disclosure of some relevant information would cause the patient serious harm. In this context, serious harm does not mean the patient would become upset or decide to refuse treatment. If a decision is made to withhold relevant information from the patient, this must be recorded in the patient's medical records and the doctor must be prepared to explain and justify the decision.

The focus of the 1998 consent guidance is on consent not being an isolated event. Consent requires a continuing dialogue between the doctors and patients that keeps them abreast of changes in their condition. The guidance advises that doctors should give clear explanations where possible and should explain the probabilities of success, or the risk of failure of or harm associated with options for treatment, using accurate data. There is also guidance for patients who have special language or other communication needs.

In the 1998 guidance there is an emphasis on "Ensuring voluntary decision making". It is for the legally competent patient, not the doctor, to determine what is in the patient's own best interests. Doctors may wish to recommend a treatment or course of action to patients, but they should not put pressure on patients to accept the advice. Where there are options the expectation is that doctors will give a balanced view of the options.

Consent: Patients and Doctors Making Decisions Together 2008

On 2 June 2008, the GMC updated its consent guidance and produced a new, updated edition entitled *Consent: Patients and Doctors Making Decisions Together*, which replaced the 1998 *Seeking Patients' Consent: The Ethical Considerations*. It also expands on the guidance in *Good Medical Practice*. This is the current edition at the time of writing this book, although as previously stated the GMC is in the process of producing updated guidance.

In deciding how much information to share with patients, doctors should take account of the patients' wishes. The information shared should be in proportion to the nature of their condition, the complexity of the proposed investigation of treatment, and the seriousness of any potential side effects, complications or other risks. The same duties are incumbent upon doctors. They are required to share with patients the information they want or need in order to make decisions, and to discuss with patients their diagnosis, prognosis and treatment.

However, this guidance also provides that doctors should maximise patients' opportunities, and abilities, to make decisions for themselves (para 2).

The 2008 guidance provides a basic model to be applied with patients who have capacity to make decisions for themselves:

(a) *The doctor and patient make an assessment of the patient's condition, taking into account the patient's medical history, views, experience and knowledge.*

(b) *The doctor uses specialist knowledge and experience and clinical judgement, and the patient's views and understanding of their condition, to identify which investigations or treatments are likely to result in overall benefit for the patient. The doctor explains the options to the patient, setting out the potential benefits, risks, burdens and side effects of each option, including the option to have no treatment. The doctor may recommend a particular option which they believe to be best for the patient, but they must not put pressure on the patient to accept their advice.*

(c) *The patient weighs up the potential benefits, risks and burdens of the various options as well as any non-clinical issues that are relevant to them. The patient decides whether to accept any of the options and, if so which one. They also have the right to accept or refuse an option for a reason that may seem irrational to the doctor, or for no reason at all.*

(d) *If the patient asks for a treatment that the doctor considers would not be of overall benefit to them, the doctor should discuss the issues with the patient and explore the reasons for their request. If, after discussion, the doctor still considers that the treatment would not be of overall benefit to the patient, they do not have to provide the treatment. But they should explain their reasons to the patient, and explain any other options that are available, including the option of seeking a second opinion.* (para 5)

It is recognised in this guidance that how much information is shared with patients will vary according to individual circumstances. The 2008 guidance provides that the approach to discussion with patients should be tailored according to the needs, wishes and priorities of the patient; their level of knowledge about, and understanding of, their condition, prognosis and treatment options; the nature of their condition; the complexity of the treatment; and the nature and level of risk associated with the investigation or treatment (para 8).

In the 2008 guidance a list is provided of information that patients want or need about diagnosis and prognosis; the uncertainties about the diagnosis or prognosis, including options for further investigations; the options for treating or managing the condition, including the option not to treat; the purpose of any proposed investigation or treatment and what it will involve; the potential benefits, risks and burdens, and the likelihood of success, for each option (this should include information, if available, about whether the benefits or risks are affected by which organisation or doctor is chosen to provide care) (para 9).

On the question of discussing side effects, complications and other risks, the 2008 guidance provides as follows:

28. Clear, accurate information about the risks of any proposed investigation or treatment, presented in a way patients can under-stand, can help them make informed decisions. The amount of information about risk that you should share with patients will depend on the individual patient and what they want or need to know. Your discussions with patients should focus on their individual situation and the risk to them.

29. In order to have effective discussions with patients about risk, you must identify the adverse outcomes that may result from the proposed options. This includes the potential outcome of taking no action. Risks can take a number of forms, but will usually be:

(a) side effects

(b) complications

(c) failure of an intervention to achieve the desired aim

Risks can vary from common but minor side effects, to rare but serious adverse outcomes possibly resulting in permanent disability or death.

30. In assessing the risk to an individual patient, you must consider the nature of the patient's condition, their general health and other circumstances. These are variable factors that may affect the likelihood of adverse outcomes occurring.

31. You should do your best to understand the patient's views and preferences about any proposed investigation or treatment, and the adverse outcomes they are most concerned about. You must not make assumptions about a patient's understanding of risk or the importance they attach to different outcomes. You should discuss these issues with your patient.

32. You must tell patients if an investigation or treatment might result in a serious adverse outcome, even if the likelihood is very small. You should also tell patients about less serious side effects or complications if they occur frequently, and explain what the patient should do if they experience any of them.

The 2008 guidance attempts to define "adverse outcome". This is described as an adverse outcome resulting in death, permanent or long-term physical disability of disfigurement, medium- or long-term pain, admission to hospital, or other outcomes with long-term or permanent effect of a patient's employment, social or personal life.

5.   The purpose of guidance issued by the GMC

In *Montgomery*, the GMC submitted to the court that the guidance was envisaged to set standards for practice to which all registered doctors were expected to adhere. The guidance was described as a professional code that is binding on doctors, even though the guidance is not strictly "binding". It is not a statutory code, nor is it a set of rules. There is no automatic link between breach of the guidance and action against a doctor in respect of registration. However, the guidance does carry significant weight and serious or persistent departures from the description of good practice set out in the guidance will put a doctor's registration at risk.

The GMC submitted to the court that doctors are expected to be familiar with and follow the guidance, and to use their judgement about how to apply the principles to the particular situations they face in practice. The use of the words "must" and "should" within the guidance allows, subject to the particular part of the guidance being considered, some flexibility to the doctor. A departure from the guidance means that a doctor must be prepared to justify the actions taken in the context of the standards set out in the guidance.

The standards set by the GMC are developed through extensive consultation in order to ensure that they reflect current expectations of the public and the profession, the currently understood law in the UK jurisdictions, and other relevant factors such as practical constraints within health and care services. It was said that the GMC is conscious that doctors may have to contend with a number of different obligations or challenges in the particular circumstances of their area of practice, and that these might impact on their ability to comply with the principles and standards set out in GMC guidance.

The guidance addresses this in two ways. The GMC will indicate where the expected standard is a "must" (an overriding duty or principle) or a "should" (where the duty or principle will not apply in all situations or circumstances, or where there are factors outside the doctor's control that affect whether or how they can follow the guidance). It places an obligation on doctors to raise concerns about problems with local systems, policies or practices that impact on their ability to adhere to GMC guidance. The example given related to time constraints. If time or resource constraints are likely to create obstacles to providing adequate information and support to patients to make decisions about treatment, steps must be taken to address this. This is consistent with doctors' legal obligations to take steps to provide information and support to patients to empower them to act as partners in decisions about their treatment and care.

It was explained that the guidance is drawn up by reference to a number of sources of evidence and information. As a UK-wide regulatory body, the GMC must ensure that its guidance takes account of not only the legal framework but also the views of its key interest groups. These include patients and the public, the medical profession, the NHS and other health care providers, medical schools and postgraduate education providers. It uses a range of engagement and consultation techniques to reach a wide audience and help identify what might be considered common ground between the profession and public about how the ethical, legal and practical considerations in health care should shape doctors' practice. The guidance development process involves a formal consultation period where draft guidance is sent to interested bodies and parties and published on the GMC website for comment and feed-back. It would be normal to involve the various Royal Colleges, patients' interest groups, NHS organisations, the BMA and defence bodies to consider proposals.

The GMC also submitted to the court that it was important to ensure, where possible, that the guidance was consistent with related guidance issue by other regulatory bodies such as the Nursing and Midwifery Council and the Medicines and Healthcare Products Regulatory Authority. They are often directly invited to contribute their views on proposed guidance.

It was explained to the court that the GMC saw a benefit to patients, as well as to doctors and those working with them in multidisciplinary teams, in achieving a degree of consistency in the standards set by regu-lators, service providers and professional bodies. The view of the GMC is that this helps to create shared understanding and clarity for everyone involved in a patient's care. Other organisations share this view. The GMC has contributed to development of the consent guidance issued by the Department of Health England, MDU, the Royal College of

Anaesthetists, and the Mental Welfare Commission (Scotland).

It was submitted that, following the consultation process, the final draft guidance will then be submitted to leading counsel to consider whether it is consistent with current law with particular reference to any statutory reference points (for example statutory obligations which regulate mental health issues) and the common law. The guidance is expressed in plain English and does not purport to be a statement or summary of the law, even where it is reflecting relevant legal requirements.

The aim is to ensure that where doctors are following GMC guidance they are also acting lawfully. The GMC routinely provides references to legal authority and summaries of the decisions of the courts in annexes to guidance, while also making clear that doctors are expected to consult their legal advisers on points of law and the law as it applies to individual cases. Such an approach permits a doctor, their advisers or any other party to appreciate the legal sources of the guidance. Doctors may, and regularly do, contact the GMC to seek advice on a proposed course of conduct or an issue in practice which they feel may not have an easy solution.

It was explained to the court that the guidance of the GMC on consent is grounded in and reflects expectations in the UK, but the underpinning principles are informed by a wider body of opinion. In addition to reflecting the position in the UK, the GMC said that it was conscious that in setting standards some aspects of professional practice may benefit from consideration of the regulatory and professional expectations established in other parts of the world. For example, the approach to patient consent in other jurisdictions, and the underpinning rationale, may support the position in the UK or provide fresh arguments and insights that suggest that a different approach may better serve the interests of patients.

It was pointed out that this approach to standard setting is widely followed in other countries. The American Medical Association and the Medical Board of Australia have adopted their own versions of *Good Medical Practice*. The Council of Europe recently published guidelines for end of life decisions drawing on related guidance from the GMC. This reflects the increasing interest in establishing a level of consistency about expected standards of practice that does not rest solely on doctors' own views about what may serve the interests of patients. That said, any doctor who practises in the United Kingdom is expected to inform themselves of the guidance referred to above, and any relevant guidance from the Colleges and employers.

6. The GMC view on patient consent

In *Montgomery*, the court was told that the GMC considered respect for a patient's autonomy to be an important principle at the heart of professional practice. This respect to underpinned professional duties and responsibilities in relation to obtaining consent to treatment, as well as consent to sharing confidential information.

It was explained to the court that the GMC's view was that doctors must respect a patient's rights to self-determination as long as they have capacity to make decisions for themselves. Fundamental to the doctor–patient relationship is the requirement that a patient with capacity to decide must be informed about treatment options open to them and be allowed to make a choice about those treatments. The GMC's position is that, although guidance has become more specific over the years, as far as how discussions with patients should be approached, and what information it may be necessary or appropriate to provide, the principle has not changed over a number of decades.

The GMC view is that by its very nature consent must be "informed". Whilst it may be suggested that there has been a move away from "paternalism", which the GMC understands to be a situation where the doctor made the decision for the patient, the GMC view is that such an approach has never been justified. Their view is that where a patient has capacity they are entitled to be informed of all clinically appropriate treatment options open, including all material risks and burdens associated with those procedures, in order that the patient may make a choice.

The GMC also explained to the court that although there had been changes over the years, with specific guidance being issued to reflect particular medical developments, none of the changes had called into question the fundamental principle of respect for patient autonomy. The view of the GMC was that that principle, inexorably bound with the right to information and the right to make a choice, is the principle which must remain constant. It was emphasised that current consent guidance makes it clear that the decisions are reached in partnership with the patient and not by the doctor alone.

The GMC view was that with reference to the *Montgomery* case there has been no change between 1999 to the present time in the expectation of doctors in respect of the patient's right to decide on a particular treatment, or to decline a particular treatment.

Mr Smith QC referred to the fact that in 1981 the World Medical Association promulgated the Declaration of Lisbon. That declaration includes the following statement:

Right to self-determination

a. A patient has the right to self-determination, to make free decisions regarding himself or herself. The physician will inform the patient of the consequences of his/her decision.

b. A mentally competent adult patient has the right to give or withhold consent to any diagnostic procedure or therapy. The patient has the right to the information necessary to make his/her decisions. The patient should understand clearly what is the purpose of any test or treatment, what the results would imply, and what would be the implications of withholding consent.

He also referred to the Oviedo Convention, to which the UK is a signatory. He quoted from the convention as follows:

Article 4 – Professional standards. Any intervention in the health field, including research, must be carried out in accordance with relevant professional obligations and standards.

Chapter II – Consent

Article 5 – General rule. An intervention in the health field may only be carried out after the person concerned has given free and informed consent to it. This person shall beforehand be given appropriate information as to the purpose and nature of the intervention as well as on its consequences and risks. The person concerned may *freely withdraw consent at any time.*

7. The GMC position on advice on risks

In the Supreme Court the GMC acknowledged that it was impractical for a patient to be advised of every conceivable risk that could ever arise from particular treatment. Some risks are of such a minor nature, in both how likely they may arise and on how minor the adverse consequences might be, that a doctor might reasonably conclude that the patient would not require to be advised.

The GMC's position was that the information a patient requires is based upon it being patient-centred, and thereby there is a shared decision-making process between the doctor and the patient. That can only be fulfilled by doctors exploring with patients their needs and expectations. The GMC view was this it should not be a passive approach by the doctor, responding to specific requests. The obligation is upon doctors to create the opportunity for dialogue.

The GMC stated that there are no distinguishing features involved in obtaining consent to treatment (or indeed lack of it) in an obstetric context, as compared to other medical procedures. Appropriate inform-ation on treatment choices must be provided to the patient. Their view was that the care "journey" involves the following components (which are clearly defined in the guidance):

(a) dialogue with the patient;

(b) discussion with the patient of the options for treatment;

(c) explanation of the risks arising from each option;

(d) ensuring that those discussions are not actively avoided; and

(e) planning ahead, to reduce the risk of decisions being taken in circumstances of urgency.

With reference to Mrs Montgomery's case, the GMC position was that if the risk of catastrophic injury was present, even at a low level of possibility, the GMC guidance at the relevant time required this to be discussed with the patient. They stated that, although a distinction appears to have been drawn by the parties as to whether an "expression of concern" is different to an inquiry about treatment, the GMC's position is that the obligation to discuss all treatment options arises automatically and without either an "expression of concern" or a specific question from the patient to the doctor. Attention was drawn to the terms of the guidance on risk, which was as follows:

> *Your discussions with patients should focus on their individual situation and the risk to them.*

The guidance makes clear that "planning ahead" should take place, in an attempt to anticipate risks and avoid decisions being taken in circumstances where the patient is distressed.

The GMC was also clear in its submissions that the obligation to inform patients about options for treatment and the risks from that treatment is not a single point in time or a "snapshot". It is an ongoing process. This is particularly so in long-term illness cases, or in obstetric cases. In the obstetric case a prospective mother may have developing needs and expectations during her pregnancy, and changes in circumstances may arise suddenly and acutely during labour. On this basis, the GMC acknowledged that it was important that those expectations and changes were kept under constant review. Where differing treatments are open to a patient, or the respective risks of one against the other (such as vaginal birth as opposed to caesarean section), these options ought to be discussed with the patient.

Guidance issued by the GMC occasionally requires clarification as to how it applies in a practical sense. Doctors are at liberty – and often do – contact the GMC directly for guidance on particular issues which are unclear to them. Such contact not only allows for the GMC to provide guidance but allows the GMC to become aware of the particular issues that are arising in practice. Doctors in doubt also have open to them the ability to seek advice from their professional bodies, defence organisations, employers or indeed colleagues.

In summary, the GMC position to the court was that the principle of consent is seen as so fundamental to the relationship between the patient and doctor that it must be at the forefront of every doctor's mind in their professional conduct. A failure to comply with the GMC's guidance may be viewed seriously by the GMC in the event of its coming to its notice.

8.   Comment

The position of the GMC was central to the issues the Supreme Court had to address in *Montgomery*. There have been many criticisms of the Supreme Court's decision. For example, it has been suggested the decision was "retrospective", that it was a decision of lawyers who were ignorant of the realities of medical practice, and that the law was changed by those who had never been at the coalface and they have now removed standard advice. It has been said a patient-focused test is unworkable in practice owing to time constraints and that the Supreme Court judges did not understand the practical difficulties for doctors in a multi-ethnic NHS.

It has also been said that it is not possible to communicate effectively with patients about issues of medicine, as they may be too complex for the ordinary person to understand. Some have even suggested that the test forces patients to have information they do not wish to have, and this may cause them further distress.

It has also been suggested that, unlike *Bolam* and *Sidaway*, where you call a colleague or check a book, having the test means there is a "loss standardisation". The reformulation, with its focus on the patient's position, has deprived doctors of the safety net of doing as others would do. There is no longer an "off the peg" consent in each case but rather a requirement for "bespoke" tailoring. There will be increased confusion, and more legal cases owing to uncertainty as there is no guidance how the test should be applied.

What the detractors appeared to have missed is that the Supreme Court simply endorsed and accepted the view of proper professional practice promulgated by the GMC since 1995. There never was standardisation with the *Bolam* approach and there now is as a result of the combination of the decision in *Montgomery* and the GMC guidance. Where doctors are unsure about their position they can take advice from their professional body or their defence union.

The GMC has always recognised the rights of the individual patient. There is no "new test". There is extensive guidance for doctors and it has been there since 1995. The guidance has been carefully thought through and revised, reviewed and discussed widely. The Supreme Court had access to all of the GMC guidance when considering the issue, and the benefit of submissions on behalf of the GMC on what they considered the correct approach should be. This was not a case of lawyers devising a test for doctors. This was the Supreme Court listening to the GMC on what it considered appropriate professional practice should be. It considers that the guidance is workable in our multi-ethnic society.

As early as October 1995 the GMC was advising doctors that they should give patients the information they either asked for or needed about their condition, its treatment and prognosis. There was recognition that doctors should respect the rights of their patients to be fully involved in decisions about their care. This is in terms of a professional standard which they describe at the outset as "basic principles of good practice". The general guidance developed over the years, but at its core was the right of respect for patient autonomy and the patient's right to self-determination.

The previous law as interpreted was out of step with proper professional practice as promulgated by the GMC. It was also out of step with many other common-law jurisdictions, which had accepted a patient-orientated test of information disclosure into their legal systems and appeared to be able to operate the principles in practice.

Sidaway permitted doctors who ignored the views of the GMC on consent to hide behind the cloak of the *Hunter v Hanley/Bolam* test should an action proceed to court. The tests derived from *Sidaway* were in fact tests devised entirely by judges without reference to the medical profession, unlike the test in *Montgomery*, where the court had the advantage of submissions from the GMC, and access to all of the GMC professional guidance to doctors.

Under the *Sidaway* test, a doctor who did not engage with the patient and provide information on alternatives and the risks and benefits of alternatives could be in direct contravention of the professional guidance issued by the GMC, yet be protected from any delictual/tortious liability should any action proceed to court. The doctor could be found by a court to have failed to provide a patient with options for treatment, and failed to provide information on the risks and benefits of the options for treatment. As a result of the *Sidaway* decision that doctor could be found in a court not to be professionally negligent, because others also failed to properly consent patients in terms of the GMC guidance.

Sam was born in October 1999. The general GMC guidance in force at that time was *Good Medical Practice 1998*. As already discussed, at that time there was also specific guidance for doctors on consent in *Seeking Patients' Consent: The Ethical Considerations* 1998. The guidance in force at the time of Sam's birth, and which Dr McLellan had a professional duty to follow, clearly provides that patients need to be advised of the options for treatment. For each option, there should be an explanation of the likely benefits and the probabilities of success.

The GMC guidance in force at the time Sam was born provides that patients should be given sufficient information to enable them to exercise their right to make informed decision about their care. Doctors were also advised that they must take appropriate steps to find out what patients want to know and ought to know about their condition and treatment. There should be a discussion about any serious or frequently occurring risks. In providing information, doctors must do their best to find out about their patients' individual needs and priorities. There is no suggestion in any GMC guidance that it would be acceptable and ethical clinical practice for a body of doctors deciding not to consent patients in this way this would be acceptable.

Most of the answers to the questions lawyers identify as raised by the *Montgomery* decision can be found in GMC guidance. The GMC guidance effectively provides a clear guide for doctors on how to apply a patient-focused test on consent as recommended in *Montgomery*. The guidance is also useful for lawyers who wish to apply the *Montgomery* principles in their cases. The guidance which would apply would be the guidance in force at the relevant time. The GMC also provides advice to doctors on how the professional guidance should be applied, which is surely preferable to the "phone a friend" approach of the past.

Contrary to the suggestions made by some *Montgomery* is not retrospective. It permits the use of a standard which has been applicable since 1995, a standard that doctors should have been aware of and should have applied in their practice. It is retrospective in the sense that lawyers can now look at previous cases in the context of the GMC guidance at the relevant time. However, it does not enforce a standard that was not promulgated at the time. It should not be a surprise for any clinician that a registered clinician should have been complying with GMC guidance on good professional practice. The fact they either chose to ignore it or were ignorant of it should be no defence.

Obtaining patient consent is not limited to "medical procedures". The GMC is clear in stating that patient consent must be obtained before a doctor undertakes *any* examination or investigation or provides any treatment. What is clear is that the GMC does not suggest that patient consent is unnecessary for minor procedures or non-invasive procedures. There is no such restriction on obtaining consent.

In 2003 Sir Liam Donaldson, the chief medical officer, said:

The patient who is armed with information, who wants to ask questions, sometimes difficult and awkward questions, should be seen as an asset in the process of care and not an impediment to it.

CHAPTER SIX
CAUSATION IN CONSENT CASES

1. Introduction

A claimant in a medical negligence claim needs to prove that the breach of duty was causative of harm. It has been said that causation is a complex, contextually variable concept in law (*United States v Oberhellmann* (946 F 2d 50) (7th Cir. 1991)).

In *R v Kennedy* ([2007] UKHL 38) Lord Bingham said that questions of causation frequently arise in many areas of the law, but causation is not a single, unvarying concept to be mechanically applied without regard to the context in which the question arises. Questions of causation are not answered in a legal vacuum but within the legal framework in which they arise (*Chappel v Hart* [1998] H.C.A. 55).

The primary question is one of fact: did the wrongful act or omission cause or materially contribute to the injury (*Wilsher v Essex Area Health Authority* [1988] A.C. 1074)? In answering this question the court must consider questions of historical and hypothetical fact. The burden of proof rests with the claimant, and the standard of proof is the balance of probabilities. The test is referred to as the "but-for" test, the "what if" test or the "counterfactual conditional". The legal burden of proof is not an insubstantial burden and in some medical contexts has been described as Herculean. It has been characterised as "the most formidable obstacle confronting health care consumers" (Russell, "Establishing Medical Negligence-A Herculean Task?" (1998) 3 SLT 17).

The concept is well illustrated in *Barnett v Chelsea and Kensington Hospital Management Committee* ([1969] Q.B. 428), where a casualty officer refused to review a patient who, shortly afterwards, died of arsenic poisoning. Although it was negligent to fail to review him, the failure was not causative of death as the claimant would have died in any event as there was no suitable treatment that could have been given.

The doctrine of material contribution has been recently developed in a number of medical cases but emanated from decisions in the 1950s and 1970s (*Bonnington Castings Ltd v Wardlaw* ([1956] AC 613); *McGhee v National Coal Board* ([1973] 1 W.L.R. 1)). The issue of material contribution was considered in the context of a clinical negligence case in *Wilsher v Essex Area Health Authority* ([1987] Q.B. 730) and *Bailey v Ministry of Defence* ([2008] EWCA Civ 883), where it was said that in a case where medical science could not establish the probability that "but for" an act of negligence the injury would not have happened, but *could* establish that the contribution of the negligent cause was more than negligible, the "but-for" test is modified and the claimant will succeed (see also *Williams v Bermuda Hospitals Board* [2016] UKPC 4; *Tahir v Haringey Health Authority* (1998) Lloyd's Rep.Med. 104; *Popple v Birmingham Women's NHS Foundation Trust* [2013] LS Law Med 47; *Telles v South West Strategic Health Authority* [2008] EWHC 292 (QB); *Ingram v Williams* [2010] EWHC 758).

A claimant in a medical case cannot succeed on the basis of a "loss of a chance" (*Hotson v East Berkshire Area Health Authority* ([1987] A.C. 750). It has been argued that it would be appropriate to apply a proportionate recovery approach in cases where it cannot be held that on the balance of probabilities there would have been a difference in outcome. The court would reflect the reduction in favourable outcome in the measure of damages recoverable. This approach was rejected by the House of Lords in *Gregg v Scott* ([2005] UKHL 2). It was felt that a robust test which produces rough justice might be a preferable test to a test that on occasion would be difficult if not impossible to apply.

In a case of negligence based on a failure to consent, the patient who complains of the breach of duty to inform must demonstrate on the balance of probability that the damage complained of was caused, or materially contributed to, by the information failure. It is arguable that the claimant in a failure to consent case is presented with a particular dilemma in relation to issues of causation. The court is asked to resolve hypothetical questions of fact. After making a finding on what advice was actually given, the judge must make a finding on what information should have been given to the patient. The judge then has to assess what would have occurred had the appropriate information been given at the time. Invoking traditional common-law principles on causation does not easily resolve the issues raised. The questions of hypothetical fact must be proved by the claimant, and given that the issues are hypothetical they require to be proved by inference.

The causal connection between the breach and the damage may be displaced where it can be shown that the occurrence of the damage was purely coincidental, or that the damage was inevitable and would have occurred without the breach, or that the event was ineffective as a cause of the damage.

There has been a recognition by the courts that in certain situations issues of causation in consent cases require to be considered in a different way. In *Chester v Afshar* ([2004] UKHL 41), traditional causation rules were relaxed to allow a claimant to succeed where disclosure would have affected the decision, even if the claimant would ultimately have given consent to the procedure at a later date.

In *Chester*, the majority adopted a liberal version of autonomy relying primarily on the work of Professor Dworkin. It was acknowledged that the purpose of the rule requiring doctors to give information is to enable the patient to exercise their right to choose. The patient decides whether to run the risk of having the procedure. If the effect of a failure by the doctor is that a patient consents to a procedure that they would not have consented to if fully advised, the purpose of the rule is thwarted if the doctor is not held responsible if that very risk material-ises.

In *Montgomery*, the claimant failed at first instance and on appeal on the issue of causation. The Supreme Court overturned the findings of the trial judge and accepted that, if properly warned, Mrs Montgomery would have proceeded with an elective caesarean section and in that situation Sam would have been uninjured. The claimant advanced detailed arguments on the nature of the test to be applied when considering issues of causation in consent cases, and also advocated that there should be a transfer of the burden of proof in such cases to the defender/defendant. The Supreme Court ultimately did not need to consider these issues and they remain to be argued at some later date. It is arguable that in the decision the Supreme Court did endorse the use of a mixed subjective/objective approach to causation in consent cases.

2.   Approaches to causation

Common-law courts have applied different tests of causation in consent cases. There are three potential ways to approach the causation question in a consent case. The first approach involves a purely subjective judgement, that is, what would the particular patient have done had they been given the information? If the test is subjective, the danger is that it may merely become a case of *ex post facto* assertion. It has been said that the subjective standard has a gross defect in that it depends on the plaintiff's testimony as to their state of mind, thereby exposing the physician to the patient's hindsight and bitterness. (*"Informed Consent-A Proposed Standard for Medical Disclosure"* (1973), 48 N.Y.U.L. Rev. 548). The test puts a premium on hindsight, even more of a premium than would be put on medical evidence in assessing causation by an objective standard.

In *Chatterton v Gerson* ([1981] Q.B.432) the court adopted a subjective approach to causation and did not accept the claim. In *Hills v Potter* ([1983] 3 All E.R. 716) it was said that the claimant's action would have failed whether the test was subjective or objective.

In *Chappel v Hart* ([1998] H.C.A. 55.) the subjective test for causation, which had been accepted for some time in the Australian courts, was endorsed as the appropriate test to apply. The court unanimously endorsed a "common sense" approach to causation as set out in *March v E & M H Stramare Pty Ltd* ((1991) 171 CLR 506). However, the court was split 3–2 on whether, applying this "common sense" test, causation was in fact established. The court delivered five separate judgements with differing views and individual reasoning.

In *Chappel* the claimant underwent surgery on her throat to remove a pouch of skin from her oesophagus. The pouch caught food occasionally when she was eating and caused problems swallowing. The claimant asked about the risks associated with the procedure and at one stage said she didn't want to end up like Neville Wran, a premier of New South Wales who had damaged vocal cords following a severe infection. It was assumed from her statement that she was referring to vocal damage. The claimant was warned about the possibility of perforation of the oesophagus but was not warned of the risk of vocal damage. A perforation occurred and she suffered from a rare complication which damaged her vocal cords and affected her voice.

In the court action, she claimed that had she been aware of the risk she would have sought a second opinion and had the operation in the hands of a more experienced surgeon at a later date. She did not suggest that she would not have had the surgery. The trial judge awarded damages and Dr Chappel's appeal was dismissed. Dr Chappel then appealed to the High Court. It was accepted that he had breached his duty in failing to warn the claimant of the potential for damage to her vocal cords. This was found to be a "material risk" she should have been warned of. Dr Chappel claimed that he did not cause the damage since the claimant would have had the operation in any event at a later date and that operation would have carried the same risk of injury. She had not lost a real chance of the risk being diminished or avoided and the injury was a random risk she had been prepared to accept. It was held that the failure to warn was the cause of damage. Emphasis was placed on the fact that the risk she should have been warned about was the risk that materialised. The minority view was that Dr Chappel had not increased the risk the claimant was exposed to.

In *Chappel v Hart* the High Court considered whether causation could be established by deferral of treatment rather than cancellation of treatment. This has some similarity with the argument advanced in the UK in *Chester v Afshar*. In *Chappel v Hart*, Gaudron and Kirby JJ attached importance to the fact that deferral of the procedure would have reduced the likelihood of the risk occurring.

In considering the subjective approach, it has been said that the subjective criterion involves the danger of the malleability of the recollection of even an upright witness. Once the event has occurred, it would be rare once litigation is commenced that a patient would not be persuaded in their own mind that the failure to warn had significant consequences for undertaking the medical procedure at all. Where a subjective test is combined with onerous disclosure obligations it could be said to put a claimant in a particularly advantageous position.

In Australia, under common law the degree of faith a patient has in a doctor has been held in a number of cases to be a relevant consideration in questions of causation. The logic is that the more trust the patient has in the doctor the more likely the patient would be to follow the doctor's advice even if they are told of risks.

In *Hribar v Wells* ((1995) 64 SASR 129) it was argued that the claimant's past medical history indicated that she did what doctors or surgeons told her to do without question and this would support the argument that she would have had the operation whatever warnings were given. The court rejected this argument, attaching significant weight to the claimant's own evidence. This was followed in *Mazurkiewicz v Scott* ((1996) 16 SR (WA) 162). However, in *Johnston v Biggs* ([2000] NSWCA 338) the New South Wales Court of Appeal agreed with the trial judge in finding that the fact the claimant had undergone various invasive surgical procedures in the course of investigation was relevant.

In Canada, there were a number of cases where patients are described as likely to follow the advice of their doctor in favour of treatment even if properly advised of risks (*Robinson v Taves* [2002] B.C.J. No. 2384 (S.C.) (Q.L.)). In *Meyer Estate v Rogers* ((1991) 78 D.L.R. (4th) 307 (Ont.Ct.-Gen.Div)) it was said that, human nature being what it is, people tend to consent to procedures recommended by their doctors.

In Australia, in *Alirezai v Smith* ([2001] NSWCA 60) it was considered relevant that the patient had received warning of risks in spinal surgery on two previous occasions and proceeded to surgery without a problem developing. It was thought unlikely, even if the warning had been given, that the claimant would have declined the operation, because a similar warning had been given previously and the claimant had proceeded. In this case the patient also had great faith in the doctor and in fact had travelled from Brisbane to Sidney to see the doctor.

In *Bridges v Pelly* ([2001] NSWCA 31) the New South Wales Court of Appeal attached significance to the fact that the claimant proceeded with cosmetic surgery at a later date despite being warned of a risk of nerve damage.

There have been similar cases in Canada where patients had previously undergone treatment which involved greater disclosed risk (*Baksh-White v Cochen* [2001] O.J. No. 3397 (Sup.Ct.Jus) (Q.L.); *Finlay v Holmes* [1998] O.J. No. 2796 (C.A. (Q.L.)); *Thibault v Fewer* [2001] M.J. No.382 (Q.B.) (Q.L.)).

In Canada, there have also been causation cases which focus on aspects of the claimant's life to justify an argument that they would have proceeded with the treatment even if warned of the risks. Factors such smoking cigarettes or taking drugs have been argued as relevant (*Brandon v Jordan* [2001] B.C.J. No.308 (S.C) (Q.L.); *Harrison v Stephany* [2002] B.C.J. No. 2648 (S.C) (Q.L.)).

In Australia, under common law the fact that the patient has asked the doctor no questions has been taken as an indication that there was trust in the doctor (see *Lawrence v Northern Territory* ([2001] NTSC 37)). This contrasts with *Hribar v Wells*, where the court attached little weight to the fact the claimant had previously accepted medical advice.

Further, also under Australian common law, if a patient is aware of the risks from other sources this can be fatal to the causation argument. In *Rosenberg v Percival* the fact the claimant was a highly experienced nurse who was well aware of the inherent risks involved in surgery and was still content to proceed was relevant (see also *Berger v Mutton* (NSW Dist Ct, Twigg DCJ, 22 November 1994)). However, in *Shead v Hooley* ((2000) NSWCA 362) causation was established even though the claimant was an intensive care nurse.

Where there are alternative treatments available, the Australian courts have approached this by considering the appropriateness of the alternative treatments, rather than the simple existence of such treatments. In *Rosenberg v Percival* the court noted there were few alternative treatments available owing to the claimant's desire for the best result.

In *Smith v Auckland Hospital Board* ([1965] N.Z.L.R. 191 (N.Z.C.A.)) the New Zealand Court of Appeal supported a subjective test. It was said that an individual patient must always retain the right to decline operative investigation or treatment however unreasonable or foolish that may appear in the eyes of their medical advisors.

An alternative approach would be to postulate a standard based on a reasonable or prudent patient, and whether that patient would have given consent when confronted with the information. This is the objective approach to causation. Where a purely objective test is used, the court cannot simply accept a claimant who states that treatment would have been refused if there had been the requisite warnings. The court must also be satisfied that the reasonable patient in the same situation would also have done so. The objective approach has been said to enable the court to mitigate the consequences of the failure to warn for the benefit of doctors.

One difficulty with the objective approach is that the issue of information and consent is particular to the individual patient. A patient may decide not to proceed with an operation for reasons that are not logical, or on the basis of views held by the majority. What if there are no common shared values, or more than one reasonable choice that could be made? A strict objective approach takes no account of these problems.

In *Reibl v Hughes* ((1980) 114 D.L.R. (3d) 1 (S.C.C.)) it was said that a vexing problem raised by the objective standard is whether causation could ever be established if the surgeon has recommended surgery. Could it be said that the reasonable person in the patient's position when proper disclosure is made would refuse to follow the surgeon's recommendation? The objective standard of what a reasonable person in the patient's position would do would seem to put a premium on the surgeon's assessment of the relative need for surgery and on supporting medical evidence of that need.

An example of the operation of a purely objective test is seen in *Mickle v Salvation Army Grace Hospital* ((1998) 166 D.L.R. (4th) 743 (Ont. Ct.)). The question for the court was whether the claimant would have undergone a termination of pregnancy. Applying the objective test, the court had to ask whether a reasonable woman in these circumstances would have proceeded with a termination. Since the risk was of minor physical disabilities the court found that the reasonable woman would not have terminated a planned pregnancy.

The Supreme Court of Canada has shown itself receptive to the argument that the causal standard can vary depending on the nature and importance of the duty breached. In Canada in *Buchan v Ortho Pharmaceutical (Canada) Ltd* ((1986) 25 D.L.R. (4th) 658 (Ont.C.A.)) and *Hollis v Dow Corning Corp.* (affirmed (1995) 129 D.L.R. (4th) 609 (S.C.C.)) there were attempts to move away from a purely objective test of causation.

In *Hollis v Dow*, a case which concerned a manufacturer's duty to warn, the court held that the imbalance of resources and information between manufacturers and patients justified a special, pro-plaintiff departure from but-for causation in the circumstances of that case. The court considered that the objective test was inappropriate and a subjective test could be applied in cases involving manufacturers. The reason given for distinguishing manufacturers from doctors was that it was thought that manufacturers, more so than doctors, tended to overemphasise the value of a product and underemphasise its risk.

In *Hollis v Dow* the claimant suffered a ruptured breast implant. She brought actions in negligence against Dow Corning, the manufacturer of the prosthetic, and also the surgeon who performed the implant procedure. She claimed that had she been properly advised of the dangers she would not have agreed to surgery. By the time the case reached the Supreme Court of Canada the question was whether causation against the corporate defendant was to be established on an objective or subjective basis.

More generally, the Supreme Court of Canada has shown itself willing to depart from but-for causation in other circumstances. In *Athey v Leonati* ([1996] 3 S.C.R. 458) and *Walker Estate v York-Finch General Hospital* ([2001] 1 S.C.R. 647) the court noted that the but-for standard was unworkable in some circumstances and, when it was, resort might be had to the material contribution test.

A third approach would be for the court to use an objective approach but qualify it by investing the hypothetical reasonable patient with the relevant special peculiarities of the individual patient. This is a combined approach or mixed approach, which involves consideration of what the particular patient, and the patient in the particular patient's position, would have decided.

In *Reibl v Hughes* ((1980) 114 D.L.R. (3d) 1 (S.C.C.)) the Supreme Court in Canada was of the view that the subjective approach was too favourable to claimants. The claimant in *Reibl* suffered a massive stroke causing paralysis following competently performed surgery for the removal of an occlusion in the left internal carotid artery. The surgeon did not advise the claimant of the chance of being paralysed during or shortly after the surgery but stressed that the chances of paralysis were greater if he did not undergo surgery. The claimant said that had he been aware of the risk he would have deferred surgery until a lifetime retirement pension had vested in a year and a half.

The court came down in favour of a modified objective approach where the starting point was to determine the extent to which the balance of risks was, medically speaking, in favour of the surgery. The failure of proper disclosure becomes therefore very material. What was also relevant were special considerations affecting the particular patient. In *Reibl* it was emphasised that it was important to take account of the patient's questions to the doctor, as this would demonstrate the individual patient's concerns and better enable the court to assess what a reasonable patient in the patient's position would have done. In this case the anticipation of a full pension would be a "special considera-tion" which emerges from the claimant's situation. It was held that there was no immediate necessity to proceed with surgery and the claimant had no neurological deficit. He was near the point when he could receive a full pension at work. There was a grave risk of stroke or worse during the surgery and, whilst there was a risk of stroke at some point in the future with no surgery, no precise time frame could be put on that other than it was three or more years ahead. On the basis of the foregoing factors it was found that a reasonable person in the claimant's position would have opted against surgery at that particular time.

It was said that the adoption of the objective standard does not mean the issue of causation is completely in the hands of the surgeon:

> *Merely because medical evidence establishes the reasonableness of a recommended operation does not mean that a reasonable person in the patient's position would necessarily agree to it, if proper disclosure had been made of the risks attendant upon it, balanced against those against it. The patient's particular situation and the degree to which the risks of surgery or no surgery are balanced would reduce the force, on an objective appraisal, of the surgeon's recommendation. Admit-tedly, if the risk of foregoing the surgery would be considerably graver to a patient than the risks attendant upon it, the objective standard would favour exoneration of the surgeon who has not made the required disclosure.*

In *Ellis v Wallsend District Hospital* ((1989) 17 N.S.W.L.R. 553 (N.S.W. C.A.)) it was found that there was negligence in failing to warn the claimant but there was a failure to establish the necessary causative link between the omission to warn and the damage sustained. The claimant failed to establish that had she been given the necessary warnings she would have rejected the operation. On appeal the New South Wales Court of Appeal stated that the test by which causation is determined in cases of medical negligence is a subjective one concerned with the particular patient.

In *Grey v Webster* ((1984) 14 D.L.R. (4th) 706 (N.B.Q.B.) the claimant wanted a tubal ligation as a means of sterilisation. She asserted that had she been aware of the failure rate for tubal ligation she would have undergone a hysterectomy. She was diabetic and it was for this reason she wished to be sure she did not get pregnant again. This argument failed as the medical evidence at that time was that a hysterectomy would not be recommended to a patient for the sole purpose of sterilisation. The court was satisfied that the claimant when faced with the consequences of alternative medical procedures and the high probability of success from a tubal ligation would have proceeded with the latter procedure. The claimant had undergone a further tubal ligation following this pregnancy.

The court reviewed the decisions in *Hopp v Lepp* and *Reibl* and stated that, in assessing whether or not the failure to disclose was a causative factor in the occasion of that risk, the court must consider what decision the patient would have made had such a risk been placed before them. In making this decision it was said the court was required to use an objective standard, namely that of the reasonable person, but putting that reasonable person in the patient's position.

In *Zimmer v Ringrose* ((1981) 125 D.L.R. (3d) 215 (Alta. C.A.) a doctor performed an ineffective silver nitrate sterilisation operation. There had been no comparison between this method of sterilisation and other methods. The claimant said she would have requested one of the more traditional sterilisation methods had she known of the novel nature of the silver nitrate method. The court found that a reasonable patient in the claimant's position would have undergone the experimental sterilisation procedure. Reference was made to *Reibl v Hughes* and it was said that an objective standard of causation should be used. However, there may be "special considerations" which the trier of fact should take into account in determining whether the patient would have withheld their consent. Reference was made to the fact that the patient in *Reibl* would have been entitled to his full pension had he deferred surgery. The court considered that the patient's particular situation must be "objectively assessed in terms of reasonableness". The "specific concerns which a patient may have with regard to the proposed therapy must be viewed objectively". In *Zimmer* it was said that a special consideration arose from the particular circumstances of the case. The claimant's primary reason for undergoing the silver nitrate procedure was that she had a new baby at home and did not wish to go into hospital. The court found that since all other methods of sterilisation required her to go into hospital it was difficult to accept her assertion that she would have continued to decline the procedure.

The Canadian Supreme Court in *Arndt v Smith* ((1997) 148 D.L.R. (4th) 48 (S.C.C.)) approved what they classified as the modified objective test as laid down in *Reibl v Hughes*. It was said that the test enunciated in *Reibl* relied upon a combination of objective and subjective factors in order to determine whether the failure to disclose actually caused harm.

In *Arndt v Smith* the claimant raised an action for costs associated with rearing her child, who had been injured by chickenpox contracted when the claimant was pregnant. She said had she been warned of the risk of injury to her baby she would have terminated the pregnancy. The trial judge dismissed the claim, and did not accept her evidence that she would have terminated the pregnancy. It was not clear what test the trial judge applied. He used the word "objectively" twice and did not mention subjective. He decided that he must determine the issue objectively, replacing the actual claimant with a reasonable and prudent expectant mother. However, some of the factors he then considered were subjective. He relied upon the facts that the claimant had desired a child, that a termination in the second trimester carried increased risks and would have required the approval of a committee, and that the claimant had a natural scepticism of mainstream medicine. There was also evidence that the risk of serious injury to the child was small and her medical advisers would have advised against termination of the pregnancy. The British Columbia Court of Appeal held that the trial judge had applied the wrong test and directed a new trial confined to issues of causation.

The majority in *Arndt v Smith* endorsed the modified objective test expressed in *Reibl v Hughes*. They found that the original trial judge had correctly applied the test and reinstated the trial judgement. The court set out how the test should be applied as follows:

> *It requires that the court consider what the reasonable patient in the plaintiff's circumstances would have done if faced with the same situation. The trier of fact must take into consideration any "particular concerns" of the patient and any "special considerations affecting the particular patient" in determining whether the patient would have refused treatment if given all the information about the possible risks. The "reasonable person" who sets the standard for the objective test must be taken to possess the patient's reasonable beliefs, fears, desires and expectations. While evidence of reasonable fears and concerns can thus be taken into account, purely subjective fears which are not related to the material risks should not be considered.*

In *Arndt v Smith* it was felt that the modified objective test struck a reasonable balance, which could not be obtained through either a purely objective or purely subjective approach. The court considered that a purely subjective approach fails to take into account the inherent unreliability of the self-serving assertion of a plaintiff, while the purely objective standard might result in undue emphasis being placed on the medical evidence, essentially resulting in a test which defers completely to medical wisdom. One difficulty with the approach in *Arndt v Smith* is that honestly held irrational beliefs of claimants are excluded from consideration.

In *Rosenberg v Percival* ([2001] H.C.A. 18) the Australian court was committed to a subjective test in determining whether a patient would have refused to undergo a medical procedure if that patient had been warned about the risk of relevant injury. If a patient is believed, they succeed even though the objective facts point the other way. If the evidence of the patient is rejected, they carry the heavy evidentiary burden of persuading the court to make a favourable finding on the causation issue solely by reference to objective facts and probabilities.

In *Rosenberg v Percival* it was said that courts frequently make findings as to states of mind based on nothing more than the objective facts and probabilities of the case. Usually such findings refer to the mental state that simultaneously accompanied some act or omission of a person. In the "what if?" situation, the relevant mental state has not accompanied any act or omission of the patient.

In *Rosenberg v Percival* the critical fact was whether the patient would have taken action – refusing to have the operation – that would have avoided the harm suffered. The court pointed out that this can only be determined by first making a finding as to what the patient would have decided to do if given the relevant information. It was not possible to find what the patient would have done without deciding, expressly or by necessary implication, what decision the patient would have made if the proper warning had been given:

> *What the patient would have decided and what the patient would have done are hypothetical questions. But one relates to a hypothetical mental state and the other to a hypothetical course of action.*

Applying the subjective test, in this case the claimant's assertion that she would not have agreed to an osteotomy if warned of the risk of temporomandibular joint disorder was not accepted. It was relevant that she subsequently underwent a further operation to alleviate pain resulting from the temporomandibular joint dysfunction.

According to McHugh J:

> *Under the Australian common law, in determining whether a patient would have undertaken surgery, if warned of a risk of harm involved in that surgery, a court asks whether this patient would have undertaken the surgery. The test is a subjective test. It is not decisive that a reasonable person would or would not have undertaken the surgery. What a reasonable person would or would not have done in the patient's circumstances will almost always be the most important factor in determining whether the court will accept or reject the patient's evidence as to the course that the patient would have taken. But what a reasonable person would have done is not conclusive. If the tribunal of fact, be it judge or jury, accepts the evidence of the*

patient as to what he or she would have done, then, subject to appellate review as to the correctness of that finding, that is the end of the matter. Unlike other common law jurisdictions in this field Australia has rejected the objective test of causation in favour of a subjective test.

It follows from the test being subjective that the tribunal of fact must always make a finding as to what this patient would have done if warned of the risk. In some cases, where there is no direct evidence as to what the patient would have done, the judge may infer from the objective facts that the patient would not have undergone the procedure. In exceptional cases, the judge may even reject the patient's testimony as not credible and then infer from the objective facts that the patient would not have proceeded. The judge might find, for example, that the patient was a person whose general credibility was so poor that no reliance could be placed on that person's oral evidence. Yet, notwithstanding the rejection of the patient's oral testimony, the judge might infer that nevertheless this patient would not have undergone the procedure. That inference would ordinarily be based not only on the objective facts but also on the tribunal's assessment of the general character and personality of the patient.

In *Richards v Rahilly* ([2005] NSWSC 352) Justice Hoeben noted that the reliability of the evidence had to be assessed by reference to other evidence.

Following a review of the law of negligence in Australia there was an introduction of civil liability legislation through the enactment of the Civil Liability Acts. With the introduction of the Civil Liability Acts there is regulation of the common-law test of causation. Where an Australian court has to consider issues of causation, the legislation requires proof of more than "factual causation" to establish liability. It also requires that the defendant be held responsible in those circumstances (the "scope of liability"). Both factual causation and the scope of liability must be satisfied before causation is established. The "but-for" test is not considered to be a comprehensive test of factual causation.

In some jurisdictions, the legislation prohibits patients testifying about what they would have done if warned of the risk in question (s5D(3)(b) Civil Liability Act 2002 (NSW)).

In *Wallace v Kam* ((2013) 297 ALR 283) the High Court of Australia emphasised the patient's right to make their own decisions, but found against the claimant on the issue of causation. Mr Wallace underwent a spinal procedure under the care of Dr Kam, a neurosurgeon. There were various risks in the procedure but the argument focused on two risks. The first was a minor risk that the patient could suffer temporary local damage to nerves within his thighs as a result of lying down on the operating table. The second was more serious in that there was a 1 in 20 risk of permanent and catastrophic paralysis resulting from damage to the spinal nerves. Neither of the risks was discussed prior to surgery. Following surgery, the claimant suffered from neurapraxia but he did not develop paralysis, the more serious of the two risks. Mr Wallace stated that if he had been warned of either of the risks he would not have proceeded with the surgery.

At the time of this case the Civil Liability Act 2002 (NSW) applied to causation questions in combination with common-law principles. (There is similar civil liability legislation in all states and in the Australian Capital Territory.) The claim was dismissed at trial. Justice Harrison found that Dr Kam was negligent in not warning Mr Wallace of the risk of neurapraxia but found that, even if warned of that risk, Mr Wallace would have proceeded with surgery. The Supreme Court of New South Wales was divided on the causation issue. Mr Wallace appealed to the High Court on the ground that the Court of Appeal had erred in holding that the legal cause of neurapraxia could not be the failure to warn of the risk of paralysis.

The decision of the majority of the Court of Appeal was affirmed by a unanimous High Court judgment. The High Court said that the underlying policy of the law on the duty to warm is to protect the patient from the occurrence of physical injury the risk of which is un-acceptable to the patient. *Wallace* was fundamentally decided upon the basis of policy considerations concerning the interrelation between the purpose of the duty to warn and the protection of a patient's right to decision-making autonomy.

The common-law principle of causation was said to be stated in s5D of the Civil Liability Act 2002 (NSW). Section 5D refers to two aspects of causation. The first is factual causation, which is a matter of fact and is determined by the "but-for" test of causation. What the patient would have done if warned is determined subjectively (s5D(3)(a)). However, under s5D(3)(b) the patient's own evidence of what he or she would have done is inadmissible except to the extent that it is against the patient's interests.

The second aspect of causation in terms of the legislation is the "scope of liability". The question is whether it is appropriate for the scope of the negligent person's liability to extend to the harm so caused. This is normative, namely whether or not and, if so, why responsibility for the harm should be imposed on the negligent party. This is properly answered by the court by the application of precedent.

The majority of the judges in the Court of Appeal considered that Mr Wallace should not be compensated for the materialisation of a risk that he would have been prepared to accept.

On factual causation, it was said that, "if warned of all material risks, Mr Wallace would have chosen not to undergo the surgical procedure at all and would therefore not have sustained the neurapraxia". However, the critical question was one of the scope of liability. In this regard, the question was whether Dr Kam's liability extended to the physical injury in fact sustained by Mr Wallace in circumstances where Mr Wallace would not have chosen to undergo the surgical procedure had he been properly warned of all material risks but where he would have chosen to undergo the surgical procedure had he been warned only of the risk that in fact materialised. Scope of liability was not made out because:

the normative judgment that is appropriate to be made is that the liability of a medical practitioner who has failed to warn the patient of material risks inherent in a proposed treatment should not extend to harm from risks that the patient was willing to hazard, whether through an express choice or as found had their disclosure been made.

The decision in *Wallace v Kam* in applying the legislation confirms that that even if doctors do not mention a particular risk they will not be held liable unless that particular risk materialises and there is evidence that the patient would not have agreed to treatment if warned of that *particular* risk. On one view this approach does undermine the duty to inform and this is not the law in the UK. Australian cases after the introduction of the Civil Liability Acts must therefore be read with care by the UK practitioner and in the knowledge that there is a different approach to causation.

Wallace was applied in *Neville v Lam [No. 3]* ([2014] NSWSC 607.) in the context of a wrongful birth claim arising from a practitioner's failure to advise of the potential for pregnancy following endometrial ablation.

3. The test of causation in the UK

The issue of which test of factual causation is employed in the UK has received little analytical attention from the courts. In *Chatterton v Gerson* ([1981] QB 432), Bristow J appeared to adopt (*obiter*) a subjective approach to causation. He stated that where a claim is based on negligence a claimant must prove not only the breach of duty but also that, had the duty not been broken, they would not have proceeded with the operation. In essence however what he did was to use a reason-able patient yardstick to test what this particular patient would have done. He rejected what the patient claimed she would have done, in favour of a reasonable inference of what someone desperate for pain relief would choose. The net effect is a hybrid test of causation.

In *Hills v Potter* ([1983] 3 All E.R. 716) the action failed on causation whether the test was subjective or objective.

In *Gold v Haringey Health Authority* ([1988] Q.B. 481) the claimant underwent a sterilisation procedure following the birth of her third child. She later became pregnant and brought an action based on the fact that she had not been warned of the failure rate of female sterilisation procedures. Had she been appropriately warned she said her husband would have undergone a vasectomy procedure. The case focused on whether the professional standard test applied to advice given in the non-therapeutic context. However, on causation the focus was on comparative failure rates between a female sterilisation and a vasectomy.

In *Thake v Maurice* ([1986] Q.B. 644) a husband underwent a vasectomy procedure and advice was given that the procedure was irreversible. There was no warning that there was a risk of re-cannulisation and that a pregnancy could occur. His wife believed that she could not become pregnant and ignored signs of pregnancy until she was five months pregnant. The argument was that if there had been an appreciation of the failure rate in vasectomy they would have realised that there was a pregnancy at such a time and it would have been possible to proceed with a termination.

In *Moyes v Lothian Health Board* ([1990] 1 Med. L.R. 463) the claimant failed to establish that she would not have proceeded with the diagnostic angiography if fully advised of the risks. The court subjected her evidence on what she would have done to scrutiny and noted that that she had accepted in evidence that she trusted the neurosurgeon's experience and judgement. She was also prepared to accept a 5% risk of anaesthetic and that risk was lower than the risk of the diagnostic angiography. She did not appear to have taken account of the effects of not proceeding with the angiography.

In the United Kingdom, this approach of blending the objective and subjective approaches found favour in *Smith v Barking, Havering and Brentwood Health Authority* ([1994] 5 Med. L.R. 285, QBD). Hutchison J adopted a subjective test but employed an objective yardstick by which to test the evidence. The claimant had undergone surgery when aged nine to drain a cyst in her spinal cord. At that point in time she had been suffering pain and a mild quadriparesis. The operation was successful in relieving her symptoms and she was able to live a normal life. When she was 18 she began to experience symptoms and her surgeon considered that further surgery was required. Without further surgery, she would have continued to deteriorate. Within three months she would have been confined to a wheelchair and within six months she would have been tetraplegic. The operation carried a significant risk in that in 50% of cases there was worsening of the condition. The operation was unsuccessful and she was immediately tetraplegic. It was accepted that the surgeon had failed to warn her of the risks of the operation. The question for the court was whether, if she had been advised of the risks, she would have undergone the procedure.

In this case both counsel submitted that the issue should be decided on a subjective basis. The judge indicated that as a matter of principle this must be right, because the question for the court must be, if this patient had been given the advice she should have been given, would she have decided to proceed with the operation or not? However, the judge recognised that there was a peculiar difficulty with this sort of case. In particular, the difficulty for a claimant in giving reliable answers after the adverse outcome is known. On this basis, it was concluded that it would be right to give particular weight to the objective assessment:

> *... there is a peculiar difficulty involved in this sort of case – not least for the plaintiff herself – in giving, after the adverse outcome is known, reliable answers as to what she would have decided before the operation, had she been given proper advice as to the risks inherent in it. Accordingly, it would, in my judgement, be right in the ordinary case to give particular weight to the objective assessment. If everything points to the fact that a reasonable plaintiff, properly informed, would have assented to the operation, the assertion from the witness box, made after the adverse outcome is known, in a wholly artificial situation and in the knowledge that the outcome of the case depends on the assertion being maintained, does not carry great weight unless there are extraneous or additional factors to substantiate it. By extraneous or additional factors I mean, and I am not doing more than giving examples, religious or some other firmly held convictions;*

particular social or domestic considerations justifying a decision not in accordance with what, objectively, seems the right one; assertions made in the immediate aftermath of the operation made in a context other than a possible claim for damages; in other words some particular factor which suggests that the plaintiff had grounds for not doing what a reasonable person in her situation might be expected to have done. Of course, the less confidently the judge reaches the conclusion as to what objectively that reasonable patient might be expected to have decided, the more readily will he be persuaded by her subjective evidence.

The court concluded that there was nothing specific to this case to differentiate the claimant from an ordinary reasonable patient. The court found that she would have agreed to have the operation as if nothing was done she would quickly have become totally disabled. The risk the operation exposed her to, if unsuccessful, was nothing worse than what could eventually occur. It would merely bring forward an earlier onset of the condition. The operation did hold out a prospect of postponement of total disability for a significant period. It was also found that she would have been influenced by the fact that her surgeon, whom she had trusted, had concluded that the chances of success were such as to justify attempting the operation.

Moreland J adopted a similar approach in *Smith v Tunbridge Wells Health Authority* ([1994] 5 Med. L.R. 334). In this case the very fact of consent and the speed of consent was held to be indicative of the fact that a clear warning of the risk of impotence had not been given.

What of the situation where a claimant cannot genuinely say what they would have done had there been a proper discussion about alternatives and risks? Can the court consider other evidence to assess whether the claimant would have declined to proceed?

In *McAllister v Lewisham and North Southwark Health Authority* ([1994] 5 Med. L.R. 343 QBD) the claimant stated that had she been advised of the dangers involved in the brain surgery she would have postponed the procedure because she had a job that was important to her and she would not have wanted to risk losing it. Beyond that she was unable to say what she would have done. It was argued by the Health Board that in this situation the judge had no basis upon which to make a finding about whether she would have proceeded or not with the operation after the initial delay:

> *The fact that the plaintiff herself, fully conscious of the distortion to her thinking likely to be caused by hindsight, is reluctant to hypothesise, should not of itself preclude a judge from the attempt, provided there exists sufficient material upon which he can properly act.*

The court looked at the evidence and concluded that it was probable that she would have continued to decline the operation. She was a sensible, rational person who would make a rational judgement. The neurological deficit she had was not advancing rapidly and there was a slight chance that it might arrest spontaneously. Given time to think, and given that it was one of the most important decisions of her life, it was likely she would have taken a second opinion. A second opinion would have been more aware of the dangers of operating and would not have been in favour of the operation and that would have tipped the balance.

In *Smith v Salford Health Authority* ([1994] 5 Med. L.R. 321, QBD) the claimant was rendered tetraplegic following spinal surgery. He brought an action based on a number of grounds and one was the failure by the surgeon to advise him of the risks of paralysis, or death arising from the surgical procedure. Ultimately the defendant was found liable on the basis of negligent surgery and the consent case failed on causation. The trial judge had found that there was a negligent failure to provide the claimant with information on the risks of the procedure but causation was not established. The court was not satisfied that had the claimant been properly advised of the risks of the operation he would have declined to proceed. It was said that had the surgeon made mention of the specific risks he would have been entitled to downplay the risks and emphasise their remote nature. The surgeon would also have been entitled to give strong advice in favour of the operation. The claimant had been intermittently in discomfort and absent from work for a period of time. On this basis, the court considered he would have followed the advice of the surgeon to proceed with the operation.

In *Newell and Newell v Goldenberg* ([1995] 6 Med. L.R. 371, QBD) the allegation was that there was a negligent failure to warn of the risk that a vasectomy could not be guaranteed to prevent a pregnancy. Mr and Mrs Newell gave evidence that had they been advised of the small risk (1 in 2000) that the vasectomy would not be successful Mrs Newell would have undergone a sterilisation procedure. The court did not accept this evidence. In assessing the question the court took into consideration evidence that patients were never advised to have joint sterilisation, and that when patients were warned of the risk of failure following vasectomy they rarely declined the procedure, or used additional contraceptive measures. The court also referred to the fact the couple had engaged in sexual relations using only condoms and the fact that a sterilisation procedure on Mrs Newell would have been contraindicated on medical grounds.

This is in contrast to *Gowten v Wolverhampton Health Authority* ([1994] 5 Med. L.R. 432) where the claimants alleged that they had not been appropriately warned of the risk of late reversal of a vasectomy. There was no dispute that even had Mr Gowten known of the risk of late reversal he would have continued with the vasectomy procedure. The argument was had they been aware of even the small possibility of late reversal Mrs Gowten would either have taken steps to be sterilised herself or would have continued to take the contraceptive pill. This would have reduced the risk of her becoming pregnant to virtually nothing. The defendants argued that given the risk of late reversal was so small it was unlikely Mrs Gowten would have sought a sterilisation procedure or taken oral contraceptives. The trial judge accepted Mrs Gowten's evidence when she said that she was desperate not to have any more children and would have taken additional precautions. She said she conceived easily and in view of the bad luck of the family it would have been just her luck to become pregnant even given the statistical probability of late reversal.

In *Chester v Afshar* ([2004] UKHL 41), causation rules were relaxed to allow a plaintiff to succeed where disclosure would have affected the decision, even if the claimant would ultimately have given consent to the procedure. Miss Chester had suffered repeated episodes of low back pain and was initially treated conservatively. By 1994 she had reduced bladder control and had difficulty walking. An MRI scan revealed marked protrusion of discs into the spinal canal. After further conservative treatment Miss Chester was referred to Mr Afshar, an eminent neurosurgeon, who recommended surgery. Miss Chester reluctantly agreed to the surgery. Three days after the initial consultation she underwent surgery and sustained serious neurological damage.

At the initial trial the judge rejected the allegation that the surgery had been performed negligently and neither the Court of Appeal nor the House of Lords was asked to rule on that question. The issue was whether Miss Chester should have been warned of the small (1–2%) unavoidable risk of serious neurological damage arising from the operation. The original trial judge held that Mr Afshar had not given this warning and the Court of Appeal did not give him leave to challenge that conclusion.

In the Court of Appeal and House of Lords the issue was what Miss Chester would have done had she been duly warned. The trial judge concluded that had she been appropriately warned she would not have undergone surgery at the time she did and would have wished to discuss the matter with others, and explore other options. He did not find (and was not invited to find) that she would not have undergone surgery at some point in time, or that there was any way of minimising the small risk inherent in the surgery. The risk that occurred was the very risk she should have been warned about. The risk was liable to occur at random irrespective of the degree of care and skill employed by the surgeon. The effect of this was that the risk would have been the same whenever and at whomever's hands she had the injury. However, on the basis of the 1–2% risk it could not be said that it was "probable" that it would occur at a later surgery.

Those acting for the surgeon argued that it was contrary to the general principles of tort law to award damages where a defendant's wrong had not been proved to have increased the claimant's exposure to risk. To succeed, the claimant must demonstrate that they would not have consented to run the relevant risk and that they would not, ultimately, have consented to run the relevant risk.

In finding for the claimant, the Court of Appeal and House of Lords relied heavily on the reasoning of the majority in *Chappel v Hart*. Lord Steyn acknowledged that there was no direct English authority permitting a modification of the approach to causation in a case such as this, however he felt that Miss Chester's right of autonomy and dignity could and ought to have been vindicated by a narrow and modest departure from traditional causation principles.

In *Birch v University College Hospital NHS Foundation Trust* ([2008] EWHC 2237 (QB)) the claimant was not informed of the comparative risk of different imaging procedures. To succeed on causation in her case she required to demonstrate that she would have declined the catheter angiography that ultimately led to her stroke in favour of an MRI. The claimant's evidence on this was accepted by the court, which noted that she appeared to be an intelligent and sensible individual well able to make decisions. The court also factored in that she had poorly controlled diabetes for many years and had previous ischaemic lesions in the past that had resolved spontaneously without the need for risk-carrying tests.

In *Wyatt v Curtis* ([2003] EWCA Civ 1779) a GP failed to advise a claimant who was pregnant and suffering from chickenpox that there was a risk to her unborn child. It was admitted that this was negligent. The child was born with serious abnormalities. What was not accepted was what the claimant would have done if she had been warned. The claimant said that she would have sought a termination of the pregnancy, which was by that time in its fourteenth week. The trial judge found that she would more probably than not have done so. The GP, Dr Curtis, was refused leave to appeal this finding. He then brought proceedings against the local hospital authority, seeking a contribution from a doctor who had seen her when she went for an antenatal check-up. These proceedings were dismissed as it was found that the hospital doctor had done enough to comply with his duty of care, and in any event the claimant would probably not at that stage have opted for a termination of pregnancy as it was in its 18th week.

In *Jones v North West Strategic Health Authority* (2010 EWHC 187 (QB)) the causation question for the court was what advice would have been given to a mother had she been referred to a doctor for review by the midwife, and what the mother would have done had she been given advice. The claimant stated that she would have proceeded with a caesarean section. The Health Board argued that the doctor would have been obliged to provide the patient with information on the risks of caesarean section, and the doctor would have advised a vaginal birth. Their position was that in 1992 most patients would usually take the advice of their doctor and it was very rare for them to go against it. One complication for the claimant was that she was a Jehovah's Witness and therefore it was suggested that the fact that she could not have a blood transfusion would have deterred her from having a caesarean section.

The court considered the question to be asked was what advice would have been given by the doctor. It was said that *Bolitho* confirmed that the hypothetical scenario must also be measured against the reasonable standards prevailing in the profession, or, where the risk was material, the significant risks about which the patient should have been advised. The court clearly considered that the evidence of professionals might assist in indicating the behaviour of patients generally and their response to medical advice. In finding against the claimant on causation in the consent case the court founded heavily on the fact that patients in 1992 normally followed the advice of doctors because "'trust in the doctor' put her in the mainstream of patients in 1992 rather than in the category of unusual patient who would take a course contrary to the doctor's advice". The court also appeared to consider the particular circumstances of the claimant and the fact that as a practising Jehovah's Witness she was less likely to proceed with a caesarean section with the increased risk of blood transfusion.

In the case of *AW, as legal representative of LW v Greater Glasgow Health Board* ([2017] CSIH 58) the Second Division of the Inner House of the Court of Session in Scotland provided some useful guidance on how a court should look at expert evidence in the context of a hypothetical scenario. This was an appeal against a decision from the Outer House of the Court of Session. The case was not a consent case but some of the general guidance on how to approach expert opinion on a hypothetical scenario does have relevance to the hypothetical causation questions in consent cases.

In *AW as legal representative of LW* there was different medical opinions on the causative mechanism of injury to LW. The Appeal Court was of the view that in such a situation the judge hearing the case has to assimilate and understand all the evidence, and penetrate the arguments to make their own decision on the hypothetical issue, applying principles found in *Kennedy v Cordia (Services) LLP* (2016 (UKSC) 59).

The Appeal Court referred to the test being one of balance of probabilities or "marginal probability". It was stated that expert evidence should be supported by reasoning if the court is to give the evidence any weight, and where conclusions are in the absence of reasoning the court should be less inclined to adopt the conclusions. The Appeal Court emphasised its opinion that where there is no direct evidence of a past event it is for the judge and not the witness to determine what is likely to have happened. The view of a witness (even an expert witness) of what was probable can never be more than an expression of opinion. A judge's view of what was probable becomes an established fact.

Where statistical evidence is used by a party this must always be considered in the context of other evidence. The Appeal Court said that weight would be given to statistical evidence according to how compelling the statistics appear, but they said that a court should normally look for other corroborating evidence to justify the statistical inference. The basis for the statistics must in all cases be subject to critical examination and statistical evidence based on defective epidemiological studies should be disregarded.

Where a claimant fails to prove that, if warned of the risk, the surgery would have been declined, there is authority for the proposition the claimant may claim damages for the shock and depression occasioned by the complication occurring.

In *Smith v Barking, Havering and Brentwood Health Authority* ([1994] 5 Med. L.R. 285 QBD) an award of £3000 was made to cover shock and depression caused when the claimant discovered without prior warning that she had been rendered tetraplegic.

In *Goorkani v Tayside Health Board* ([1991] 3 Med. L.R. 33) (Court of Session, Outer House) the claimant did not know that a side effect of the drug he was taking would make him infertile. It was held that he would still have taken the drug, as his disease could have proceeded to blindness without the drug. He was awarded £2,500 in damages for the distress and anxiety occasioned.

In *Laferriere v Lawson* ((1991) 78 D.L.R. (4th) 609 (S.C.C.)) the claimant was awarded damages for psychological damage occasioned by a failure to advise her that she had breast cancer, which ultimately resulted in her death. The main issue before the court was whether the claimant should be compensated for the loss of a chance of obtaining treatment and avoiding death. Her belief was that had she known about the diagnosis earlier something could have been done to prevent the illness becoming terminal.

In *Snider v Henniger* ((1992) 96 D.L.R. (4th) 367) a claimant was awarded a sum for post-hysterectomy stress and anxiety when she was not advised that there was a risk if a suture inserted broke down a hysterectomy would be required (see also *Rodney Crossman v St George's Healthcare NHS Trust* [2016] EWHC 2878 (QB).

It is important to note that it is questionable whether in law damages are recoverable for shock or distress if there is no physical injury or diagnosed psychiatric illness.

4. *Montgomery* – causation

In the Outer House and the Appeal Court in Scotland Mrs Montgomery failed on causation. Her position in her written case, and in
evidence, was that had she been appropriately warned about the risks of
shoulder dystocia and mechanical problems in labour she would have
proceeded to elective caesarean section rather than vaginal delivery. The
law required her to prove this fact on balance of probabilities.

In the Outer House Lord Bannatyne did not accept Mrs Montgomery's
evidence, applying the traditional "but-for" test on causation. The
Appeal Court did not consider it could overturn this decision as plainly
wrong. The Supreme Court did overturn the decision of the Lord
Ordinary and in doing so did not have to consider some of the arguments advanced by the claimant on new approaches to causation
principles in consent cases detailed below. These remain to be argued at
some later date.

a. Montgomery – causation in the Outer House of the Court of Session

Mrs Montgomery's evidence on what she would have done had she
been offered a caesarean section was in fairly short compass:

> *If you had been told there was a risk of shoulder dystocia, what
> would your reaction have been?- I think I would have wanted her to
> explain to me what that meant and what the possible risks of the
> outcomes could be, and if it was a significant risk to me, as it was, I
> would have asked her to performed a caesarean section.*

> *Now, during the, the time that you spent in, in hospital, up until the
> time Sam was delivered, if at any stage you had been offered a
> caesarean section, what would your attitude have been?- I would
> have bit her hand off for it.* (para 265)

In the Outer House of the Court of Session the claimant submitted to the court that her evidence should be accepted that had she been properly advised of the options for delivery and the risks of mechanical problems in labour and shoulder dystocia, she would have proceeded with an elective caesarean section. The claimant argued that the traditional "but-for" test of causation was satisfied on the evidence of the claimant, however she could also succeed on the basis of policy and corrective justice following the decision in *Chester v Afshar*.

The Health Board argued that the "but-for" test of causation should be applied and that the principles in *Chester* had no application to the circumstances of the case. Its focus was on the fact that the risk to be considered was the risk of significant harm should shoulder dystocia occur. This risk was small. Had the very small risk of shoulder dystocia causing significant problems been explained to Mrs Montgomery, the Health Board asserted that it was unlikely as an intelligent person she would have proceeded to caesarean section.

Lord Bannatyne in the Outer House of the Court of Session concluded that the first question for the court was whether "given the very small risks" involved in vaginal delivery the claimant would have proceeded to caesarean section had she been properly advised. He said that, despite what could be described as definitive answers to the questions, he required to consider the evidence in more detail before he could conclude that the "but-for" test was satisfied.

He considered that Mrs Montgomery's answers had to be viewed in the light of knowing that had she undergone a caesarean section Sam would have been born healthy. He formed a view that "It could be said therefore, that she was bound to answer the said question in the way that she did." He concluded, "At least at an unconscious level it could be said she was altering her position in evidence and that would not have been her position at the time." He did not however suggest she was deliberately lying when she gave this answer.

He considered it was not simply a case of accepting or rejecting the claimant. He needed to look at the evidence in more depth to see whether there were any factors that could be said to negate or support the position Mrs Montgomery expressed in evidence. In doing so he appeared to accept that he had to do more than simply accept or reject the evidence of the claimant. He had to consider what she said she would have done in the light of the evidence.

He concluded that the following facts pointed against Mrs Montgomery opting for a caesarean section:

(a) the minimal risk of adverse outcome should shoulder dystocia occur;

(b) the risks of caesarean section, which would have been explained to her as part of the consent process;

(c) the fact that Dr McLellan would have remained of the view that Mr Montgomery should proceed to try to deliver vaginally, and would have continued to put that view to her;

(d) the fact that Mrs Montgomery had said in evidence that she was not arrogant enough to demand a caesarean section.

He concluded:

> *I regard these factors as powerful evidence pointing towards a conclusion that had she been aware of the risks of shoulder dystocia she would nevertheless have proceeded to attempt vaginal delivery. I am unable to identify any factors which would have pointed towards her not adopting that course. I accordingly do not accept her evidence she would have had a caesarean section and she accordingly fails the "But For" test.*

He gave consideration to the decision of the House of Lords in *Chester v Afshar* and concluded that this did not assist the claimant in this case.

b.   Montgomery – causation in the Appeal Court in Scotland

In the Appeal Court the claimant argued that the court should set aside the decision of the Lord Ordinary. The Appeal Court in Scotland will seldom disturb the finding of a first instance judge on an issue of credibility of a witness. Traditionally the credibility of a witness is considered to be a matter best left to the judge who has seen and heard the witness. In this case the claimant argued that Lord Bannatyne had not made the decision on causation on the basis of credibility. He concluded that she was being honest when she said she would have elected to proceed with a caesarean section, but felt that her view had been coloured by what had happened to Sam. On this basis, the claimant was able to argue that the Appeal Court could review the causation finding.

The primary argument was that Lord Bannatyne's decision on causation was predicated on an erroneous assumption that the risk with the option of vaginal delivery was small. He had also set himself a test to assess the evidence and consider whether the evidence supported or negated the proposition that she would have proceeded to caesarean section had she been properly advised. The claimant did not suggest that he could not assess the evidence in this way but argued that he had failed to properly analyse the evidence available and apply this test.

The claimant submitted in his assessment that Lord Bannatyne had failed to include factors which clearly supported the claimant's position. He had also founded on facts which he said were against a caesarean section which were clearly wrong. The claimant suggested a mixed subjective/objective approach to causation.

It was submitted that:

•   Dr McLellan accepted in evidence that had she advised Mrs Montgomery of the risks of shoulder dystocia she would have no doubt requested a caesarean section. This evidence was not included within the assessment in the Outer House. In evidence Dr McLellan stated:

since I felt the risk of her baby having a significant enough shoulder dystocia to cause even a nerve palsy or severe hypoxic damage to the baby was low I didn't raise it with her, and had I raised it with her then yes, she would have no doubt requested a caesarean section, as would any diabetic today.

- Dr McLellan did not say in evidence that she would have continued to suggest a vaginal delivery in the context of a patient requesting a caesarean section. She accepted that if a diabetic woman with a big baby had asked her for a caesarean section she would have agreed to it. In coming to his decision Lord Bannatyne had relied on the fact that Dr McLellan would have continued to advise a vaginal delivery. It was submitted to the Appeal Court that he was not entitled to do so on the basis of the evidence he had heard.

- Dr McLellan said that she would have offered a caesarean section if the baby was over 4kg. A proper assessment of the projected weight of the baby at the time of anticipated delivery would have placed him over the 4kg limit. This would tend to support that Dr McLellan would have agreed to perform a caesarean section if asked.

- Weight was placed on the fact that Mrs Montgomery stated she was not arrogant enough to demand a caesarean section. This answer was taken out of context in the evidence and given undue emphasis.

- Lord Bannatyne failed to place sufficient emphasis on the fact that Mrs Montgomery was an anxious first-time mother clearly concerned about the size of her baby and her ability to deliver it vaginally. This could be seen as "special considerations" in respect of this claimant. This anxiety could be said to be something which would tend to support the fact she would have opted out of a vaginal delivery had she been given the opportunity to do so.

- Lord Bannatyne failed to take account of the evidence of Dr McLellan when she said that no woman would want to encounter shoulder dystocia in any form. She also stated that if women knew of the risk most women would say they would prefer a caesarean section.

- No expert witness had said that a caesarean section was not a suitable alternative.

- The experts supported the fact that if a woman in this situation said "I'm not prepared to go through labour" they would agree to delivery by elective caesarean section.

- There was no detailed evidence about risks of caesarean section and how any such risks would have impacted upon Mrs Montgomery's decision.

- The minimal risk of adverse outcome was a factor Lord Bannatyne considered negated the option of caesarean section. This assessment was incorrect as it was not based on the risk of shoulder dystocia occurring.

- Lord Bannatyne failed to consider the significant risk of shoulder dystocia occurring and the fact that there were many consequences should it occur. It was an occurrence that could not be predicted, nor could the doctor reliably predict which cases would resolve with no problem for the mother and baby.

- If the court accepted that the risk of mechanical problems in labour/shoulder dystocia are significant or material risks, this in itself would support the proposition that the claimant would have opted for an elective caesarean section.

On behalf of the claimant it was submitted that on a proper analysis of her evidence it was clear she would have proceeded with a caesarean section if properly advised. This is a subjective approach to causation. An alternative proposition is to assess what a reasonable person in the claimant's position would have done (objective approach). The claimant submitted a proper approach to causation in this situation is to apply a hybrid or mixed approach to causation and require that the evidence of the claimant is tested against some test of reasonableness to inject a check on the resort of hindsight. On a proper analysis of the evidence, and proper application of the appropriate test, the finding should have been that the claimant would have opted for a caesarean section had she been properly advised of risks.

The Appeal Court did not set aside the finding of the Lord Ordinary on causation. In its view the Lord Ordinary was entitled to conclude that even if advised of the relevant risks the claimant would have been persuaded by Dr McLellan to attempt vaginal delivery in the first instance.

c.   *Montgomery* and strict liability – a new approach

In *Montgomery* in the Appeal Court in Scotland it was argued on behalf of the claimant that the "but-for" test of causation should be replaced by what is essentially a strict liability test should a failure to consent be proved.

It was said in *Fairchild v Glenhaven Funeral Services Ltd* ([2002] UKHL 22) that causal requirements for liability often vary, sometimes subtly, from case to case. Since causal requirements for liability are always a matter of law, these variations represent legal differences, driven by the recognition that the just solution to different kinds of case may require different causal requirement rules. It was argued that the traditional test on causation should be considered in the context of principles of justice and legal policy.

In terms of the decision in *Chester v Afshar*, a claimant may establish causation without satisfying the "but-for" test. In *Chester* Lord Bingham of Cornhill said (para 8):

It is now, I think, generally accepted that the "but for" test does not provide a comprehensive or exclusive test of causation in the law of tort. Sometimes, if rarely, it yields too restrictive an answer.... More often, applied simply and mechanically, it gives too expansive an answer.… But in the ordinary run of cases, satisfying the but for test is a necessary but not sufficient condition of establishing causation.

There are situations in which justice requires the wrongdoer to be strictly liable for the outcome. Courts have power to override causal considerations in order to vindicate a right in cases where the claimant's rights have clearly been infringed by a defender/defendant. The principle is one of vindicating rights that have been violated. Where a claimant has lost the opportunity of making an informed decision this could be regarded as an injury in itself. A negligent failure to disclose a material risk increases the likelihood of the patient deciding to undergo the treatment. There is a fundamental breach of the patient's right to make their own decision.

Causation in consent cases necessarily hinges on the resolution of a hypothetical situation. The courts require to protect the right of the patient to a fully informed choice. The wrong is an infringement of a basic human right. The right is to be informed of all material and unusual risks before consent is given to any medical treatment, or before a decision is made to forgo treatment. The interest deserves protection in its own right and should be compensated.

In Canada, the courts have accepted that alternative approaches to causation may be justified in specific circumstances. In 1931 in *Kenney v Lockwood* ([1931] O.R. 438 at 446 S.C.: [1932] O.R. 141 (C.A.)) the Ontario Court of Appeal analysed the surgeon–patient relationship as fiduciary in nature, requiring honesty on the part of the surgeon. Although the decision of the trial judge on liability was overturned on appeal, the Court of Appeal did not address the temporal aspect of the original trial judgement. The case was cited with approval in *Hopp v Lepp* ([1980] 2 S.C.R. 192).

Where a fiduciary duty is breached in not supplying sufficient information, harm that flows from such a breach is worthy of compensation. Where a fiduciary duty is breached, other contributing factors can be ignored. The claimant can receive compensation for her full losses, despite the presence of other contributing factors or the materialisation of harms that seem outside the scope of the duty.

In the Canadian approach the focus is on the breach itself and not the subsequent procedure or event. The fiduciary approach was followed by Lambert JA in his dissent in *Arndt v Smith* ([1995] 7 W.W.R. 376 at 386–87 (B.C.C.A)):

> *the duty of disclosure of material or of special or unusual risks is not like an ordinary duty of care in negligence, because it is not set by the standard of a reasonable medical practitioner, but is more similar to a fiduciary duty of disclosure, where the standard is set by utmost good faith in the discharge of an obligation by a person in the position of power and control to a person who is vulnerable, in a position of dependency, and is known by the doctor to be in a position of reliance.*

In *Arndt v Smith* Lambert JA relied upon the judgement of Lord Thankerton in *London Loan & Savings Co. of Canada v Brickenden* ([1934] 2 W.W.R. 545), a Privy Council judgment analysing causation following a breach of fiduciary obligation in the commercial context. It was said that, when a party holding a fiduciary relationship commits a breach of duty by not disclosing material facts which their constituent is entitled to know in connection with the transaction, he cannot maintain that disclosure would not have altered the decision to proceed with the transaction. Once the court has determined that the non-disclosed facts were material, speculation as to what course the constituent on disclosure would have taken is not relevant.

On this approach the sole limitation would be that the non-disclosed facts would need to be material. It would also seem likely that there must be some form of injury. This fiduciary approach was not discussed in *Chester v Afshar*, although there was recognition that the duty to warn had a special significance. The legislature should intervene to create a recovery mechanism for patients who have had their dignity right infringed by a doctor's negligent failure to disclose a risk. The standard as to what risks should be disclosed should remain all material and unusual or special risks.

In *Seney v Crooks* McIntyre J held that the doctor had failed to live up to the standard of care with respect to communication, disclosure and discussing options with his patient. He said that in a fiduciary relationship the fiduciary cannot suggest that the fully informed beneficiary would have acted the same way. With reference to *Arndt v Smith*, he said that a fiduciary in breach of duty to disclose and discuss cannot in law maintain an argument that the beneficiary would have acted in the same way if the fiduciary's obligation had been discharged.

A distinction can also be made in a situation where a patient did not require to be exposed to a risk if properly informed. In *Rogers v Whitaker* ([1994] 4 Med. L.R. 79) Mrs Whitaker elected to have eye surgery on her bad eye. She would not have elected to do so had she been warned of the dangers of sympathetic ophthalmia in the good eye. The chance of sympathetic ophthalmia was 1 in 14,000. In that case, although the risk to which she was exposed was small, she was not obliged to run it at the time of the operation, or indeed at any time.

In *Chappel v Hart* the advice related to a risk that Mrs Hart was bound to run, sooner or later. Dr Chappel violated Mrs Hart's right to choose for herself, but he did not make an alteration of the risks to which she was exposed. If she had chosen to have the same operation at a later date the same risks would have been present, although her argument was that with a more experienced surgeon the probability of the risks occurring were significantly less.

In *Montgomery*, the risk of mechanical problems in labour, shoulder dystocia and brain damage were risks that the claimant was not obliged to be exposed to at any point in time. Her position therefore differed from the patient who may require the same operation, with the same risks at some later point in time. It was argued that the court did not have to enter into an analysis of the probability of the risk occurring at some later date. Had Mrs Montgomery been informed she had options for delivery, she could have chosen a path which did not involve vaginal delivery. It was agreed that had she chosen that path of vaginal delivery the shoulder dystocia would not have occurred and Sam would not have been injured.

If the court agreed that Dr McLellan failed to give Mrs Montgomery the option of removing herself from the category of persons exposed to the risk of mechanical problems in labour, shoulder dystocia and brain damage, liability would be established without further proof. In this case, the very risk the claimant should have been warned about did in fact materialise. She had a baby in excess of 4kg (as should have been predicted) and the baby sustained brain damage as a result of shoulder dystocia. Dr McLellan was responsible for the outcome as a result of her failure to warn. The court should give sanction to an underlying moral responsibility for causing injury of the very sort Mrs Montgomery should have been warned of.

In *Chester* Lord Hope recognised that the law which imposes on the doctor a duty to warn has at its heart the right of the patient to make an informed choice as to whether, and if so when and by whom, to be operated on:

> *The function of the law is to enable rights to be vindicated and to provide remedies when duties have been breached. Unless this is done the duty is a hollow one, stripped of all practical force and devoid of all content. It will have lost its ability to protect the patient and thus to fulfil the only purpose which brought it into existence.*

In *Chester* Lord Steyn recognised that a departure from traditional causation principles was justified where a patient's right of autonomy and dignity needed to be vindicated. He said that one of the most basic aspirations of the law was to right wrongs. The expectation of society was a factor that could be relevant in determining whether a departure from recognised principles of causation was justified.

The Appeal Court decided that on reading the speeches of the majority in *Chester* it was not apparent that they intended that the modification of causation principles which they were prepared to make in Miss

Chester's case should apply generally to all cases in which a medical practitioner had failed in a duty to advise of risks. It was their view that the concern in *Chester* was to supply a causal link in the rare case in which a patient's reaction could not be established in evidence.

In *Montgomery*, the court was of the view that this was not a case of truly elective surgery. The birth of a baby could not be put off or postponed. In such a situation, the case was not within the ambit of what their Lordships had in mind in *Chester v Afshar*. They were not prepared to consider a different approach to causation in the consent case. This argument was made within the written case before the Supreme Court in *Montgomery* but was not advanced in the oral argument.

d.   *Montgomery* and the burden of proof – a new approach

In clinical negligence cases, it is accepted that the burden of proof remains upon the claimant. The standard of proof is "balance of probabilities". What of the situation in a consent case where obtaining the patient's consent is an essential prerequisite to proceeding with treatment? Establishing a causal link between a breach of duty and harm can at times be a difficult challenge for a claimant.

It has been suggested that if evidence relating to a particular element is apt to be within the control of one party, theirs should be the burden of proving it. The argument is that consent is a defence, and like other defences this should be raised and proved by the defender/defendant.

In *Nowsco Well Service v Canadian Propane Gas & Oil Ltd* ((1981) 122 D.L.R. (3rd) 228) it was said:

> *If causation is overwhelmingly difficult to prove or impossible to prove then it is a matter of public policy or justice that it is the creator of the risk who should be put to the trouble of hurdling the difficulty or bearing the consequences.*

In *Chappel v Hart* all but one member of the court endorsed the application of the rule whereby the burden of proof switched to the defendant in a failure to warn case when the claimant had shown *prima facie* causation. This was based on the principle originally espoused by Lord Wilberforce in *McGhee v National Coal Board* ([1972] 3 All ER 1008). Where a defendant exposes a claimant to an increased risk of injury and injury results, the burden of proof might shift to the defendant to disprove causation.

In *Hart v Herron and Chelmsford Private Hospital* (unreported jury trial in the Supreme Court of NSW No. 12781 of 1979) it was said on the basis of the decisions in *McHale v Watson* ((1964) 111 CLR 384) and *Blacker v Waters* ((1928) 28 SR (NSW) 206) that the burden of proving consent lay upon the defendant. The judge appeared to accept the view that consent is in the nature of a defence.

In *Seney v Crooks* ((1998) 166 D.L.R. (4th) 337 (Alta. C.A.)) the Alberta Court of Appeal confirmed that the duty of disclosure is not confined to risks but extends to other material information – such as any alternatives to the treatment being proposed and the risks associated therewith – which a reasonable patient would want to have. Conrad JA suggested that, once a claimant proved that she would have opted for an alternative treatment, the burden of proof should shift to the defendant to establish that this treatment would not have made any difference.

Swiss law has recognised that when a patient submits to medical treatment the risks they normally bear shift to a doctor who negligently fails to provide the patient with sufficient information to make the decision to submit to a procedure.

In *Montgomery* in the Appeal Court, and in the Supreme Court it was argued on behalf of the claimant that there should be a shift in the burden of proof. Where a claimant had established that there had been a failure to provide full information on alternatives and the risks and benefits of the alternatives, and where the non-disclosure substantially reduced the likelihood of the patient declining the treatment, or was a factor in inducing the patient to proceed, the onus of establishing that real consent would not have altered the course of events should lie with the defender/defendant.

In *Clark v McLennan* ([1983] 1 All E.R. 416, QBD) it was said:

> *where there is a situation in which a general duty of care arises and there is a failure to take a precaution, and that very damage occurs against which the precaution is designed to be a protection, then the burden lies on the defendant to show that he was not in breach of duty as well as to show that the damage did not result from his breach of duty.*

The Appeal Court in Scotland did not disturb the finding of Lord Bannatyne on traditional grounds and did not consider that there was justification for introducing a new approach to causation.

e.   *Montgomery* – causation in the Supreme Court

In the Supreme Court the primary argument was that Lord Bannatyne had failed to apply the proper test on causation, and had failed to properly analyse the evidence when applying the causation test. This was the same argument advanced before the Appeal Court in Scotland.

It was asserted that his reasoning was predicated on an erroneous assumption, namely that the claimant faced a very small risk. This was plainly incorrect. The Lord Ordinary had also set for himself a test to scrutinise the evidence of the claimant on what she would have done but failed to properly apply this test. He founded on a number of factors he considered would have pointed against the claimant opting for a caesarean section and stated that he could find no factors that supported her evidence. This was plainly incorrect.

The claimant renewed the argument made before the Appeal Court that there were a number of crucial factors Lord Bannatyne had failed to include in his assessment (as detailed above). Had he included these factors he could not have made the finding he did. Importantly he failed to take account of crucial expert evidence, and evidence from Dr McLellan that would support the proposition that Mrs Montgomery would have proceeded to elective caesarean section.

The claimant submitted that the failure to warn created a situation wherein the sequence of events leading to Sam's birth occurred. Mrs Montgomery was placed in a position by the negligent failure where she could never demonstrate as a fact what she would have done if properly advised. She was also exposed by the failure to a risk to which she need never have been exposed. It is for this reason that questions of causation in such cases require to be treated differently from the traditional "but-for" test of causation.

The Scottish courts had wrongly focused on the issue of "elective surgery". The question was not whether surgery was "elective" but whether there were options. It is correct to say that she needed to deliver her baby, but she had options for delivery. The proper approach should focus on whether there were options or alternatives for treatment/surgery.

The claimant also argued that the proper approach to causation in consent cases should be a mixed subjective/objective approach. This is a test which provides fairness to all parties in assessing the hypothetical actions of a claimant deprived of information to enable them to make an informed decision.

Had the court applied a mixed subjective/objective approach to the facts it would have had to conclude that Mrs Montgomery would have proceeded to caesarean section.

Mrs Montgomery said that she would have proceeded to caesarean section if she had been properly advised of the options. Applying a subjective approach the court should look at the particular patient involved, and the particular circumstances relevant to her situation. The court should consider whether there are any facts or "special considerations" particular to her case which would support her in her contention she would have proceeded to elective caesarean section. It was submitted that there were a number of facts that would support her:

- Mrs Montgomery said in evidence that she would have proceeded to caesarean section had she been warned of the risks, and she was not challenged on this point.

- She was a young, anxious first-time mother who was concerned about the increasing weight of her baby. It was agreed in evidence that Dr McLellan cancelled the last scan for weight as she felt that the scans were making Mrs Montgomery more anxious.

- She did raise concerns at the 36-week clinic about the risk of her ability to deliver vaginally. This is evidence of what was concerning her at that time and such evidence can be relevant in assessing what her hypothetical response would have been.

- Dr McLellan accepted in evidence that had Mrs Montgomery requested a caesarean section she would have agreed this was appropriate. She never suggested that she would have refused it on the basis of any risk involved in the caesarean section procedure risk.

- Dr McLellan had said in evidence that in Mrs Montgomery's case at a weight above 4kg there were risks to the fetus. At a weight above 4kg Dr McLellan considered a caesarean section to be appropriate. On her own evidence a caesarean section required to be seriously considered at projected weights of 4kg and above.

Applying the objective approach the following can be said:

- The risks of shoulder dystocia/mechanical problems in labour/brain damage were all significant risks. The risk of brain damage to the fetus is a significant risk and also a serious consequence.

- There was an option to elect for a caesarean section, where the claimant would not have been exposed to these risks at all.

- The risks associated with a caesarean section were small and did not include shoulder dystocia or brain damage. This is an elective procedure offered to mothers who simply do not wish to deliver vaginally and who have no risks.

- Shoulder dystocia in itself, even if resolved without injury to mother and baby, is a significant obstetric emergency. Labour ward drills and protocols have been devised to deal with this emergency.

- Dr McLellan agreed that no parent would wish to encounter shoulder dystocia in any form. Dr McLellan stated in evidence that diabetic women and women in general would request a caesarean section if warned of the risk of shoulder dystocia. She gave that as one reason why she would withhold information from them.

- The experts agreed that when you tell mothers about risks they opt for a caesarean section. This is important evidence on their experience of what mothers generally will do.

Applying this mixed subjective/objective approach to the above facts it was submitted that a reasonable patient in Mrs Montgomery's position would have proceeded to caesarean section if properly advised of the options and the risks and benefits of each option.

The claimant did not proceed with the argument advanced in the Scottish Appeal Court that there should be strict liability where a failure to consent is proved. The claimant did ask the Supreme Court to consider the question of burden of proof in a case where a failure to consent is held proved as detailed above. It was submitted that the onus of establishing that Mrs Montgomery would not have proceeded with a caesarean section should rest on the Health Board. If the onus was accepted as being on the Health Board, there was a failure to discharge that onus.

f.   *Montgomery* – the decision of the Supreme Court on causation

The Supreme Court recognised that appellate courts should exercise restraint in reversing findings of fact made at first instance (*McGraddie v McGraddie* ([2013] UKSC 58); *Henderson v Foxworth Investments Ltd* ([2014] UKSC 41)).

The Supreme Court, taking into account Australian case law, noted that the issue of causation, where an undisclosed risk has materialised, is closely tied to the identification of the particular risk which ought to have been disclosed. They found that both Lord Bannatyne and also the Appeal Court in Scotland, had proceeded on the basis the relevant question was what the claimant would have done if advised of grave consequences arising should shoulder dystocia occur, rather than what she would have done if she had been advised of the risk of shoulder dystocia and the potential consequences of that complication.

The Supreme Court concluded that the evidence from Dr McLellan to the effect that diabetic women, and women in general, would request an elective caesarean section if made aware of the risk of shoulder dystocia was not appropriately considered by the Lord Bannatyne or the Appeal Court. They noted Dr McLellan's evidence that it was her position that it was precisely because most women would elect to have a caesarean section if informed of the risk of shoulder dystocia that she withheld the information from them. They also commented on the fact that this was the view of one of the experts for the Health Board, Mr Mason. Mr Mason gave evidence that if doctors were to warn women at risk of shoulder dystocia "you would actually make most women simply request a caesarean section". This evidence was not appropriately considered by the Lord Ordinary or the Appeal Court.

More fundamentally it was said that:

> the consequence of our holding that there was a duty to advise Mrs Montgomery of the risk of shoulder dystocia, and to discuss with her the potential implications and the options open to her, is that the issue of causation has to be considered on a different footing from that

on which it was approached by the Lord Ordinary and the Extra Division. They had in mind the supposed reaction of Mrs Montgomery if she had been advised of the minimal risk of a grave consequence. The question should properly have been addressed as to Mrs Montgomery's likely reaction if she had been told of the risk of shoulder dystocia. On that question, we have Dr McLellan's unequivocal view that Mrs Montgomery would have elected to have a caesarean section. The question of causation must also be considered on the hypothesis of a discussion which is conducted without the patient's being pressurised to accept her doctor's recommendation. In these circumstances, there is really no basis on which to conclude that Mrs Montgomery, if she had been advised of the risk of shoulder dystocia, would have chosen to proceed with a vaginal delivery.

Having considered the question of causation on the traditional "but-for" test, the Supreme Court set aside the decision of the Lord Ordinary and the Scottish Appeal Court and found that had she been given information about the risks of shoulder dystocia she would have proceeded with an elective caesarean section and Sam would have been unharmed. In these circumstances the court found it unnecessary to consider whether the claimant might have established causation on some other basis.

g.   Causation cases post-*Montgomery*

There have been a number of cases following the decision in *Montgomery* where the courts have had to assess causation.

In *David Lee Barrett v Sandwell and West Birmingham Hospitals NHS Trust* ([2015] EWHC 2627 (QB); 2015 147 B.M.L.R. 151) the claimant suffered from diabetic retinopathy and had raised intraocular pressure. Relying on *Montgomery* the claimant argued that he should been advised that there were two options for treatment of the intraocular pressure in the left eye. The risks and benefits of the options, including urgent operative treatment, should have been discussed. Had this been done it was said the claimant would have chosen to have urgent surgical treatment. The claimant had however qualified his evidence by saying that he would have followed medical advice. The defendants argued that this was not a case previously pleaded and in any event neither surgeon would have recommended the claimant undergo surgery (even if there was an obligation to discuss the option).

Interestingly the court accepted the submission from the defendants that the question of what the claimant should have been told was qualified by what a reasonable vitreoretinal surgeon would have advised. This appears to be a use of the *Bolam* test to qualify what advice should be given to a patient, which is contrary to *Montgomery* principles. The court also focused on expert evidence on what they would have advised as a treatment method and what advice the "hypothetical reasonable ophthalmologist" would have given and said that would be to treat medically. It was found that the claimant would have followed that advice. At no point was there a discussion on what a reasonable patient would wish to know, or reference to the GMC guidance on consent, which sets the standard for information.

In *SXX (By Litigation Friend NXX) v Liverpool Women's NHS Foundation* ([2015] EWHC 4072 (QB)), S was a twin who suffered an intracerebral haemorrhage, hydrocephalus and permanent neurological disability following a forceps delivery. The allegation was that his mother should have been referred by midwives to discuss the mode of delivery with a consultant. The parents' evidence was that had there been such a referral they would have sought to elect for a caesarean section. The consultant who would have reviewed them (had there been the referral) accepted that had the parents requested a caesarean section he would have agreed to this, despite the fact it would probably have been safe to aim for vaginal delivery. Of relevance was that that there was a family history of a death of one twin during vaginal delivery. It was agreed by the parties that if it was accepted there should have been such a referral then causation was made out. The court found there should have been such a referral.

In *Mrs A v East Kent Hospitals University NHS Foundation Trust* ([2015] EWHC 1038 (QB); 2015 Med. L.R. 262) the claimant's action was based on a failure to advise her at a consultation on 13 May 2009, or at a consultation on 3 June 2009 that her baby might be suffering from a chromosomal abnormality. She alleged that had she been advised of the risk of chromosomal abnormality she would have undergone an amnio-centesis, which would have proved the abnormality and she would have terminated the pregnancy. Her baby was ultimately born with chromo-some abnormalities which caused severe disabilities. The court found that the risk of chromosomal abnormality was not a material risk which should have been communicated. The claimant also failed on the causa-tion arguments. It was said that, in the light of a negligible, theoretical or background risk of chromosomal abnormality, and the real risk of amniocentesis provoking premature delivery, the claimant would not have proceeded with the test. Such a decision, it was said, would have been illogical. There was also the question of whether the claimant would have opted for a termination if an amniocentesis had demon-strated a chromosomal abnormality. The court rejected the parents' evidence on this on a subjective basis.

In *FM (by his father and Litigation Friend, GM) v Ipswich Hospital NHS Trust* ([2015] EWHC 775 (QB)), the defendants accepted that there should have been a discussion with the mother about the mode of delivery prior to her labour and that this did not occur. Shoulder dystocia occurred and her child suffered a brachial plexus injury. It was not accepted that had such a discussion taken place the mother would have elected to proceed with a caesarean section. It was argued on behalf of the defendants that she would have been advised to proceed with a vaginal delivery, with the reassurance that she would have been under the care of a consultant and senior staff. They asserted that she would have accepted that advice.

The claimant said that had she known all the material facts she would have recognised the significance of the potential size of the baby and discussed this with the obstetrician. She would have wanted as much information as possible, which would include an ultrasound scan to assess weight. This was a non-invasive test that posed no risk to her baby. The court accepted that she would have requested an ultrasound scan and this would have been done. Had this been done the scan would have suggested that the estimated weight at term would have been between 4.5 and 5.5kg and would suggest the baby was likely to be substantially larger than either of her previous babies. It was accepted that she would have proceeded with a caesarean section even if the advice from the obstetrician had been to proceed with a vaginal delivery. The claimant had had previous problems with her deliveries and also that she was accepted to have been risk-averse.

In *Tracy Holdsworth v Luton and Dunstable University* (2017 154 B.M.L.R 172) the claimant underwent a right unicompartment knee replacement. In the consent case, she alleged that she was not warned of the risks of persisting and continuing pain if she underwent surgery. She said that she was not advised that she might require further knee surgery. Her position was that had she been so warned she would not have proceeded with surgery. The trial judge applied a purely subjective test to causation and found that the claimant was determined to have surgery and she would have gone down the route of surgery whatever was said to her.

In *Rodney Crossman v St George's Healthcare NHS Trust* (2017 154 B.M.L.R 172) the claimant had widespread degenerative changes and narrowing of the spinal canal. He was advised that conservative management with physiotherapy was appropriate and if the symptoms persisted a cervical foraminotomy would be performed. Despite this the claimant was put on the list for surgery and surgery was performed. During surgery, he suffered radicular nerve root injury. The risk of this occurring was less than 1% and probably in the order of 0.5%. Had there been conservative management and he then had surgery at a later date the level of risk would have been the same.

It was accepted that there was a negligent failure to follow the plan of conservative management, and a failure to pick up that he should have had conservative management before surgery. It was argued that there was no causal link between the admitted negligence and the claimant's injury. While surgery would have been delayed, this would not have materially affected the risk of damage to the C5 nerve root. There was also a case that the claimant was negligent in not raising the fact that he had been advised to have conservative treatment with hospital staff. It was found that, since the risk at a later operation was not one that was more likely than not to have been realised, the claim could succeed on conventional principles. The claimant also argued applying principles found in *Chester v Afshar* that the claimant was also deprived of an opportunity to have physiotherapy before surgery and on this basis his right to make an informed decision was infringed. The court considered that it was appropriate to apply only traditional principles in the case.

In Scotland, in *Britten v Tayside Health Board* (2016 G.W.D. 37-668) the claimant required treatment with steroids but he was on lithium for bipolar disorder. The claimant was not advised that he could have treatment by steroid injection or by oral steroids. He commenced oral steroids and he suffered a relapse of his bipolar disorder and required admission to hospital. The court found there was negligence in failing to discuss the reasonable alternative of a steroid injection with the pursuer, and in failing to discuss the risks and benefits of this treatment against treatment with oral steroids. However, on causation the claimant failed. It was found that the breach did not cause the claimant's loss as he would still have opted for the same treatment even if fully informed. The court considered that the claimant's characterisation of the choice he would have made was based on false premises and was flawed. It was found that it was likely the claimant would have followed the clinical judgement of the doctor on what was the most effective treatment. Treatment with oral steroids carried a recognised risk of causing mental health problems but the risk was small and there was no research evidence to suggest that this risk was greater than in someone who had not previously suffered from a mental health disorder.

In *Diamond v Royal Devon & Exeter NHS Foundation Trust* ([2017] EWHC 1495 (QB)) the court applied a subjective/objective approach to the issue of causation. This was a clinical negligence action relating to spinal fusion surgery in 2010 and an abdominal hernia surgery performed in June 2011. The consent issue related to the hernia repair operation, which was performed with mesh. It was agreed that there had been no discussion about the potential implications of a mesh repair in terms of a future pregnancy, and that if there was a potential of a future pregnancy this required to be discussed. The claimant argued that had she been appropriately counselled she would not have undergone a mesh repair but would have had a suture repair as she did wish to consider a future pregnancy. It was not suggested that she would not have had treatment. She was at that time desperate to have the hernia repaired. It was accepted that there was a higher risk of recurrence of the hernia with a suture repair. It was said the risks of a future pregnancy posed by mesh were both *objectively* and *subjectively* serious.

The claimant was found to be a credible and truthful witness but:

> ... *recalling specific events or conversations is markedly different from attempting to reconstruct what her response would or might have been if given certain information. Expert witnesses, lawyers and others are trained not to use the benefit of hindsight to inform their opinion of what might or should have happened. It is, however, human nature for people to permit that which eventuated to influence their thinking on what they might have done if warned about a particular risk. To my mind, it would be quite impossible for the Claimant to divorce from her thinking, the fact that she was subsequently told by Mr Jones that it would be inadvisable for her to become pregnant because of the mesh and that, in the event, she has not had another child. Unquestionably, in my view, this sad outcome colours and informs her view of what she would have done if she had been appropriately warned.*

The court weighed up all the evidence (both objectively and subjectively) on the issue. Having done so, it concluded that even if she had been given all information she would have proceeded with the mesh repair. The court provided a list of subjective and objective reasons for coming to this view.

In *Correia v University Hospital of North Stafforshire NHS Trust* (2017 Med. L.R. 292) the claimant underwent surgery for a painful recurrent neuroma in her right foot, following which she developed chronic regional pain syndrome. The recorder found that the operation had been performed negligently but that the negligence had not caused the pain and suffering. On appeal the issues raised related to consent and causation. The claimant argued that if she could bring herself within the causation principle established in *Chester v Afshar* she would not need to demonstrate the negligence caused the damage. It would be sufficient to show that the injury was within the scope of the duty to warn when consent was obtained. The claimant had consented to a three-stage procedure and had not been warned of the material risks of an operation which omitted the third step. In this case the surgeon did omit the third step, which involved dealing with the nerve endings. It was argued that if she had been warned she would not have undergone a procedure that omitted the third step. This failure entitled her to damages since the risk of damage from the material omission was something she should have been warned of. This argument was rejected on appeal. It was found that the negligent omission of the third stage did not negate consent as it did not make it a different operation for the purposes of consent.

In *Thefault v Johnston* (2017 Med. L.R. 292) the claimant alleged that she gave consent to the performance of discectomy without full and accurate information. The surgeon accepted that he had failed to give the claimant full information. The court found that had she been given the proper information she would not have consented to the operation. Mr Justice Green addressed causation by first considering the position from a predominantly objective standpoint "to arrive at a prima facie position". Then he inserted more subjective criteria to test the *prima facie* position. He considered that the hypothetical patient would make a decision on surgery as a means of achieving accelerated pain relief. Without surgery, a full recovery and dimming of pain was expected over time. He therefore considered the increased risks of surgery and/or reduction in the prospect of pain relief were important factors to consider. He concluded that a reasonable patient with Mrs Thefault's condition would have declined surgery, or at least deferred it pending a second option. He then considered precisely which of the risks and benefits in practical terms were most important to this particular patient. He analysed her evidence and accepted her evidence that had she been appropriately warned she would not have gone ahead with surgery. The defenders also unsuccessfully argued on causation that Mrs Thefault was suffering from Weakened Back Syndrome and as a result she would still be suffering her present problems regardless of the advice given or surgery.

In *Malone v Greater Glasgow and Clyde Health Board* (2017 G.W.D 8-118) the Lord Ordinary applied a subjective test to the causation question of whether the claimant would have attended for an ECG appointment if it had been made. He noted her evidence that she would have attended such an appointment but rejected that on the basis of her non-attendance at medical appointments over a long period of time and on his general view of her reliability as a witness.

In *Sebastian Webster (A Child and Protected Party, By His Mother and Litigation Friend, Heather Butler) v Burton Hospitals NHS Foundation Trust* (2017 Med. L.R. 113) the claimant's case was that Ms Butler should have been offered induction of labour at term, and had this been done the subsequent brain damage suffered by her child would have been avoided. On the question of causation, the test applied was a purely subjective one. The claimant was accepted in her assertion that had she been given the information that there were risks she would have wanted delivery. Reference was made to the fact that she had a university degree in nursing and to her willingness to take responsibility for her pregnancy. She had been unwell during the pregnancy and it looked as if she would require induction in any event.

5.   Comment

In *Montgomery* Lord Bannatyne considered Mrs Montgomery's evidence on the hypothetical question of what she would have done if properly advised. His view on causation was predicated on his finding that there was a small risk of harm should she proceed with a vaginal delivery. Given this small risk he considered that Mrs Montgomery would not have proceeded with a caesarean section. He applied a subjective approach to causation but did consider other objective evidence as a test of the reliability of her evidence.

When the Supreme Court decided that in fact the risk that should have been discussed was the significant risk of shoulder dystocia occurring, this changed the landscape. Causation then required to be considered on the basis of this different factual finding. The question became what she would have done hypothetically had she been advised of the significant risk of shoulder dystocia occurring in the vaginal delivery option, when compared with the option of elective caesarean section. The Supreme Court faced with this significant risk found that she would have proceeded to elective caesarean section and would have rejected the option of proceeding to vaginal delivery, even with the option to resort to caesarean section should difficulty be encountered.

The decision in *Montgomery* highlights that questions of hypothetical causation in consent cases must be closely and carefully linked with the correct options, the risks of each option and the potential risk of adverse occurrence.

It was argued in the Appeal Court and in the Supreme Court that the court should apply a combined or hybrid approach to the question of causation in a consent case, however in applying the test there must be priority given to the right of the individual patient to choose.

It is counter-intuitive to seek subjective truth by means of only of objective criteria. The aim in the failed information case is to assess how this particular patient would have reacted to proper disclosure. For this reason, great care must be taken when attributing weight to what a hypothetical patient in that situation would do. The court should not disallow fears or concerns of the particular patient simply because the reasonable patient would not have had them. If on the basis of irrational beliefs a claimant would have refused treatment that a reasonable person would have accepted, the objective test incorrectly concludes that an injury was not causally connected to the omission. The determination of such a matter must take the patient seriously and must reflect decisions that would have actually occurred.

There is no doubt that if a court applies a purely subjective approach to causation in consent cases there is the danger of self-serving testimony.

Where treatment is unsuccessful a patient may genuinely believe, and may also be tempted to say, that they would not have opted for the treatment had they been appropriately warned.

A purely objective approach to causation requires the court to ignore the individual patient's view if it does not correspond with the hypothetical reasonable patient. A court has no means of assessing the hypothetical reasonable patient, or what factors were relevant to that patient in making their decision. Is evidence from doctors about what patients normally do reliable? If there is recourse to decisions made by patients in a pre-*Montgomery* era, those decisions may be based on wrong information. There is no method of understanding what factors were operating in the decision-making process of the hypothetical reasonable patient. The courts have recognised that there is a basic problem in ascertaining the nature and reactions of the hypothetical reasonable patient.

It has been said that the objective test is in fact not operating as a test of causation but performing an evidentiary function in that it provides a test of the credibility and reliability of the claimant's testimony. In the information context, where a patient can make an irrational decision for reasons peculiar to their own situation, any test which is purely objective can lead to injustice. What about the situation where there is more than one reasonable decision?

What then is the fairest way forward to ensure justice to all? The law recognises the right of the patient to make individual choices. There is the right to self-determination. An individual patient has the right to decline treatment, however unreasonable or foolish the decision may appear to others. The right to self-determination includes the right to be objectively unreasonable. The patient's right to self-determination is not qualified by what other patients may think is a reasonable approach or what doctors consider is a reasonable approach. The claimant's personal reasons for refusing treatment should be treated with respect and not be ignored. To apply only the objective standard of the hypothetical reasonable patient undermines the right to choose. It ignores the idiosyncrasies of the individual. Where patients are being asked to make a decision on medical care they do not do so based on what the hypothetical patient might do but on factors affecting their medical situations, their families and their lives.

Courts routinely assess the reliability and credibility of witness evidence by the use of objective factors. The claimant in *Montgomery* urged the court to clarify that a modified subjective/objective test was the appropriate test to be applied to causation in consent cases. In doing so, the court should however use as a starting point what the particular patient in question would have done, factoring in all that was relevant to their decision-making process.

The primary evidence must be the subjective evidence of what the particular claimant stated that they would have done. The facts peculiar to the decision of that patient must be determined and given due weight. It was accepted that to ensure fairness a court may wish to consider other factors in determining whether this evidence can be accepted. However, the court should consider only evidence relevant to that particular patient. The court could also consider what a reasonable patient in the particular claimant's position would do. Objective facts can be used by the courts as a test of the statement of the claimant but this must be done with great care. No "generalising yardstick" should be used. Importantly, the court should not permit the medical profession to say what the appropriate choice would be. The *Hunter v Hanley* and *Bolam* tests are removed from this area of the law and should not be reintroduced by the back door.

It has been said that the modified objective test in *Reibl v Hughes* was pro-defendant in its adoption of a modified objective test to questions of causation in consent cases. The Supreme Court of Canada did reaffirm the modified objective test in *Arndt* in 1997. There was however a powerful dissent in favour of a purely subjective approach. The majority judgement did accept that a number of very subjective factors should be taken into account in applying the test. One of the difficulties with the modified objective test in *Reibl v Hughes* was the way the courts applied it. Different judges considered different ranges of subjective factors to be relevant to the causation question. This diversity of approach is explained by the lack of proper guidance given on how the modified test should be applied and which particular personal factors are relevant.

In Canada, in *Arndt* the majority emphasised that the patient's reasonable beliefs, fears, desires and expectations are appropriately considered in the modified objective test. However, idiosyncratic or irrational fears and concerns are not considered. To appropriately apply a modified test to a consent case it is suggested that fears particular to the patient (even irrational) must be considered by the court.

Following *Montgomery* there is a commitment to uphold the right of the patient to choose. This cannot be upheld by a court applying a causation standard in consent cases that is capable of only recognising the patient's right to autonomy only to the extent that the choices are reasonable.

One obvious problem with the modified objective test is the complete absence of a means to deal with the situation whereby there are two potential courses of action, either of which could be chosen by a reasonable person in the patient's position.

It is also worth noting that in the consent case a claimant does not need to prove that they would never have treatment. Applying *Chester v Afshar* principles, a patient may say that had they been properly informed they would not have submitted to treatment at that particular time. The patient may have wished to conduct research on the procedure, or on alternative procedures. The patient may wish to seek the advice of another surgeon. The patient may wish to defer treatment to seek an opinion from a specialist in the field. This aspect should not be forgotten when considering causation in consent cases. In such a situation, the fact that a risk has materialised does not mean that deferred surgery at a later date would produce the same result. Consideration must be given to the likelihood of that risk materialising, and it may be possible to argue where the risk is small on balance of probability the risk would not materialise at a delayed or later procedure (*Crossman v St George's Healthcare NHS Trust*).

In *Montgomery*, the claimant also asked the Appeal Court in Scotland to accept that where there had been a failure in disclosure a material risk and thereafter resulting damage this should be sufficient for a claimant to succeed given the nature of the doctor–patient relationship. There is recognition following *Chester v Afshar* that in consent cases there can be a different approach to causation. In *Fairchild v Glenhaven Funeral Services Ltd* the but-for test was seen to be unworkable. The but-for test was workable in *Chester v Afshar* but the court departed from it. The duty of the doctor to provide information to patients is a particularly important duty. If the relationship between the doctor and the patient were to be categorised as a fiduciary relationship it could be argued that the failure to advise a patient of a material risk harm flowing from that breach should be compensated. This argument was rejected by the Appeal Court and was not advanced in the Supreme Court.

The claimant also asked the Scottish Appeal Court and the Supreme Court to consider a shift in the burden of proof in consent cases. If a court finds the claimant's evidence that they would not undergo treatment to be plausible at the time, it should then be incumbent upon the defender/defendant to prove the contrary.

The Supreme Court accepted that Lord Bannatyne should have found that Mrs Montgomery, properly advised, would have proceeded with a caesarean section. Having made this finding, the Supreme Court did not need to consider the detailed arguments on whether a subjective or objective approach to causation was appropriate, and how that should be applied. However, in deciding the original question of causation, the court does appear to have adopted a mixed objective/subjective approach. They considered what Mrs Montgomery said she would have done and then tested it against the evidence, including the evidence of what women generally would do in that situation. They did however particularise the question to the circumstances of Mrs Montgomery.

It is interesting on a review of the cases on causation since *Montgomery* that there does not appear to be any consistency in the approach used to approach causation in consent cases. In many of the cases in coming to a decision on what a patient would have done, great weight has been placed on what a doctor would persuade or advise a patient to do. On a review of the Australian cases, this is an argument that was also advanced under common law. Some courts have considered what was the "right medical decision" according to the doctors or experts. Some courts appear to form the view that patients normally do what doctors recommend.

In *Reibl v Hughes* there was a recognition by the court that that merely because medical evidence establishes the reasonableness of a recommended operation that did not mean that a reasonable person in the patient's position would agree if proper disclosure was made of the risks. Recent cases such as that of Charlie Gard demonstrate that patients no longer are prepared to follow medical advice without question. Mediation is now offered in many hospitals in an attempt to resolve conflict between health professionals and patients.

In *FM v Ipswich Hospital NHS Trust* the defendant's expert stated to the court that he was "able to persuade most of his patients not to elect for caesarean sections" and that his experience was that most patients did not elect for caesarean section following his discussion. A defendant should not be able to rely upon the fact the procedure was medically indicated as that undermines the principles of patient self-determination. Nor should a defendant be able to rely upon the fact a doctor would have pressurised them or persuaded the patient to follow a particular approach.

The GMC guidance on consent makes it clear that the role of the doctor is to provide patients with balanced information to enable them to make the decision that is the correct decision for them. The GMC guidance provides:

> *The doctor uses specialist knowledge and experience and clinical judgment, and the patient's views and understanding of their condition, to identify which investigations or treatments are likely to result in overall benefit for the patient. The doctor explains the options to the patient, setting out the potential benefits, risks, burdens and side effects of each option, including the option to have no treatment. The*

doctor may recommend a particular option which they believe to be best for the patient, but they must not put pressure on the patient to accept their advice.

The patient weighs up the potential benefits, risks and burdens of the various options as well as any non-clinical issues that are relevant to them. The patient decides whether to accept any of the options and, if so, which one. They also have the right to accept or refuse an option for a reason that may seem irrational to the doctor, or for no reason at all.

In *Montgomery*, the Supreme Court said: "The question of causation must also be considered on the hypothesis of a discussion which is conducted without the patient's being pressurised to accept her doctor's recommendation."

Great care must be taken to prevent the professional practice test slipping back into consent cases by means of causation, with courts allowing doctors to make the decision on what the correct treatment would have been, and what the patient would have done if properly informed, with the views of the patients ignored on the basis that it must always be self-serving testimony.

CHAPTER SEVEN
CASES ON CONSENT
SINCE MONTGOMERY

1.   Introduction

There have been a number of cases since the decision of the Supreme Court in *Montgomery*. There have also been a number of cases settled out of court. In the course of litigation there have been attempts to understand and define the test set out by the Supreme Court. In this chapter the reported cases have been analysed in date order to ascertain whether there has been a move towards the formulation of the test envisaged by the Supreme Court.

2.   Cases in 2015

Tasmin (By Her Father & Litigation Friend Almas Ali) v Barts Health NHS Trust [2015] EWHC 3135 (QB) Jay J

This case considered the issue of materiality in the context of *Montgomery*. The claimant suffered an acute profound hypoxic-ischaemic injury in the minutes before her delivery consequent on her umbilical cord tightening around her neck. She suffered a severe brain injury and serious disabilities. The question for the court was whether she should have been delivered earlier than she was delivered by caesarean section.

The defendant admitted that following a pathological CTG tracing there should have been a fetal blood sample (FBS). However, they argued that caesarean section was not mandatory and it was appropriate to perform an FBS prior to this to assess fetal well-being. Their position was that had an FBS been performed it would have been normal, in which case the labour would have been allowed to continue and the injury would not have been avoided.

The claimant argued that caesarean section was one of a range of reasonable management options prompted by the CTG trace which should have been offered to the parents in accordance with the principles flowing from *Montgomery*. The parents stated that they would have accepted a caesarean section if offered.

The court appeared to accept that if a patient made an express wish for a caesarean section this would have to be respected, but in this case at no stage during the labour did the parents express a wish to have an earlier caesarean section.

The court applied the RCOG and NICE guidance. This guidance provides that there was no obligation to offer a caesarean section as an alternative to an FBS. The RCOG recommendation was to proceed first to an FBS, not to immediate caesarean section. It was noted that the guidance made no express reference to parental wishes and consent, nor does it explicitly recommend offering caesarean section as an alternative to FBS. Following *Montgomery*, it must be open to argue that this guidance is deficit in failing to recognising the rights and choices of the patient.

There does not appear to have been any reference in the arguments to the GMC *Guidance to Doctors on Consent to Medical Treatment* or the GMC documentation on duties of a doctor when considering the issue. In *Montgomery*, the focus in the Supreme Court was on that guidance as providing a basis for the professional duty.

The defendant's expert also gave evidence that it was not good obstetric practice to proceed to caesarean section in this situation without an FBS. The relevant risks could not be specified until the FBS had been performed. It follows from this that there could be no obligation to offer a caesarean section until the FBS had been performed. The FBS was not a "treatment" and even if it could be described as such it carried no risk. In any event the risk here was negligible, being in the region of 1 in 1000.

It was argued for the claimant that the principles in *Montgomery* served to trump both the RCOG guidance and Dr Tuffnell's expert evidence. Whatever the standard obstetric practice was, it failed to reflect fundamental and overriding legal obligations.

The court held that in this situation there could be no sensible discussion before the results of the FBS were known. The FBS procedure was quick and carried no risk and the doctor had a duty to obtain all relevant information prior to the decision being made. It was also held that a risk of 1 in 1000 was not a material risk. It was recognised that the Supreme Court in *Montgomery* had eschewed characterising risk in percentage terms but it was thought that this was in the context of "defining the borderline between materiality and immateriality". In this case the court decided that the risk was below that borderline.

SXX (By Their Litigation Friend NXX) v Liverpool Women's NHS Foundation Trust [2015] EWHC 4072 (QB) Mr Elleray QC

The claimant was born the first of a twin delivery and he was delivered by forceps. His sister was delivered subsequently by caesarean section. During the forceps delivery he suffered an intracerebral haemorrhage and hydrocephalus, as a result of which he had a neurological deficit. Prior to the birth the parents had some concern about proceeding with a vaginal delivery. They said that they wished to proceed to caesarean section but the midwife had not taken their concerns seriously. Had she done so it was said that the mother would have proceeded to caesarean section.

It was held that the advice given by the midwife was protocol-compliant. The midwife should have made a referral to the consultant and at that stage the risks of vaginal delivery would have been explained. Had this been done the mother would not have proceeded to vaginal delivery.

Connolly v Croydon Health Services NHS Trust [2015] EWHC 1339 (QB)

This case considered the provision of inaccurate information on risks and withdrawal of consent. The claimant suffered from a range of medical conditions and had a dislike of medical procedures. In April 2009, she complained of symptoms that were suggestive of angina pectoris. She was referred to hospital for further investigation. Following review the clinical diagnosis was possible angina and she was referred for an echocardiogram and an ETT. Following these tests an angiogram was recommended.

The claimant underwent an angiogram on 19 June 2009. She signed a consent form and she was given an information leaflet explaining the risks of the procedure. She stated that she was told the test was a "brilliant and safe test … that there is only a risk to someone with diseased arteries". Her evidence was that from this she understood that there was no risk to her as she knew that her arteries were healthy. Had she been told there was a risk that healthy arteries could be damaged by the performance of an angiogram, she would not have proceeded with the procedure. The defenders doctor did not accept this and did not accept that they would have advised her arteries were normal.

The initial procedure was performed under local anaesthetic. During the course of the procedure it was noted that the left descending artery was occluded. A decision was made to proceed with an angioplasty. A catheter was inserted and this caused her arm to spasm, and after a further attempt a decision was made to access via the femoral artery, which was successful. The claimant's position was that she told the doctor that she did not want him to go in through her leg (femoral artery route). She said she repeatedly asked the doctor to stop.

The doctor indicated that she may have asked him to stop at some point but it was necessary to continue the procedure since they had detected an occluded left descending artery and this is a life-threatening condition. It was argued that the situation was a medical emergency. At some point the claimant sustained a dissection of the left descending artery. It was unclear whether the dissection had occurred at the time of the angiogram via the radial route or following the change to the femoral route.

The claimant's case was that the hospital failed to obtain her consent for the procedure and had failed to stop the procedure when she required it to be stopped, and the continuance of the procedure in this situation amounted to battery. She alleged that she did not provide valid consent for the angiogram as she was provided with misleading information prior to the commencement of the angiogram. She also alleged that she withdrew her consent prior to the change to the femoral route, and prior to the dissection occurring.

The defendants disputed that misleading information was given to her, but stated that even if she had been given misleading information this did not vitiate her consent. They did not accept that her consent was withdrawn in the course of the procedure. They asserted that she did not have capacity to withdraw consent as the medication she had received would have affected her capacity. They also argued that there was an event that threatened her life and in such a situation they were entitled to ignore a withdrawal of consent.

The claimant failed in this claim on both negligence and causation. The court rejected the claimant's evidence on the issue of consent and accepted the evidence of the doctor. It was held that the information in the sheet did not vitiate consent. It was considered that she lacked capacity to withdraw consent owing to the effects of the drugs she had been given. Once the occlusion had been identified it was considered appropriate to proceed because it was said that the consequences of the failure to proceed would have been death.

A v East Kent Hospitals University NHS Foundation Trust [2015] EWHC 1038

The decision in *Montgomery* was issued five days before the start of the trial in this case. The question for the court was whether at the 32- or 35-week clinic there was evidence from which it might be inferred that there was a material risk that the fetus might be suffering from a chromosomal abnormality. If so, it was common ground that the doctors ought to have raised the material risk with Mrs A.

Mrs A alleged that had she been advised of the risk she would have undergone further investigation by amniocentesis, which would have proved the abnormality and in those circumstances she would have terminated the pregnancy.

The court noted that, following the decision in *Montgomery*, the question was whether a reasonable person in her position would be likely to attach significance to the risk or whether the doctor was or should reasonably be aware that she would be likely to attach significance to the risk. It was concluded (accepting the defendant's expert evidence) that the risk of the chromosomal abnormality was 1 in 1000 or theoretical/negligible. The claimant's experts suggested that the risk was between 1–3% but this evidence was not accepted.

The court said:

> *In my judgment the decision in Montgomery affirms the importance of patient autonomy, and the proper practice set out in the GMC Guidance and the proper approach set out in Pearce and Wyatt. It is not authority for the proposition that medical practitioners need to warn about risks that are theoretical and not material.*

On the issue of causation, it was decided that the mother would not have opted for an amniocentesis if she had been told about the negligible risk because the risks of a disabled baby would have been greater from amniocentesis than from continuing with the pregnancy. It was also felt that, given her reaction to being told about the risks of an imminent delivery on 13 May, even if she had such a test and the abnormality had been detected, it was unlikely that she would have terminated the pregnancy.

FM (By His Father and Litigation Friend GM) v Ipswich Hospital NHS Foundation Trust [2015] EWCH 775 (QB)

The decision in *Montgomery* was handed down during the course of the trial in this case. The claimant's parents had two older sons. The first baby was delivered by means of a venteuse vacuum extraction after a long painful labour. The claimant's mother considered the second labour rapid and uneventful, although it was recorded that the delivery was complicated by a "moderate degree of shoulder dystocia".

It had been identified that the claimant was a potentially large baby. When he was born, his delivery was complicated by shoulder dystocia, causing a brachial plexus injury to his right shoulder resulting in permanent damage. The claimant argued that his mother should have been advised of the risk of shoulder dystocia and the possibility of caesarean section discussed. If she had been warned of the risk, she would have opted for a caesarean section and the brachial plexus injury would have been avoided.

The Trust did accept that there should have been a discussion regarding delivery given the occurrence of shoulder dystocia during the second son's birth. However, had that discussion taken place, it was argued that the claimant's mother would have been advised to proceed with a vaginal delivery and the claimant would therefore have suffered the brachial plexus injury in any event. The focus therefore was on causation issues.

The court held following *Montgomery* principles that if there was a significant risk in any treatment or procedure which would affect a reasonable patient's judgement, the doctor had a responsibility to inform the patient of that significant risk. On the evidence, it was felt that if the claimant's mother had been advised of the risk of shoulder dystocia she would have opted for a caesarean section rather than run any risk of repeating the birth she had experienced with her first son, even if this would have been against the advice of the obstetrician, and the claim succeeded.

David Spencer v Hillingdon Hospital NHS Trust [2015] EWHC 1058 (QB)

Following surgery for an inguinal hernia, the claimant suffered a deep-vein thrombosis, followed by a pulmonary embolism on each lung. The consent form he signed for the operation warned him of the risks of "bleeding, infection, scar, recurrence of problem, conversion to open procedure, injury to bowel". The claimant argued that he had not been advised of the risk of a thrombosis or embolism and that he had not been made aware of the signs and symptoms, or the importance of seeking medical help.

The court appeared to consider in light of the decision in *Montgomery* the test that should be applied was the *Bolam* test, with the added gloss that the court should pay regard to what the ordinary sensible patient would expect to have been told. It was said the test was whether the ordinary sensible patient would be justifiably aggrieved not to have been given information at the heart of this case when fully appraised of the significance of it? Applying that test the court found in favour of the claimant.

The court expressed a view on the significance of the decision of the Supreme Court in *Montgomery*:

> *Montgomery is clearly a decision which demonstrates a new develop-ment in the law as it relates to the law on informed consent and strictly the ratio decidendi of the decision is confined to cases involving the adequacy of otherwise of information given to a patient upon which they are to decide whether or not to undergo a particular type of treatment. It is not of central importance to consideration of the facts of this case. However, there is force in the contention advanced by Mr Skelton that the basic principles – and the resulting duty of care – defined in Montgomery are likely to be applied to all aspects of the provision of advice given to patients by medical and nursing staff. Insofar as the judgement in Montgomery emphasises the need for a court to take into account a patient's as well as their doctor's point of view as to the significance of information for a*

patient. I consider it relevant to a consideration of the facts of this case.

Caution must be exercised when referring to this decision. In *Thefaut v Johnston* ([2017] EWHC 496 (QB)) consideration was given to *David Spencer v Hillingdon Hospital NHS Trust* and it was said that it was not accepted that the *Montgomery* test was a variant of the *Bolam* test or that the test could be limited to the reaction of the ordinary sensible patient since this has resonances of the patient on the Clapham omnibus and underplays or ignores the subjective element which the Supreme Court has explained is a component of the test. It was also said that the test for what has to be disclosed is not what would leave the patient feeling "justifiably aggrieved".

Shaw v Kovac [2015] EWHC 3335 (QB)

This was a claim for damages brought by Mrs Shaw on behalf of the estate of her late father, who had died following an operation for a transaortic valve implant (TAVI procedure). The defendant doctor and the Trust had consented to judgment being entered against them. Mrs Shaw argued that her father had not been informed that the procedure was newly developed and the subject of clinical trials, and that the prosthetic valve used in the procedure was not approved for public use, nor was it fully or adequately evaluated in terms of safety and performance. It was argued that he did not give consent to the TAVI procedure. There were alternatives of either open-heart surgery or conservative treatment.

In addition to a claim for personal injury, a claim was sought for "loss of life without having been given informed consent". Damages were sought on the basis that he died in circumstances where he was deprived of the opportunity to make an informed choice as to whether undergo the TAVI procedure.

Reference was made to *Montgomery* and *Chester v Afshar* and it was said in both that the court clearly recognised the importance of a patient's autonomous right, including the right to choose what treatment to accept. If there was a breach of that right as a result of negligent non-disclosure of information by a doctor, then that of itself would create a right in the patient to claim damages. This right is free-standing and does not depend on any other loss being proved. It is a claim for damages for the removal of the right to make a free choice as to treatment.

The argument was rejected by the court. It was said that *Montgomery* dealt with the issue of informed consent in the context of the standard of care and *Chester* with issues of causation. It was said that on *Montgomery* principles the claimant still required to prove the breach of duty had caused a loss.

The claimant appealed the decision ([2017] EWCA Civ 1028) without success. On appeal, it was argued that the trial judge should have acceded to the claimant's arguments and should have made an additional award of damages to reflect the wrongful invasion of the deceased's personal autonomy.

Jones v Royal Devon & Exeter NHS Foundation Trust (2015 CC Decision, Recorder David Blunt QC)

In November 1999, the claimant was referred with a history of low back pain to Mr Daniel Chan, consultant orthopaedic surgeon. She was put on the waiting list for bilateral decompression surgery, which she understood would be performed by Mr Chan. Whilst on the waiting list her pain had increased and she had been offered earlier surgery performed by a different surgeon but she stated that she wished to wait for Mr Chan. Mr Chan had an impressive reputation as a spinal surgeon in the south-west and even nationally. Her operation was performed on 29 July 2010 by a more junior clinician.

The claimant stated that she was unaware that Mr Chan would not perform the surgery until the day of surgery, when she was ready for theatre and asked where Mr Chan was. She felt at that stage she had no option but to proceed. The Trust argued that she was aware that Mr Chan would not perform the surgery when she signed the consent form, because she was told then. The consent form also stated there was no guarantee of surgeon. During the course of surgery, a dural tear occurred which left the claimant with permanent numbness, bladder and bowel problems and a significant loss of mobility.

The recorder found that there was a breach of duty by the Trust in failing to inform her that there would be a change of surgeon. He didn't accept the evidence that the claimant had been advised earlier that Mr Chan would not perform the procedure. It was held that had she been so advised it was likely she would not have proceeded, having turned down the opportunity previously to undergo surgery under the care of a different surgeon.

The recorder found that the injury would not have occurred had surgery been performed by Mr Chan. Mr Chan was a more experienced surgeon and the risk of occurrence was small. There was no pre-existing condition likely to increase the risk whoever performed the operation.

Barrett v Sandwell and West Birmingham Hospitals NHS Trust [2015] EWHC 2627 (QB); 147 BMLR 151

The claimant's position was that he was rendered effectively blind after treatment at Birmingham and Midland Eye Centre. A central issue at trial was whether surgery should have been carried out to relieve excessive post-operative intraocular pressure in the claimant's eye within 24 hours of the beginning of medical treatment, or whether the condition was appropriately managed medically. At that time, it was argued that there were two options for treatment of the intraocular pressure of the left eye. The benefits and risks of, in particular, urgent operative treatment should have been discussed.

In the consent case *Montgomery* was referred to and in particular the passages in the judgment which deal with the assessment of whether a risk is material, the doctor's advisory role involving dialogue, and the degree of unpredictability inherent in the decision being tolerated as a consequence of protecting patients from exposure to risks of injury which they would otherwise have chosen to avoid. It was not possible to consider a particular medical procedure in isolation from its alternatives.

It was argued that causation must be considered on the hypothesis of a discussion which is conducted without the patient being pressurised to accept the doctor's recommendation. Advice on risks should be given dispassionately, explaining the potential consequences and alternatives. The question was to be answered by reference to what a reasonable vitreoretinal surgeon would have advised, rather than by reference to a particular individual, and the court appeared to accept that submission as correct. There was no reference to the duties of advice contained within the GMC guidance on consent. There was no submission that, following *Montgomery*, the test of which information should be given to patients is not grounded within professional practice (*Bolam*). In fact, it appears to have been accepted that the professional practice test was relevant to an assessment of what risks should have been discussed.

The defendant's evidence was that the surgeon would not have discussed surgery because he did not think that any course other than medical treatment was appropriate. The evidence was that surgery was an alternative at that time and, on that basis, a breach of duty was established. The claimant had given evidence that he would have wanted surgery had he been told of it. However, he qualified his evidence by saying he would have followed medical advice. The court found that he would have followed medical advice and a breach of duty was not established. The court invited the parties to make submissions on whether a more broadly based causative approach might be available based on the decision in *Chester v Afshar*. The parties agreed that this decision was inapplicable to the facts of the case.

Grimstone v Epsom and St Helier University Hospitals NHS Trust [2015] EWHC 3756 (QB)

The claimant had been suffering from pain and stiffness in both hips. She was a keen sportswoman. She was referred to a specialist in the field of hip replacement surgery. Following surgery, she suffered from a series of problems that required repeated surgical intervention. She did not suggest that there was any negligence in the performance of surgery. Her claim was based on a failure by the surgeon to adequately advise her of the surgical options available to her. It was argued that he also failed to advise her of the alleged lack of data on the failure and survival rate of the components used in the procedure.

Reference was made to the decision of the Supreme Court in *Montgomery*, which was said to provide "definitive guidance". Following review of *Montgomery*, the court held that the claimant had a fundamental right to be properly informed of the nature and risk of the proposed procedure. The information should have been provided to her in a way that was comprehensible to her. This was not a case where there was any justification for withholding information about risk on clinical grounds.

Despite the decision in *Montgomery* the defendants led expert evidence to the effect that a responsible body of orthopaedic surgeons would not have discussed the respective merits of similar resurfacing designs and would simply have discussed their own preferred resurfacing device and a "conventional" stemmed total hip replacement.

The court found that the claimant had consented to the procedure. The evidence of the surgeon was accepted on the advice and information he gave to her. The fact that there were letters to the GP and a full record made by the surgeon was of crucial importance. The claimant was found to be an intelligent and competent woman and, on this basis, it was said that no special measures were required. Given what the claimant wanted from surgery, it was found that in any event it is likely that she would have chosen the procedure she ultimately did have.

3. Cases in 2016

Crossman v St. George's Health Care NHS Trust [2016] EWHC 2878 QB

The claimant suffered symptoms of numbness in the left arm, and pain and restriction of movement in his neck. He underwent a MRI scan and was referred to Professor Papadopoulos at St George's Hospital. He discussed various management options in light of the MRI scan with the claimant and explained the potential risks and benefits of surgery. He advised conservative treatment, with physiotherapy and review in three months. Despite this, the claimant was put on the waiting list for surgery. He then received two letters from the hospital asking him to attend for preoperative assessment and the other giving him a date for admission. He contacted the hospital believing there had been a mistake and they indicated that if he did not attend he would be put back the waiting list.

The claimant attended for surgery on 10 April 2011 and gave consent to surgery. However, it was suggested that he defer surgery at that time as a result of concerns about the ability of his blood to clot. The claimant did not want to do so. During the course of surgery, he suffered a radicular nerve root injury. It was agreed by the experts that the risk of this as a result of the operation was less than 1% and was probably around 0.5%. Had surgery been deferred he would have suffered the same risk.

The parties agreed that there was negligence in failing to follow the plan for conservative management, failing to pick up that the original plan had not been followed, and failing to advise him that he should undergo conservative management. The defendant's position was that, although surgery would have been delayed, this would not have materially affected the risk of damage to the nerve root. It was also suggested that the claimant was negligent in failing to raise the fact that he had been advised to undergo conservative treatment.

Reference was made to the decision in *Montgomery* and the provision that the duty of the doctor was to provide the patient with information and to advise the patient of the material risks inherent in the treatment. It was not the duty of the patient to ask questions. It was the duty of the doctor to inform and without information a patient could not be expected to ask questions:

> *… an approach which requires the patient to question the doctor*

disregards the social and psychological realities of the relationship between a patient and her doctor, whether in the time-pressured setting of a GP's surgery, or in the setting of a hospital. Few patients do not feel intimidated or inhibited to some degree.

It was held that the claimant could not be found at fault for not raising the change in the treatment plan with the hospital. One expert was of the view that even if surgery had been performed some three months later the injury would still have occurred and the other was of the view that it was improbable that it would have occurred at a later date. The court found that given the magnitude of the risk it was not one that was more likely than not to be realised, and on that basis the claim succeeded on conventional "but-for" principles. There was an argument based on *Chester* principles but the court found that the case should be decided on conventional principles.

KR v Lanarkshire Health Board [2016] CSOH 133; 2016 Scot (D) 18/9
Lord Brailsford

This was a cerebral palsy case brought by KR, the mother of BHR. The court found in favour of the pursuer. As a result of injury sustained during birth, BHR suffered from significant disabilities in the form of dystonic athetoid cerebral palsy. It was agreed by the parties that BHR suffered an acute hypoxic event in the 30 minutes proceeding birth, and that had she been delivered at any time before 7.14pm on 1 December 2007 she would have been unlikely to suffer any injury.

There were several duties averred to be incumbent upon the registrar who was managing the labour. The thrust of the argument was that she had a duty to deliver the baby earlier, either by caesarean section or assisted delivery. It was also averred, applying the principles in *Montgomery*, that the registrar had a duty to discuss with KR the non-reassuring features on the CTG, and the options for management of the labour, including urgent delivery by caesarean section and assisted delivery to enable KR to make an informed decision and give her consent to proceed with the labour.

At the outset of labour KR was tachycardic and thereafter there was persistent tachycardia and meconium. There were abnormalities in the CTG tracing, although the experts disagreed on the interpretation of those abnormalities. Fetal blood samples were performed during the course of the labour and they were within normal range and not suggestive of fetal hypoxia. In this situation, the defender's experts' view was that it was reasonable to continue with the labour. The pursuer's expert was of the view at KR should have been delivered earlier, and in particular she should have been transferred to theatre for assisted delivery at 6.18pm given the backdrop of pyrexia, an abnormal CTG and meconium-stained liquor.

KR gave evidence that there was no discussion with her at all during the course of the labour and she had been unaware of the reason to perform a fetal blood sample. She said in evidence that she had heard mention of meconium at one point and she knew what that was and that caused her concern. She said that at that time she had asked for a caesarean section.

On the issue of consent, it was accepted that the registrar did not offer KR a caesarean section at any time, nor did she offer the option of an assisted vaginal delivery. The pursuer's expert had stated that it was reasonable to offer these options. There did not appear to be any evidence that the registrar had involved KR in any part of the decision-making process of this labour.

It was asserted by the pursuer that it was for the court to address what was a "material risk" in the context of what is important to the particular patient. It was submitted that the question was whether there was a risk about which the pursuer should have been advised, and which would have resulted in her accepting an option of an alternative mode of delivery. The focus appeared to be on the first limb of the *Montgomery* test. It was suggested that the registrar had adopted a paternalistic approach to the decision-making process in that she determined what options were to be given as opposed to what options were available. On the issue of causation, KR stated in evidence that had she been offered the option of a caesarean section/assisted delivery she would have taken that option.

The defenders submitted that this was not a case where *Montgomery* applied having regard to the facts and circumstances of the particular case. It was accepted following *Montgomery* that a doctor was under a duty to exercise reasonable care to ensure that a patient is aware of any material risks involved in any recommended treatment and of reasonable alternative or variant treatments. The defenders asserted that the test of materiality was whether in the circumstances of the case a reasonable person in the patient's position would be likely to attach significance to the risk. They also accepted that the court, armed with a full and proper understanding of the risk and benefits of a course of action, was entitled to reach its own view as to whether failure to advise on the comparative risks and benefits constituted a failure of reasonable care. The defender submitted that since the registrar had performed two fetal blood samples and given that these were not abnormal there was then no concern or risk that required to be discussed with the patient. There was no material risk to be identified.

The court did not agree with the pursuer that there should have been earlier delivery prior to 6.18pm. However, in the immediate period prior to 6.18pm there had been a sudden bradycardia and a prolonged deceleration and this gave rise to a risk of the fetus developing hypoxia. At this stage the fetus was deliverable. It was held at this stage that there were two approaches to the management of labour. The first was assisted delivery and the second was fetal blood sample with a view to determining whether labour should proceed. It was held that the two alternatives should have been explained to the KR.

MC & JC (A Child Proceeding by His Mother and Litigation Friend MC) v Birmingham Women's NHS Foundation Trust [2016] EWHC 1334 (QB)

In this case, it was recognised that the proper approach in law to the issue of consent is found in the decision of the Supreme Court in *Montgomery*. A decision was made to induce a mother owing, it was said, to the risk of her developing pre-eclampsia. There was criticism of the consultant for not discussing the risks and benefits of induction directly with the mother and for leaving the discussion to a junior doctor. It was also questioned whether the mother should have been advised prior to induction that necessary support would not have been available on the ward or that a delivery suite may not have been immediately available. The court concluded that it was "reasonable" to advise the mother to undergo induction and, in any event, even if the pros and cons of induction had been explained to her she would have proceeded. The pros and cons focused upon appeared to be questions of availability of facilities rather than any medical consequences of induction.

Miss Joanna Lunn v Dr Prapakaran Kanagaratnam [2016] EWHC 93 (QB)

The trial in this case was limited to disputes of fact concerning the consent procedure and issues of causation were not addressed. The claimant collapsed on the ward following surgery and an eight-minute sinus pause was recorded and a vasovagal collapse was diagnosed. The claimant was advised to have a pacemaker inserted. As a result of the insertion of the pacemaker she suffered a very rare complication of the surgery, comprising a pericardial effusion. This then lead to development of Dressler's syndrome, an inflammation of the pericardium surrounding the heart, which resulted in chest, neck and arm pain.

The claimant accepted that the surgery was carried out with due skill and care. She asserted that she should have been advised that the insertion of a pacemaker was not mandatory and that there was a division of medical opinion regarding the efficacy of pacemakers. She also argued that she was not advised that there were other non-invasive treatment options which could have been tried prior to surgical insertion of the pacemaker.

On causation, she argued that had she been appropriately advised she would have chosen one of the options that did not require the insertion of a pacemaker. In such circumstances, she would not have undergone pacemaker surgery and would have avoided the complications of that surgery. Even if she had undergone pacemaker surgery at a later date, she argued that she would not have suffered from the complications that she did in fact suffer. The defender argued that even if she had chosen an alternative option that would have been unlikely to be effective and she would have undergone pacemaker surgery at a later date. As a matter of law the claim failed on causation as the risk of the complication would have been the same at that later date.

On the question of consent reference was made to *Montgomery* and to the relevant GMC guidance. It was accepted that the GMC guidance set out the essential information a patient was entitled to expect. Following evidence the court found that the defendant did not fail to advise the claimant that the surgery was not mandatory. It was also found that it was not the defendant who had caused the claimant to believe the surgery was urgent. However, the court found that there had been a failure to advise of alternative courses of action to treat her vaso-vagal syncope, including non-invasive options.

Ian Francis Britten v Tayside Health Board [2016] SC DUN 75 Sheriff Collins QC

The pursuer had suffered from bipolar disorder for many years and in around 2001 he started to experience pain, photophobia and inflammation in his left eye. He was referred to hospital and diagnosed with acute anterior uveitis in the left eye. In 2005 he was diagnosed with panuveitis in the left eye and he was advised that this was a serious condition and if left untreated there was a serious risk of permanent loss of vision. Continued treatment with steroid drops was said to be no longer appropriate. It was said that treatment with oral steroids was required.

Treatment with steroids is well recognised as being associated with adverse psychiatric events in around 10–15% of cases. Where a person suffers from bipolar disorder there is a risk that the condition will be exacerbated, although the fact that the patient was taking lithium did not make treatment with oral steroids inappropriate. Administration of steroids by injection was thought to create a lower risk of precipitating an adverse psychiatric event than taking oral steroids. The extent of the lower risk had not been quantified. There were risks in using steroid injection.

In this case the pursuer was not advised of the possibility of treatment by steroid injection as an alternative to treatment by oral steroids. He was not advised of the relative potential risks and benefits between the two treatments. It was said that the advice was not given because, having been advised of the risk to his mental health when using oral steroids, the pursuer was dismissive of this risk and made it clear he just wanted the problem with his eye fixed.

The pursuer did not respond well to the dosage of oral steroids and the dosage was increased. At that time the pursuer was not offered the alternative of treatment by steroid injection. He eventually was given a steroid injection. The pursuer then became increasingly mentally unwell and delusional and was admitted for treatment to hospital.

The court found that there was a failure to advise the pursuer of the availability of steroid injection as a reasonable alternative for the condition of panuveitis of the left eye. There was a failure to fully explain to him the potential and relative risks and benefits thereof as against treatment with oral steroids. On the issue of causation, the court held that, even if properly informed, the pursuer would have opted for treatment by oral steroids, which he in fact received, with the same consequences.

Abdul Mutalib bin Mohamad Gani v Dr Kuladeva Ratnam & Another [2016] 2 AMR 117

The claimant was the husband of a women who died of sepsis following burns sustained following a gas explosion. The High Court of Malaysia was referred to the decision of the Supreme Court in *Montgomery* but ultimately the court made no findings other than to set out the decision.

In Malaysia, the *Bolam* test is used to assess the standard of care expected of a medical practitioner. In *Foo Fio Na v Dr Soo Fook Mun &*

Another ([2007] 1 MLJ 598) the claimant become totally paralysed following neck surgery. One of the arguments was that she should have been advised of the risk of paralysis. The Federal Court departed from the *Bolam* test in respect of the duty to advise but maintained that it was applicable to medical negligence in all other respects. The court was of the opinion that the *Bolam* test has no relevance to the duty and standard of care of a medical practitioner in providing advice to a patient on the inherent and material risks of a proposed treatment. The court adopted the test set out in the Australian case of *Rogers v Whitaker*. The court was of the view that the *Rogers v Whitaker* test was a more appropriate and viable test in this millennium than the *Bolam* test.

Scott Inglis v Susan Brand [2016] SC EDIN 63

This is a dental case in which the pursuer failed on the merits and causation. The pursuer attended his dentist in 2001 complaining of pain in the left side of the gum area. It was noted that there was dental decay in the lower left wisdom tooth and the recommendation was that the tooth could not be restored and required to be extracted.

The defender argued that the pursuer was given the option of either extraction or leaving the tooth in situ. It was also argued that the defender advised the pursuer of the risk of pain, and the lesser risk of temporary or permanent numbness of the lower lip or tongue, in the event that the procedure developed into a surgical extraction or if the root of the tooth were to put pressure on a nerve during extraction.

The tooth was extracted, following which the pursuer returned with pain in the socket and some bone was removed. The pain continued and the claimant was eventually referred to the Edinburgh Dental Institute, where his submandibular gland was removed. Thereafter he was diagnosed as having suffered damage to the lingual nerve.

Reference was made to *Montgomery* and it was argued that there were no reasonable treatment options other than extraction. Further the pursuer was warned of the risk of permanent nerve damage. Focus was on what a reasonable person in the patient's position would consider material. The focus was only on the first limb of the *Montgomery* test.

In the first instance the court appeared to consider the practice of presenting the options of extraction, or doing nothing in the context of the *Hunter v Hanley* test not *Montgomery*. It was held that there was no negligence in terms of the test since the options were presented. The court then applied the principles found in *Montgomery* to the question of discussion about the treatment and risks of injury. It was stated that the duty incumbent upon the defender was "to take reasonable care to ensure that the patient is aware of any material risks involved in any recommended treatment, and of any reasonable alternative or variant treatments. The test of materiality is whether, in the circumstances of the particular case, a reasonable person in the patient's position would be likely to attach significance to the risk." It was held that there had been discussion of the risks and the pursuer had consented.

Tracey Holdsworth v Luton and Dunstable University Hospital NHS Foundation Trust [2016] EWHC 3347 (QB)

The claimant underwent a right unicompartment knee replacement (UKR) in 2010, and then a right total knee replacement in 2011. She had further revisionary surgery but her pain had increased and she was heavily reliant on a wheelchair. One of the arguments in the case was that she did not give consent to the UKR. She said that she was not warned of the risks of persisting and continuing pain or that she might require further knee surgery.

The court held that the surgeon did have a long consultation with the claimant. It was noted that the consent form identified the "serious or frequently occurring risks", although not the fact there could be ongoing pain. The surgeon had given evidence that he would have advised her of the possibility of continuing pain. This was accepted by the court. On the causation question it was decided that even if she had not been informed about the risks she was determined to have surgery and would have gone down that route no matter what was said to her.

Regina (M and Another) v Human Fertilisation and Embryology Authority [2016] EWCA Civ 611

In this case a terminally ill young woman undertook IVF treatment to remove and store eggs. As part of her treatment she signed a consent form in which she consented to storage and usage of the eggs after her death. After her death, in accordance with informal instructions her mother applied for authority to export the eggs to the USA. Her plan was to use an anonymous sperm donor and bring up any child as her grandchild. The application was refused on the ground that effective consent to treatment and disclosure of relevant information were integral provisions of the Human Fertilisation and Embryology Act 1990. It was argued that although she had consented to the storage and use of her eggs after her death she had not given effective consent to the precise use which was now proposed.

A claim for judicial review was dismissed and the mother appealed. The Appeal Court considered *Montgomery* and concluded that the mother's evidence of conversations with her daughter, in which they had discussed her wishes on death could not be ignored as evidence of her consent. The HFA had stated that a person undergoing treatment should receive "such relevant information as is proper". They did not say that a person must receive all information.

The court held that an analogy could be drawn with the duty of the doctor as set out in *Montgomery*. The court recognised that the test established by the Supreme Court involved an assessment of what would be material to someone in the patient's position and depends on the facts and circumstances and characteristics of the patient. Information therefore would vary according to the particular circumstances. The HFA applied the same test of sufficiency of information to all cases. The appeal was successful as it was stated that the committee needed to assess consent based on what level of information was appropriate based on the totality of the evidence in the case. It was only in this situation that a decision could be made on whether consent was given.

4.   Cases in 2017

Sebastian Webster (A Child Protected by His Mother and Litigation Friend, Heather Butler) v Burton Hospitals NHS Foundation Trust [2017] EWCA Civ 62

This was a cerebral palsy case in which the breach of duty was admitted. The child was born on 7 January 2003 and it was common ground that his disabilities were caused by an injury to his brain which occurred between 72 and 48 hours prior to delivery. It was agreed that had he been delivered before 4.09pm on 4 January 2003 he would have avoided brain damage and consequent disabilities. The injury sustained was a hypoxic-ischaemic insult to the brain caused by a relatively short period of cord compression.

During the course of the pregnancy on 18 November 2002 an ultra-sound scan had been performed and it was noted that the fetus was small for gestational age. There was also asymmetry and polyhydram-nios. Following the scan the mother was reviewed by the consultant, who noted that she should be reviewed at 41 weeks with a view to induction of labour. It was agreed that the consultant was negligent in failing to arrange further ultrasound scanning.

On 26 December 2002 the mother went into hospital as she felt unwell and she was kept in overnight and observed. Her expected date of delivery was 27 December. She was reviewed on 27 December by the consultant and he indicated that she should go home. The claimant's case was that she should have been offered induction on 27 December and had this been done the injury would have been avoided. The defendant's position was that if the omitted scans had been performed they would have provided reassurance and there would have been no necessity to discuss induction at that point in time. Ultimately the labour was induced on 7 January 2003.

At first instance, it was found that had the mother been advised she should proceed to induction of labour, or that there were increased risks in waiting until January she would have wanted to be delivered.

The decision of the Supreme Court in *Montgomery* was decided after the judgement in the case. On appeal, it was noted that the judge at first instance followed the *Bolam* approach, basing his opinion on whether the consultant acted in accordance with a responsible body of expert medical opinion. It stated that following *Montgomery* this was unacceptable. The doctor's obligation is to present the material risks and uncertainties of different treatments, and to allow patients to make decisions that will affect their health and well-being on proper information. The significance of the risks and uncertainties was relevant, including the possibility of alternative treatment, being sensitive to the characteristics of the patient.

The court considered that the mother should have been told about the emerging incomplete material showing increased risks of delaying labour in cases such as hers. Had she been given this information the court considered that she would have wished to be delivered on 27 December and this would have been so even if the information had been couched in terms of contrary arguments in favour of non-intervention. She had given evidence that she would have wished her baby delivered if there was any suggestion of risk and she had shown a willingness to take responsibility for her pregnancy. She also held a nursing degree and all these factors were relevant in addressing causation.

Thefaut v Johnston [2017] EWHC 497 (QB)

In this case the claim succeeded on the basis of the consent case and failed in relation to the case of negligence in relation to performance of the surgery. There was disagreement with the test applied in *Spencer v Hillingdon Hospital NHS Trust*.

In the consent case the complaint was that the surgeon, Mr Johnston, had failed to give the claimant full and accurate advice about the risks and benefits of the proposed surgery, which was a discectomy. The surgery was unsuccessful and as a result the claimant sustained nerve damage and as a result suffered from constant back and leg pain. She asserted that Mr Johnston had given her comforting and optimistic advice, which had reassured her and led her to give her consent. Mr

Johnston had sent out written advice to Mrs Thefaut but accepted in evidence that the advice he had given was substandard.

The court considered the decision of the Supreme Court in *Montgomery*. It was said that under the test the doctor must communicate material risks and this should include reasonable alternatives or variants. On the question of "materiality" the court applied the first part of the test and said "The test is whether … in the circumstances of the particular case, a reasonable person in the patient's position would be likely to attach significance to the risk." It was said that this test combined subjectivity with objectivity. Having decided that this was the test the Supreme Court had advocated in *Montgomery*, the court then questioned the extent to which subjective factors relating to the actual patient were relevant.

On the issue of causation, it was said that it was common ground between counsel that the test was a mixture of subjective and objective. It was said that what was less clear was the actual extent to which subjective factors relating to the actual patient were relevant owing to the greater degree of subjectivity inserted into the assessment the further one departs from the standard of the reasonable patient.

It was concluded that a reasonable patient with Mrs Thefaut's condition would have declined surgery if properly advised, or at least deferred it pending a second opinion. Thereafter, the evidence of Mrs Thefault was tested carefully against the intrinsic logic of the case and the actual documentary and scientific evidence. Her subjective evidence was entirely consistent with the analysis of how a reasonable patient, similarly placed, would have reacted.

Correia v University Hospital of North Staffordshire NHS Trust [2017] EWCA Civ 356

On appeal, it was argued that the claimant had consented to a three-stage procedure and this was not the procedure that was performed. The claimant had not been warned of the material risks of an operation which omitted the crucial step of relocation. It was argued that if she could bring herself within the causation principle established in *Chester v Afshar* she would not need to establish that the negligence caused the pain and suffering. It would be sufficient to show that the injury was within the scope of the doctor's duty to warn when he obtained her consent to the operation. The argument was unsuccessful on the causation point.

Lucy Diamond v Royal Devon & Exeter NHS Foundation Trust [2017] EWHC 1495 (QB)

The claimant underwent spinal fusion surgery, following which she developed an abdominal hernia. The consent issue in the case related to an alleged failure to properly secure her consent before proceeding to repair the hernia with mesh. Following the surgery, she continued to have abdominal pain and swelling and she was advised to undergo abdominoplasty. The mesh was removed and the hernia was repaired with a single stitch and a full abdominoplasty was performed.

It was common ground that the doctor only offered a mesh repair, with prolene mesh, or, if the muscle damage was too extensive, a biological mesh. He made no reference to a primary sutured repair. The claimant stated that she was not asked about any future pregnancy prior to surgery. The doctor's position was that she had made it clear that she was not contemplating a further pregnancy in the immediate or foreseeable future. There was no reference to this in the clinical notes or in the letter following the clinic visit and the court did not accept the doctor on this issue. It was agreed that there was no discussion about the implications of a mesh repair in the content of any future pregnancy.

Despite the decision in *Montgomery* the court appeared to consider expert evidence relevant to the question of what risks should be disclosed to a patient. The court said "On the basis of the expert evidence from both the Claimant's expert … and the Defendant's expert … there is general consensus that a Claimant should have been counselled about the potentially adverse effects of a mesh being present in pregnancy". The defendant doctor appeared to agree that, if there was a risk of future pregnancy, the risks associated with the mesh repair would need to be discussed.

The court held that there was a failure to advise the claimant of the risks of a mesh repair in a future pregnancy. She should also have been advised that there was an alternative of a primary suture repair as opposed to mesh repair even if there was a higher failure risk in that procedure.

On the causation issue, the court appeared to consider that it had to assess what the doctor would have in fact have told the claimant and then it should apply the *Bolam/Bolitho* test and decide whether, objectively, that would have complied with the duty owed to the claimant. On this basis it was decided that had she been given appropriate information she would have gone ahead with the repair.

It was also argued on behalf of the claimant that if there had been a negligent non-disclosure by a doctor then that of itself could create a right for the patient to claim damages. This argument was said to be based upon *Montgomery* and the principles in *Chester v Afshar*. The court did not accept this argument.

Melissa Malone v Greater Glasgow and Clyde Health Board 2017 Scot (D) 12/3; [2017] CSOH 3

The pursuer had attended her GP between 2001 and 2002 with a number of non-specific symptoms and he referred her to the Haematology Department at Glasgow Royal Infirmary for investigation as she was anaemic. In fact, the pursuer had atrial myxoma, a rare, non-malignant tumour of the heart.

In 2002 as part of the general investigations an ECG was ordered. The purpose of the ECG was to exclude sub-acute endocarditis. It was common ground that had an ECG been performed at the time the diagnosis of the tumour would have been made. The ECG was not performed and the pursuer suffered a stroke in 2006 as a result of small pieces of the tumour breaking off.

The pursuer stated that she was unaware that the ECG test was to be performed. Her position on the basis of the decision in *Montgomery* was that there had been a failure to advise her that there was an alternative treatment or investigatory option (ECG) open to her on two occasions. There was a failure to explain the risks if she did not undergo an ECG.

The defenders founded on the pursuer's failure to attend her hospital appointments and her failure to engage with the those treating her. By the time she did attend it was considered that there was no ongoing requirement for an ECG, an infective cause for her anaemia having been eliminated.

The pursuer was unsuccessful as the court found that the pursuer had failed to attend hospital for appointments and by the time she did attend there was no ongoing requirement for an ECG.

Hii Chii Kok v Ooi Peng Jin London Lucien and Another [2017] SGCA 38

In this case the Court of Appeal in Singapore considered *Montgomery* and its application to their law on consent. The claimant had pancreatic lesions, which were diagnosed as possible tumours, and various treatment options were proposed but ultimately he underwent major pancreatic surgery. During the course of surgery an anastomosis was performed to join the remaining tract and preserve the integrity of the gastrointestinal tract. A known complication of the procedure was anastomotic leakage. Following surgery, it was confirmed that he had hyperplasia and did not have tumours.

In Singapore, since the case of *Khoo James and another v Gunapathy d/o Muniandy and another* ([2002] 1 SLR (R) 1024) it has been accepted that the *Bolam* test applies to all actions of doctors, although the practices must be logically defensible applying *Bolitho* principles. It was described as applying a physician-centric approach, placing emphasis on peer review. In the High Court the *Gunapathy* test was applied and the court found that there were no failures in care in relation to advice given.

In the appeal, one question was how the court should assess the standard of care in relation to medical advice and whether Singapore should gravitate towards a more patient-centric approach. The attorney-general deemed the issue to be of such public interest that he applied for leave to file submissions in the appeal. The claimant argued that the test that should be applied was the test as set out in *Montgomery*.

The court did not find in favour of the claimant but did consider that it was appropriate to move towards what they described as a patient-centric approach when prescribing the standard of care in relation to the doctor's duty to advise the patient and provide the patient with the requisite information to enable them to participate meaningfully in decisions affecting the medical treatment they will receive. *Gunapathy* would still apply in cases of diagnosis and treatment.

The test formulated by the Court of Appeal draws heavily on the test in *Montgomery* with a few significant alterations. It is important to note that, whilst the test does contain many of the elements identified as important to the issue of consent in *Montgomery*, the court conducted its own analysis of the law in other jurisdictions and formulated its own test. It described the test as "the modified *Montgomery* test".

The test devised has a number of components. First, the patient must identify the exact nature of the information they allege was not given to them and establish why it would be regarded as relevant and material. The court stated that it did not confine the scope of information in question to material risks concerning the recommended treatment and any reasonable alternatives of variant treatment.

In their judgment, the information which doctors ought to disclose is:

(a) information that would be relevant and material to a reasonable patient situated in the particular patient's position, or

(b) information that a doctor knows is important to the particular patient in question.

It was said:

> *We are satisfied that this stage of the inquiry should be undertaken essentially from the perspective of the patient, because the autonomy of the patient, who has an interest in being furnished with sufficient information – in terms of both quantity and quality – to allow him to arrive at an informed decision as to whether to submit to the proposed therapy or treatment, demands nothing less.*

"Materiality" is assessed from the vantage point of the patient, having regard to matters that the patient in question was reasonably likely to have attached significance to in arriving at their decision, or matters which the doctor in fact knew or had reason to believe that the patient would have placed particular emphasis on. Materiality is not restricted to risk-related information. It is necessary to contextualise materiality and judge it from the patient's perspective. Expert evidence and guidance may be useful in assisting a court to determine what would be material.

The court also held that the advantages and disadvantages associated with alternative procedures and the consequences of forgoing treatment also needed to be disclosed since patients cannot measure risks in the abstract.

If the court is satisfied that the information was both relevant and material, the court then must proceed to the second stage of the test, which is to determine whether the doctor was in possession of that information. If the doctor was not aware of the information, they cannot pass that information onto the patient. On whether they were/should have been aware of the information, the court concluded that this would continue to be determined, applying the *Bolam/Bolitho* test.

The court would then proceed to the third limb of the test, which is to assess why the doctor chose to withhold the information from the patient. Justification for withholding information, although informed by medical considerations, would not be determined by the *Bolam* test, although there will be specific contexts where the *Bolam* test would continue to be relevant. At this stage the burden would be on the doctor to justify the non-disclosure and this might involve supportive expert evidence.

5. Attempts to introduce a consent case based on *Montgomery*

Georgieve v KCH [2016] EWHC 104

Initially, permission was refused to allow a consent claim to be added, though it was then granted. The claimant suffered from cerebral palsy as a result of a period of hypoxic ischaemia in the course of a home birth. Six months before the trial there was an application to amend the claim to include an allegation applying *Montgomery* principles that the claimant had not been advised of the risks of a home birth.

Jones v Royal Wolverhampton NHS Trust [2015] EWHC 2154 (QB)

The case was about to proceed to trial three months after the decision in *Montgomery* was handed down. The claimant was permitted to amend to bring in a consent case.

The original basis of the claim was that it was negligent to fail to start anticoagulant treatment within sufficient time to prevent the stroke. Following *Montgomery* the claimant wanted to argue that the nurse's failure to warn of the risk of stroke amounted to a breach of duty. Prior to *Montgomery* the failure to warn would not have been negligent, applying the *Bolam* test. The defender argued that it was too late to introduce this argument. The court allowed the amendment as it was considered that the claimant should be allowed to amend to take account of the development of the law.

Clark v Greater Glasgow Health Board [2016] CSOH 24

In Scotland, the pursuer unsuccessfully attempted to introduce an amendment to introduce a consent case after the case had been heard by the court but before the judgment was issued. The pursuer (Jill Clark) sustained a profound and irreversible hypoxic brain injury at birth. She is however competent and able to instruct her lawyers and bring an action on her own behalf. This is important when considering issues of time bar. The motion was made 23 years after the injury was sustained, 10 years after the action was raised and after the case had proceeded to proof.

The object of the amendment was to introduce a new "risk disclosure" case and reopen the case. It was argued that following *Montgomery* the clinicians had a duty to discuss the options for delivery with Mrs Clark (Jill Clark's mother) and the risks and benefits of each option. The claimant sought to introduce arguments that vaginal birth after caesarean section carried the risk of rupture of the uterus, and should this occur the consequences could be potentially serious for the fetus and mother. There was also the risks associated with the use of Synto-cinon should a mother elect to proceed to a trial of vaginal delivery. It was argued that if proper advice had been given Mrs Clark would have opted for caesarean section, and in that situation there would have been no vaginal birth and no brain damage. The pursuer also submitted that if she were not permitted to amend to introduce the consent case she could in fact raise a separate action based on a failure to consent.

The Lord Ordinary, Lord Stewart, did not agree that the pursuer could bring a new action based on a consent failure as he was of the view that this action would be time-barred, since the birth was on 2 March 1992 and Jill Clark was not incapax (Prescription and Limitation (Scotland) Act 1973). (In law, where a person does not have capacity (where they are incapax) there is no set period within which an action can be raised. However, where a person does have capacity there are strict legal time limits for raising an action in court.) He also refused leave to amend to allow the pursuer to bring in the new case to the existing action. His decision appeared to be based on his view that *Montgomery* had not in fact made any great change to the landscape of consent, and that the pursuer had the benefit of legal advice from experienced practitioners for many years. He also referred to the fact the original senior counsel in the case was also the senior counsel for the defenders in *Montgomery* and in that sense must have been well aware of the arguments advanced as the case proceeded in the Inner House and to the Supreme Court.

The claimant appealed against the refusal of Lord Stewart to allow the minute of amendment to bring in a consent case ([2017] CSIH 17). The pursuer did not appeal against Lord Stewart's decision on the merits of the original action. Following the refusal of the amendment Lord Stewart had issued a decision finding in favour of the defenders. The Appeal Court considered that Lord Stewart's assessment of the impact of *Montgomery* was correct and refused to overturn the decision. The court was of the view that a consent case could have been brought in the original action on the same grounds as *Montgomery* had they chosen to do so. Reference was made to the dictum in *Pearce*, which it was said supported such a claim.

Opbroek bhnf Crittall v Australian Capital Territory [2016] ACT SC 64

In this case the claimant in Australia sought to amend her statement of claim and added in allegations in relation to failure to inform of risks, and reasonable or alternative forms of treatment. There was reliance on the decision in *Montgomery* and it was said that this was a developing area of the law.

In refusing to allow the amendment, the court stated that the decision in *Montgomery* in effect brought the law in the UK into line with Australian law rather than being a new development of the law, which could not have been brought earlier by the claimant. It was said that the significance of the decision was the abandonment by the Supreme Court of the statement of a doctor's standard of care in *Sidaway v Board of Governors of the Bethlem Hospital*: "In doing so, the members of the Court adopted the approach that has been adopted by the High Court in *Rogers v Whitaker*". It was said:

> *While providing a useful articulation of the duty of a doctor to his or her patient (see in particular [81]) and, in the judgement of Lady Hale an articulation of how that relationship applies in the context of decisions about methods of giving birth, the substance of the decision*

is one which reflects Australian law as articulated since Rogers v Whitaker.

6. *Montgomery* and solicitors' negligence

<u>*Scumann v Veale Wasbrough* [2015] EWCA Civ 441</u>

This case concerned solicitors' and a barrister's negligence in relation to a clinical negligence action. An attempt was made to use the decision in *Montgomery* to set the standard to be applied for advice and information in other disciplines. The court noted that *Montgomery* was decided after the date when the advice was said to have been negligently given and did not apply it. In any event, it was found that the claim was statute-barred.

<u>*Baird v Hastings (Practising as Hastings & Company, Solicitors)* [2015] NICA 22</u>

Mrs Baird claimed damages against her solicitor for negligence and breach of contract in relation to the conduct of a conveyancing transaction. There was a finding of negligence and the solicitor appealed against this. In the appeal reference was made to *Montgomery* and it was said:

> *The doctor/patient relationship is not a full or true analogue of a solicitor/client relationship since the therapeutic duties owed by a doctor to a patient raises different questions from those arising between a solicitor and client. However, a solicitor is bound to take reasonable care to ensure that the client understands the material legal risks that arise in any transaction which the client has asked the solicitor to handle on his behalf. As in the doctor/patient relationship the test of materiality is whether a reasonable client would be likely to attach significance to the risks arising which should be reasonably foreseeable to the competent Solicitor. As in the medical context, the advisory role of the solicitor must involve proper communication and dialogue with the client.*

Darrell Healey GSE Investments Limited v Shoosmiths (a firm) 2016 EWHC 1723 (QB)

In this professional negligence case, counsel for the claimants referred the court to *Baird v Hastings* ([2015] NICA 22), which had referred to *Montgomery*. It was noted that in *Baird* the court accepted that the doctor–patient relationship is not a full or true analogue of a solicitor–client relationship. It was argued that in this case there was a belief that there was no way to get out of the particular contract. There should have been a discussion and it should have been made clear that there was a choice available.

7.   Comment

There has been a flurry of cases since the decision of the Supreme Court in *Montgomery* in 2015. This also occurred in Australia and Canada when those jurisdictions introduced a patient-focused information test.

There are those in the UK who have said that the decision in *Montgomery* was not required since the decision of Lord Woolf MR in *Pearce v United Bristol Healthcare NHS Trust* had already moved the UK law forward since the House of Lord's decision in *Sidaway*. In England, there had been application of a "reasonable patient" test in cases decided prior to *Montgomery*. In Scotland, in the Inner House in *Montgomery* it was argued by the claimant that the test set out by Lord Woolf in *Pearce* had advanced and informed the test found in *Sidaway*. The Scottish Appeal Court rejected this and held that could not advance the law beyond the decision in *Sidaway* given that *Sidaway* was binding upon the court in *Pearce*.

In *Pearce v United Bristol Healthcare NHS Trust* the test as formulated by Lord Woolf MR is focused only on a significant risk which would affect the judgement of a reasonable patient. This not a test which truly recognises the particular importance of individual patient autonomy. Lord Scarman in *Sidaway* explicitly did not go as far as a particular patient test. The test formulated by Lord Woolf is a one-step test with emphasis on what a reasonable patient would do:

> *In a case where it is being alleged that a plaintiff has been deprived of the opportunity to make a proper decision as to what course he or she should take in relation to treatment, it seems to me to be the law, as indicated in the cases to which I have just referred, that if there is a significant risk which would **affect the judgement of a reasonable patient**, then in the normal course it is the responsibility of a doctor to inform the patient of that significant risk, if the information is needed so that the patient can determine for himself or herself as to what course he or she should adopt.*

He does not say a risk that would affect the judgement of a reasonable patient in the patient's position. However, this passage has been interpreted in England as extending the *Sidaway* test to a reasonable patient in the patient's position.

In *Montgomery*, it was said that:

> *An adult person of sound mind is entitled to decide which, if any, of the available forms of treatment to undergo, and her consent must be obtained before treatment interfering with her bodily integrity is undertaken. The doctor is therefore under a duty to take reasonable care to ensure that the patient is aware of any material risks involved in any recommended treatment, and of any reasonable alternative or variant treatments.*

On the test of "materiality" the Supreme Court quoted directly from *Rogers v Whitaker* and said:

> *The test of materiality is whether, in the circumstances of the particular case, a **reasonable person in the patient's position** would be likely to attach significance to the risk, **or the doctor is or should reasonably be aware that the particular patient would be likely to attach significance to it**.*

The test is focused in the first instance on a reasonable patient in the patient's position. However, the *Montgomery* test has a second limb which does not appear in *Pearce*. To understand the test formulated consideration requires to be given to how the patient-centred test was developed in Australia following the decision in *Rogers v Whitaker* and also the Canadian cases, which follow a similar line. These are dealt with in detail in Chapter 3.

The first limb of the *Montgomery* test is the objective limb. This is what a reasonable person in the patient's position would have done. This limb of the test focuses on the requirements of the reasonable person in the patient's position. The second, subjective limb recognises that a patient may not be reasonable and allows the courts to consider the particular patient and their requirements or fears (reasonable and unreasonable). This is subject to the caveat that the medical practitioner is or ought to be aware of those considerations. If a patient had special needs or concerns and this was known to the doctor, this would indicate that special or additional information is required.

Following *Montgomery*, Singapore has adopted what they described as a "modified *Montgomery* test", which is a three-stage test to be applied in consent cases. It is interesting to note that the Court of Appeal of Singapore in refining its test in the light of *Montgomery* recognised the two-step test formulated by the court with reference to *Rogers v Whitaker*.

In Singapore, the Court of Appeal directed that materiality is assessed from the vantage point of the patient, having regard to matters that the patient in question was reasonably likely to have attached significance to in arriving at their decision, or matters which the doctor in fact knew or had reason to believe that the patient would have placed particular emphasis on. This is remarkably similar to the test formulated in *Rogers v Whitaker* and *Montgomery*, although Singapore has retained *Bolam* as applicable to certain aspects of the test they have devised. The court recognised in doing so they were not adopting the decision in *Montgomery* without reservation.

It is also interesting that the court recognised and highlighted the misuse of the term "informed consent". In *Sidaway* Lord Scarman had condemned the use of this term to qualify consent.

Following the decision in *Montgomery* it seemed obvious that there was scope to use the *Montgomery* principles in cases of information, advice and choice in other areas of professional negligence. There have been cases where attempts have been made to do so. There has been a suggestion that the doctor–patient relationship is a particular relationship with patient autonomy at its core. However, it is important to consider the link between professional codes and guidance and the question of information and advice similar to the use of the GMC guidance to define the scope of the professional duty of the doctor in *Montgomery*. Solicitors are given professional guidance on the provision of information to clients to enable the clients to make an informed decision on how to proceed.

In *Montgomery*, the Supreme Court said that the correct position now in information disclosure is that substantially adopted in *Sidaway* by Lord Scarman, and by Lord Woolf in *Pearce*, **subject to the refinement made by the High Court of Australia in *Rogers v Whitaker*.** On an analysis of cases post-*Montgomery*, it does appear that the test has not always been applied with consideration given to the formulation defined by the Supreme Court.

What has been applied in many of the post-*Montgomery* cases is simply a test linked to a reasonable person in the patient's position, which appears to be a gloss or extension of *Pearce*. In many cases, the second limb of the test found in *Rogers v Whitaker* is given no consideration at all. A full reading of the Canadian and Australian cases and the approach to materiality is required to understand the test formulated by the Supreme Court in *Montgomery*. There also appears to be confusion on the application of the *Bolam* test and the role of experts in information disclosure cases in this new era. A full reading of the Australian and Canadian cases referred to in Montgomery (*Rogers v Whitaker, Reibl v Hughes, Rosenberg v Percival*) will assist those struggling to grapple with these issues.

MORE BOOKS BY
LAW BRIEF PUBLISHING

A selection of our other titles available now:

'A Practical Guide to Holiday Sickness Claims, 2nd Edition' by Andrew Mckie & Ian Skeate
'A Practical Guide to Inheritance Act Claims by Adult Children Post-Ilott v Blue Cross' by Sheila Hamilton Macdonald
'A Practical Guide to Elderly Law' by Justin Patten
'Arguments and Tactics for Personal Injury and Clinical Negligence Claims' by Dorian Williams
'A Practical Guide to QOCS and Fundamental Dishonesty' by James Bentley
'A Practical Guide to Drone Law' by Rufus Ballaster, Andrew Firman, Eleanor Clot
'Practical Mediation: A Guide for Mediators, Advocates, Advisers, Lawyers, and Students in Civil, Commercial, Business, Property, Workplace, and Employment Cases' by Jonathan Dingle with John Sephton
'Practical Horse Law: A Guide for Owners and Riders' by Brenda Gilligan
'A Comparative Guide to Standard Form Construction and Engineering Contracts' by Jon Close
'A Practical Guide to Compliance for Personal Injury Firms Working With Claims Management Companies' by Paul Bennett
'A Practical Guide to the Landlord and Tenant Act 1954: Commercial Tenancies' by Richard Hayes & David Sawtell
'A Practical Guide to Personal Injury Claims Involving Animals' by Jonathan Hand
'A Practical Guide to Psychiatric Claims in Personal Injury' by Liam Ryan
'Introduction to the Law of Community Care in England and Wales' by Alan Robinson
'A Practical Guide to Dog Law for Owners and Others' by Andrea Pitt
'Ellis and Kevan on Credit Hire, 5th Edition' by Aidan Ellis & Tim Kevan

These books and more are available to order online direct from the publisher at www.lawbriefpublishing.com, where you can also read free sample chapters. For any queries, contact us on 0844 587 2383 or mail@lawbriefpublishing.com.

Our books are also usually in stock at www.amazon.co.uk with free next day delivery for Prime members, and at good legal bookshops such as Hammicks and Wildy & Sons.

We are regularly launching new books in our series of practical day-to-day practitioners' guides. Visit our website and join our free newsletter to be kept informed and to receive special offers, free chapters, etc.

You can also follow us on Twitter at www.twitter.com/lawbriefpub.

INDEX

Printed in Great Britain
by Amazon